NOT DEAD YET

SECOND EDITION

by
Oisin Hughes

NOT DEAD YET

You can find a series of videos uploaded to accompany this book on YouTube at the following link:
http://www.youtube.com/user/roguebikers

I'll be adding a video hopefully every 10 days or so up until June 2014.

SECOND EDITION

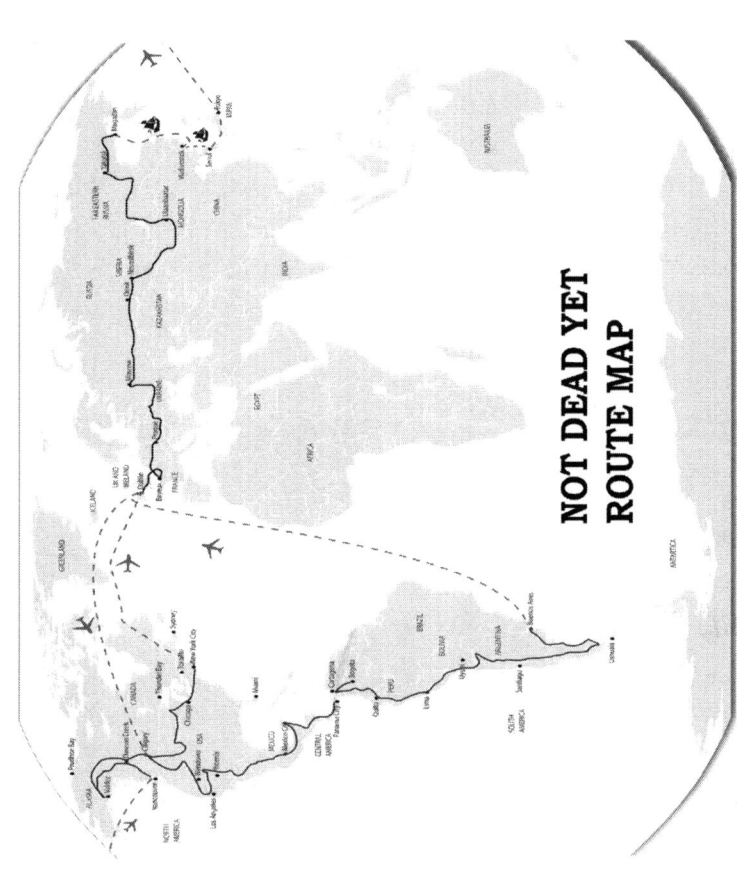

NOT DEAD YET

Hi there! My name is Oisin and this is my story. It's anything but boring, I promise. This book is mostly about riding around the world on a motorcycle. It's also about attempting to make a documentary about the trip and in smaller part about growing up in Ireland in the 1970's and 1980's.

Interlaced between some of the chapters recounting the journey are very short stories about growing up in Ireland. I added these stories because while I was traveling, I thought so much about them, they became a huge part of the emotional journey I went through. In the worlds truly isolated locations, all you do is think, and I thought mostly about this stuff, so I think they belong in the tale.

Finally, thanks to Ewan McGregor and Charlie Boorman for inspiring me to do the trip in the first place.

Why a second edition?

There's a couple of reasons. First, I've added all the route information into the appendices as well as added a large FAQ and kit section, which will hopefully prove a good resource for people who are thinking of taking on a similar trip. Secondly, the first edition was way too emotional, I wrote it too soon after coming back from the journey and it was written more like a personal journal, rather than a book written for the reader to enjoy, in summary it was bad! I wanted to do a better job of it, so it was something I was very proud of.

I really hope you like it.

Ships that pass in the night, and speak each other in passing, only a signal shown, and a distant voice in the darkness; So on the ocean of life, we pass and speak one another, only a look and a voice, then darkness again and a silence.

Henry Wadsworth Longfellow

CHAPTER 1
THE IDEA

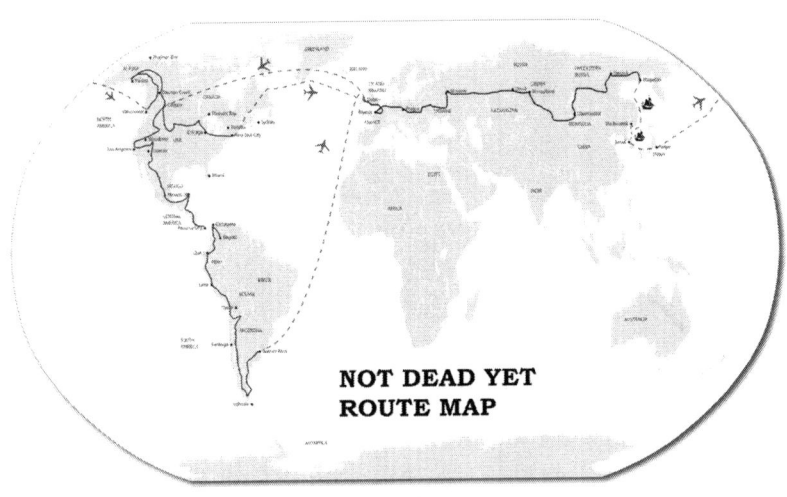

I once read a book called "Trail to Titicaca." It tells the story of three English lads who, many moons ago rode their bicycles from the town of Ushuaia in Southern Argentina, all the way North to Lake Titicaca in Peru. All told, that's a journey of over 6500 miles and their account of how they did it is a wonderful read. I read the new edition of the book, where the author circles back to the guys who did the trip to find out how they were getting on and what they were up to, almost ten years on. I was depressed to find out that they all went back to living very normal lives. I couldn't believe it. How, after doing such an incredible journey could they adjust to the hum drum of normal living again?

Little did I know that when I finished my own "Big Trip" in 2008, recounted in the book "That I May Die Roaming," that is exactly what was waiting for me. In the second half of 2008, Ireland had, in only a few short months, descended into the worst economic collapse the country had ever known. Everyone you talked to was either getting let go from their job, or found their hours of employment cut. Adjusting from, "The trip of a life time" to going back to work in a country that seemed to be moaning itself to death, was a brutal shock to the system. I knuckled down and got on with it as best I could, telling myself I was lucky to have a job. In only a few short weeks, the 34,000 mile Pan American Trip I'd completed the previous December, seemed like a distant memory. So much for the trip changing my life, I felt like I was right back at square one.

Early in 2009, I was talking online to one of the guys I'd met in Alaska on the bike trip. He was hatching a plan to go to South America on a motorcycle and was keen to try and make a documentary about the experience. He was looking for someone to come along. His plan was to buy a couple of cameras and film as he went and then when the whole thing was done, hopefully cut the thing together and sell it to the Discovery channel. I was back in work and having just completed the identical trip he was talking about, I wasn't overly interested. I would however have been interested, if he was going Dublin to New York. I had spent a lot of time thinking about someday doing a mirror trip to the Long Way Round and when he mentioned the plan, my ears definitely pricked up.

We threw emails back and forward and eventually a very fuzzy plan hatched to do the Pan American highway combined with riding from Dublin to New York heading east. A quick back of the envelope calculation showed the trip coming in at 46,000 road miles, and it would take almost a full year. It was just a pipe dream at that stage and I'd no serious intention of doing it, but as time wore on, the seed slowly grew in my head.

While all this was going on, my employer was offering redundancies and with fifteen years service under my belt, I'd walk out with a large wedge of cash. Very quickly, the conversation I was having in my head turned to, "Do I stay and continue my career or do I head off on another adventure and in the process maybe film a documentary?" It seemed perfect. It was my chance to do a version of the Long Way Round.

Giving up a good job in a recessionary economy was a big risk. Joe (name changed to respect his privacy) was self-employed so he could work from the road. All he needed to keep his business afloat was an internet connection, although to be fair, he had worked his ass off for years to build up his product offering and was risking at least as much as me by giving the documentary a go. He worked in the special effects industry in Los Angeles and was a keen photographer. His ambition was to produce his own shows. He saw this trip potentially providing him with the opportunity to break into that line of work. I kept going back and forwards on the idea in my head. We were both motorcyclists, we got on very well with each other, being of similar age and having lots of the same interests. I was starting to look at it as an opportunity to take the road less travelled. Then I would start rationalizing it in my head. I knew nothing about filming a documentary and even less about editing or producing one. I was just back from a massive trip, it was too soon to go again. I had a good job and had responsibilities in Ireland which I needed to tend to. This new trip was like going back to the tattoo parlor before the ink dried on your first tattoo. It was a bad idea.

What eventually pushed me over the edge and made me commit to doing it? The answer will seem silly. For as long as I can remember I've had the same reoccurring dream. A big fly or a wasp comes into my bedroom while I'm lying in the bed trying to enjoy a lie on. It's normally a Saturday morning and I've nowhere special to go, just the sort of morning that you'd like nothing better than to spend an extra few hours in the nest. However, the pesky intruder has other ideas, as it rattles around the room creating a major din. It's always a blue bottle, or a big wasp, normally just big enough so that you can't ignore it. I always seem to get up to take care of it. I stand there armed with a size 15 hob nail boot waiting for the sound of buzzing wings to give its location away, but by this time it's already gone. I'm up and fully awake so there's no point in getting back into bed. I've always taken these little visits as a signal that I've lingered too long and it's time to start moving again. The dream, I think is telling me that I'm stagnating and that I'm in a rut. In some ways I think I feel like I'm dying or rotting and that the fly is attracted by the smell of a dying person. I know it sounds a bit grim, but like I said it's a dream and you can't control what you dream about. I'd done the same job for 15 years and had moved my way up through the organization at a reasonable pace. I knew deep down though, that in another 15 years I'd be a little wealthier, but a lot older. One of the things we all have in common is time. The sun will rise and set every day for the rest of your life no matter what you decide to do with the time you have left, all we get is about 30,000 sunrises. I was 38 years old, kicking the shit out of 40, it was now or never. If the purpose of life is to continuously strive and improve, I felt that the best way for me to grow as a person was to take a chance at something new. Opportunity was knocking.

A few emails later I made up my mind that I was going to do it, assuming we could work out a plan that passed the sniff test. We talked about the route and decided that we'd leave Los Angeles in September 2009. After a tour of the South Western United states, we'd head south for Argentina via Mexico and Central America finally ending up in Rio de Janeiro in time for the Carnival in February. Once complete, we'd leave for Dublin Ireland, and ride from there to New York.

Fucking Easy!

NOT DEAD YET

CHAPTER 2
TRIP PREP AND GOING TO LOS ANGELES

Having decided to go on the trip, the first purchase I made with my redundancy check was a 2006 BMW GS Adventurer. It was black and grey, a super looking machine. The next job I had was to add modifications to the bike, to help it with the upcoming 46,000 miles. Given it wasn't my first time to get a bike ready for such a trip, I had all the upgrades done in fairly short order with the help of my buddies in Ireland, Barry Dunne and Conor Moran.

With the projected cost for the trip being so high, Joe and I decided it would be a good idea to hang out for a week or so before we started the trip. We wanted to make sure we both wanted the same things out of the project. We needed to talk about what the project "was" and crucially for me, what it "wasn't". From the outset, I wanted it to be clear that it was a documentary about riding our motorcycles around the world, and a commentary about the things we saw along the way. We would go with the flow, but the project had a start (LA), Middle (Dublin) and end (New York). None of that was negotiable in my eyes. (If you are thinking that I should have had this conversation before I left my job - You're absolutely right! This classes as one of the worlds finest examples of letting the heart rule the head). If we were going to make a documentary the target market would be "us", every guy or girl who was stuck in an office and wanted nothing more than to head off on an adventure, but for whatever reason couldn't.

Joe around this time was in Europe on a bike trip and we had originally planned for him to fly to my place in Ireland so we could do our project leveling session. For whatever reason he couldn't, it would mean I'd have to fly out to Los Angeles swallowing a thousand euro flight in the process. The early signs of a problem were there to see, but I was so blinded by the opportunity to make a documentary and everything that went with it, I bottled it up thinking "Things will work out." He said he didn't have time to stop in Ireland on his way back from Europe, I guessed that he must have had a lot on his plate so I let it slide.

When I got to LA, I was surprised to find that Joe was sharing a house, sleeping on a futon in his friend's spare bedroom. When I got there they offered me the couch but the house was cramped owing to the fact that the owners daughter was in town, so I got a hotel. If roles were reversed, I was certain that I'd have made sure I'd a place for Joe to stay, especially if he'd just flown over 5,000 miles to get there. Joe's office was a converted downstairs apartment in Torrance, where he worked alone. I'd taken "company" to mean something more. I'd misjudged the situation, but none of that was Joe's fault. I'd built him up to impossible heights in my head based on what he'd told me, the reality was a lot different, but that wasn't enough for me to pull the plug on the project. I had already left my job so it was going to take something huge to derail things.

I think that your initial perception of a person will fill the vacuum created by any gaps in the information you have about them. If you think they are really cool, all the gaps will be filled with positive thoughts, and the opposite is also true. I told myself, "Nobody lied, it is not Joe's fault you assumed he was a rich entrepreneur, get over it and get on with it."

We quickly evolved the understanding that as far as the project went I would own the route through Mexico, Central and South America leveraging the experience I had gained on my previous Pan American trip to take us to the most "photogenic" locations. Joe would look after the technical aspects of how we would put together the film for the documentary. Joe was also very mechanical, fantastic at fixing stuff and a brilliant photographer. He also knew an awful lot about the process of making movies. The fundamentals of the partnership were still ok. We had agreed that we would split costs and profits right down the middle so money was never going to be an issue.

We started to build up a huge amount of photographic equipment. We had cameras on our helmets, Canon HD diary cameras and we also went out and purchased a really expensive production camera for all the panoramic shots we intended taking. We were both also packing Digital SLR Cameras. On top of that there were chargers, spare batteries, portable hard drives, lenses, filters, on and on it went, and up and up went the cost.
We agreed a plan which would see me flying into Calgary on August 12th and over the course of the following

ten or so days, make my way to Los Angeles for about the 22nd of August. We'd then take a week to get everything set up and do any final modifications to the bikes, leaving LA on September 1st. The rough plan that we'd follow, would be to make our way to Ushuaia in Argentina and back up to Rio De Janeiro in time for the carnival in February, this would give us about six months, which was plenty of time. We would then ship our bikes to Ireland and get them fixed up so we could ride from Dublin to New York, heading east. We calculated that we needed to leave Ireland no later than the start of May, otherwise we wouldn't get through Russia and out of Alaska and the Yukon before the onset of winter. It also gave us enough time to suck up any delays which might occur for whatever reason. This also however, automatically put a constraint on the first leg of the trip in terms of time, i.e. we had to be out of Brazil by the end of February so we could take care of the visa paperwork for

Russia and Mongolia in time to get going for the start of May.

CHAPTER 3
GETTING TO CANADA

The date was August 12th and I was leaving Ireland for Calgary in Canada to start "Another" once in a life time adventure. The plan was to take about 12 days to ride to Los Angeles, California where I'd meet up with Joe. Once there, we'd spend a little over a week getting the bikes ready so we could film our journey from LA to Rio via Cape Horn. When we'd completed that portion of the trip, it would be Dublin to New York overland via Europe, Russia, Mongolia and Siberia. It was too big to think about when you looked at it as a whole, I kept saying to myself, "Take one day at a time." I got up early and did some final checks around the house to make sure I wasn't forgetting anything. I closed the door behind me and jumped in the car with my Dad who had stayed over to give me a lift to the airport.

Ireland's economy and general mood was at an all-time low. Talk of redundancies, plant closures, shortened work weeks, increased taxes and mortgage foreclosures were the chief topic of most people's conversations, in many ways I was glad to be leaving. As we got closer to the airport, it started to dawn on me that I was going away for a very long time, and my mind filled with thoughts of friends and family and how much I would miss them. I said goodbye to my Dad and while walking into the departure area, did my best to put the feelings of loneliness to the back of my mind. I had shipped my motorcycle out of London about ten days earlier with James Cargo so I was reasonably confident that if I got into Calgary early enough, I might be able to clear the bike through customs that day and maybe even get on the road by that evening. No sooner was I checked in, when an announcement came through the hall that the flight was delayed by five hours and with that went my slim chance of getting on the road that day in Canada. Reading back the sentence now, I'm wondering why I was in such a hurry anyway. One of my friends, Kasia who worked in the airport came down to meet me for lunch which helped me pass a couple of hours. We'd such a great time yapping that a part of me was sorry to be leaving.

The flight eventually boarded and I was seated beside Sean and Patricia from Lethbridge, a town to the South west of Calgary in Alberta, Canada. Sean was originally from County Down in Northern Ireland and at a young age had set out to travel to the world. When he got to Lethbridge he liked it so much that he never left, this was the first time he'd been home in 45 years. I've a theory about people who go off traveling the world. They only do it because there's something missing in their lives, they feel restless, somehow incomplete. If life was perfect for them, they wouldn't set off traveling in the first place, at least not for protracted periods and they certainly wouldn't do it alone. Hmmm, did I just describe myself?

Calgary, Alberta

I got to Calgary, cleared myself and my bags through customs and took a taxi to a Hotel. As the Taxi pulled up outside the hotel, I noticed a Tony Roma's, thinking to myself "That'll do nicely!" I quickly showered and went back down to Tony's for some ribs and beer. I ended up talking to a guy from Scotland who was protesting that his son was a good enough footballer to play for Celtic, and whose other son was "no doubt about it" going to be a world champion boxer. I was biding my time for a comma, whereupon I'd make my excuses and bolt out the door.

I walked back to the hotel and turned on the TV flicking through news channels all completely dominated by the health care debate in the US. I turned on my mobile phone and it was stuffed with messages from well-wishers which sent me off to sleep smiling. I woke up at 2am as fresh as a daisy and a wicked dose of jet-lag quickly ensued.

Feeling a bit groggy I left the hotel around 8am, it was time to free Sam Gamgee 2 (nickname for the bike) from customs. I'd done very little research on how to get the bike back from customs in Calgary, but having done this sort of thing before, I knew that the shipping and customs buildings would be reasonably close to each other.

I took a taxi to Lufthansa who had shipped the bike then paid for the storage and signed for the bike. Then it was just a quick skedaddle back with the forms to customs who stamped them after being convinced that I was "absolutely" leaving the country. With all the paperwork in hand, I went back to Lufthansa, uncrated the bike and burned off west in the direction of Canmore on the Trans Canada highway, Highway 1.

Canmore, Alberta

I'd been in Canada on the same date the previous year and it was in the 80's temperature wise, this time round, it was freezing. I was rattling with the cold on the bike and was delighted not to have too far to go as I approached the town of Canmore. I booked into a motel and after a roasting hot shower, headed into the town for a walk. The "Alberta Rockies" part of Canada is very expensive, probably 50% more expensive than its equivalent in the USA and is packed out with tourists. As I was meandering around the town it started to piss rain so I drifted into Murietta's Bar and grill and whiled away a couple of hours writing postcards and drinking beer while watching people walk by in the pouring rain. Every now and then mountains would peek out through the mist and rain and then hide again. I've always felt there's something very comforting about looking out into the pouring rain, it's not quite as good as looking into an open hearth fire blazing away in a dimly lit room, but it is up there.
As I walked around I met quite a few folks who were up traveling from the lower 48. North America is a brilliant

NOT DEAD YET

place and the people there for the most part are the best in the world. However, as in any large population center you can get plenty of bottom feeders too, and the saying, "If only people with closed minds came with closed mouths" is apt for some.

A minor pet peeve of mine regarding the culture is the handshake. Nowhere on earth, do they put more value on the simple handshake and nowhere else on earth are you as likely to get the shit shook the fuck out of your hand. I suppose it's the home of the power handshake. "My handshake says a lot about who I am" are words I actually heard a guy say.
I said to myself that from tomorrow, I'd try to get myself into a rhythm. I'd get up early, ride, stop often to enjoy the scenery and then as it was getting dark find a place to get a door between me and the night, then rinse and repeat for the next year or so! Yippee.

Banff, Alberta

After doing as much in Canmore as there is to do on a wet rainy autumnal afternoon, I headed back to the motel and turned on the news and flicked till I found the weather channel. The bad news was the weather wasn't going to change for the next five days, it was to be unseasonably cold and piss rain every day. "Feck it anyway" I said to myself. I consoled myself with the fact that although it might be raining, it didn't mean that there wouldn't be great things to see. Even in the rain there would be mountains with mists rolling over their shoulders and it would look completely different that it did the previous time I visited, and besides a bit of rain never hurt anyone.
I got up the next morning, the plan being to head out for the Icefields parkway. It's a road which cuts through the Alberta Rockies joining the towns of Banff and Jasper. Most articles which talk about the "World's top ten plac-

es to visit" include this area of the world. Emerald lakes, snow-capped mountains, glaciers, even bears were all on the docket and as I packed the bike up that morning, I couldn't wait to get going.

Unfortunately, Mother Nature had other ideas and what started as a bit of drizzle as I was leaving Canmore, turned into a relentless downpour by the time I was twenty miles out the road. After two hours battling through the elements, I gave up and turned back for Banff. I checked into ridiculously expensive accommodation (Nowhere is cheap in Banff) and soaked in a hot bath till the heat returned to my bones.

As it turned out, retiring from the road early that day was a blessing in disguise. I went out walking to see what the town had to offer and to my surprise it was stuffed full of things to see and do. My first port of call was a

NOT DEAD YET

Free Masons temple, normally Masonic Halls are not open to the public but the town had told the Masons the only way they could keep the temple open was to convert it to a museum, which they did. The place was full of old photographs and unusual furniture and the sense of ritual and tradition in the building as I walked around was palpable. I didn't know much about these guys beyond the fact that they were a secret society set up originally by stone masons, who in recent years had tried to come out in the open a bit more.

I popped into a couple of the other museums in the town which were full of photos from when Banff and Jasper were frontier towns on the edge of civilization. I was struck by many things, mostly though and it will probably sound very shallow, the women were all brutal looking. There were lots of pictures of Indians from the turn of the century, the women were really malnourished looking and very small in stature, similar to what you would see if you were to visit modern day Ecuador. There wasn't a single picture from the era with a woman who you'd say, " Now that's a fine thing!". It's so shallow I know, supposed to be looking at history and only looking to see what the women looked like back then. Lads, I'm not the only one right?

Banff is a great place to visit, outrageously expensive and starting to get crammed with memorabilia stores, but it still has enough going on to more than warrant a visit. I hit a bar that evening for a couple of beers and all the talk was of Brett Favre and the Minnesota Vikings, they were looking like they had a shot to get to the Superbowl.
As I sat slugging down a couple of beers I reflected on

the end of the third day, it had been mostly rain and that was all that was to come for four more days. The real reason I'd come to this part of the world before going to Los Angeles was, having watched The Horse Whisperer just before I left, I wanted to spend a bunch of time in Montana. Touring around the Rockies was just the icing on the cake so I made my mind up to do a quick loop around the Alberta and British Colombia Rockies, then cut south to try and get out of the changeable weather. I made my way initially west in the direction of Revelstoke and then south towards Creston and then back East towards Glacier National Park. As soon as I started to head south the weather improved and while it was still too cloudy and misty to see the mountains, at least I wasn't getting pissed on.

I had been through this part of the world twice before and didn't mind rolling through it relatively fast. However, if you find yourself here on a single visit, take my advice and stay till you get good weather. It is truly one of the worlds most scenic and naturally beautiful locations. There are only a handful of locations that can compare to it, so don't miss out on it. I met a guy who had come down from Alaska, and all he had seen the whole trip was rain. Like most places, if you get the weather the Great Northwest is utterly spectacular, but it can be misery if the weather is poor.

I talked with Joe later in the day. He had an almost identical experience while in Canada the year before. When I told him about the bad weather and high prices he said, "That's Canada Man, That's Canada!"

CHAPTER 4
HUNGRY HORSE TO LOS ANGELES

NOT DEAD YET

Glacier National Park, Montana

Two sisters Cafe, Babb, Montana

As I went south the clouds gradually cleared and the sun started to shine, I took it as a good omen that I'd made the right decision by leaving Canada. I took the "Road to the Sun highway" through Glacier National Park which crosses over the Continental Divide at Logan Pass.
The road climbs its way through beautiful mountains and for long periods the road is flanked with a vast gorge on the left and a solid rock cliff face to your right. The whole place is breath taking. Most of the mountains in the park, despite it still only being August, were capped with snow and it gave the air a chill that made sure you were fully awake to appreciate the astonishing views. When you ride in this sort of landscape, you cant help but feel more alive. I parked up the bike to take a couple of pictures and as I turned, a snow capped mountain was having its snow capped peak blown to bits by the wind in the distance. The road continued to rise higher and higher as I left the clouds far below me. I crossed the continental divide and started to go down the other side and all of a sudden I found myself looking out onto a vista of yawning green valleys half filled with clouds hemmed in with glistening white mountains. The road descended on the other side through forests on a road that wound and wound its way out of the mountains. As the land flattened out I pulled up alongside a lake not far from the town of Hungry Horse. The Lake was surrounded by mountains with thick black clouds standing ominously in the distance. I shot at least twenty pictures of the exact same photo, as if with every picture, I was moving the image deeper into a place in my mind where I would always remember it. If you're planning on coming this direction, remember that the last day you can ride the

Road to the Sun Highway is the 21st of September. I pulled into the Mini Golden Inns Motel, the same

one I'd stayed in a year previously with my Venezuelan buddy, Rafael. I'd ridden over 400 miles through some of the best countryside anywhere in the world and I was emotionally and physically full up, thinking to myself, "It'll take a lot to top today." It was a carbon copy of how I felt when I passed through the same location a year previously and once more, If I'm honest about it, the two reasons I went to Hungry Horse were first because it's one of the places Ewan and Charley stayed in, on the Long Way Round, and second because myself and Rafael had such a good time when we stayed there. A part of me felt that by riding the same journey and doing the same things we'd done a year previously, that somehow I wouldn't feel so lonely. It was almost as if he was there with me and things seemed to make sense. I also knew that I'd stop there one more time when it came time to come through that way on the Dublin to New York leg, so it was an important way point for me. The fact that the town is surrounded by some of the worlds most spectacular sights in Glacier National Park obviously helps too.

I went a couple of hundred yards up the road and had some grub in Eleanor's grill. It's a typical small town American grill with ok food and friendly service, after a long day on the bike it was perfect. This was the first day I started to feel a rhythm in the journey, things were starting to come together.

The motel was almost full and they only had a disabled room, no big deal, the only difference is more room around the shower and toilet. There was a bar across the top of the toilet at about neck height, no doubt used by people to pull themselves up off the toilet and back to their wheelchairs. During the night, when I slumbered into the bathroom to take a number one, while half asleep, I managed to clothes-line myself off the bar, ending up on the flat on my back. "This is the sort of thing that didn't happen to Charley and Ewan", I thought to myself as I picked my fully awake ass up off the cold tiles. The next morning I spent a bit of time moving stuff around on the bike because no matter where I looked for something, it always seemed to be someplace else. The 50-50-90 rule was breaking my heart. I'll explain. On the bike there are two big storage panniers where most of your gear is kept. So if you go looking for something, and can't remember exactly where you put it, you've a 50% chance of getting it right by picking either the left or

the right pannier, or so you'd think. "It's gotta be in this pannier" I'd say to myself. Well, the "90" in the rule refers to the fact that if you have a 50/50 chance of getting something right, 90% of the time you'll get it wrong.
I was also trying to get the hang of filming myself talking about where I was, and taking stills of the countryside. When you aren't used to this sort of thing, you tend to not film yourself especially if there are people around purely out of embarrassment. I kept telling myself, "You are trying to make a production, Pony up and get on with it." Looking back at some of my early attempts, they were simply awful!

Great Falls, Montana

I left Hungry horse and rode towards Great Falls in Montana riding mostly Highway 89. I caught the tail end of the weather system I'd been in while in Canada and for the first half of the day it was back to being wet and miserable. The ups and downs and changes in circumstances on these trips are all part of the experience, at least that's what I told myself as pools of water filled my boots and funneled down between the cheeks of my arse. You can't have the ups without the downs — but I could have done without the River Shannon flowing through my nether regions.
As the Rocky's flatten out into prairies, you can see an unobstructed view of the horizon in every direction, and as far as I could see, it was all black rain clouds. I puckered up and continued to head south knowing that eventually the sun would shine, "The rain don't fall on the same dogs ass every day". I arrived in Choteau and

stopped for some hot food and to take the opportunity to dry off a bit. I sat in the corner of the restaurant people watching as I waited for my grub to arrive. Two booths up, what seemed like the dumbest girl in the world was having a conversation with a contender for the fattest person in the world. For the record, I'm a fat bastard and I could do with dropping 30lbs but in certain places in North America they have a unique brand of fat bastard, people that look like oversized bean bags. As their conversation wore on without any appreciation for the volume they were talking at, it became clear that these two people represented a threat to the gene pool of all humanity. They kept going on and on about some guy called Hank and whether he would, or would not call round with the truck. While they were talking, I made eye contact with one of the other folks in the restaurant, we both looked at each other as if to say, "Thick as planks!" I got to Great Falls later in the evening and after a shower I went out for some grub. I was served by a girl called Cody. She had a really sexy walk that accentuated an incredible figure, and made her blonde pony tail swing left and right across her back like a metronome. Even as I'm writing this nearly eighteen months later, I can remember her vividly. The husband and wife in the booth next to me ended up having a fight because the guy was ogling her too much. They left and I ogled Cody enough for the two of us, I nicknamed her "hypno-hoop". I hadn't had a girl friend in a very long time any my forecast was looking very bleak.

Billings, Montana

The plan for the next couple of days was to ride around Montana and get all, "Horse Whispery" so with that in mind, the next morning I set off in the general direction of Billings. They coined the nickname "Big Sky Country" for Montana, but to just call it that would be an injustice. It also has massive tracts of huge mountains, lakes, rivers and forests and wonderful rolling prairies. My first port of call was to drive through the Lewis & Clark forest, named after the same two lads who drew the Dixie line and did a huge amount of exploring and mapping of the Great North West in the early 1800s. It's lovely country to ride in and the roads were full of motorcyclists, all of whom waved as they passed. The state gets its name from the Spanish for mountain, Montaña and is the 4th largest state in America. It's about the size of Germany, so not surprisingly, getting anywhere in it, takes a long time. I was surprised by how much poverty there was in the

state, when I checked over 150,000 people or about 15% of the people living there lived below the poverty line. Most of the small towns had murals about Crystal meth destroying their communities so as beautiful as the state is, it seemed to have its fair share of problems. I pulled up at a highway intersection where people from all walks of life were pulling in to fill up. I sat on a bench downing some cold soda watching as they went about their business. There were hunters, farmers, city folk, Asians, African Americans, Indians but the strangest of the lot was a woman trying to get her Chihuahua to take a crap before they got back into the car. The whole time I sat there, country music blared out over the sound system and even though the song changed four or five times, the melody seemed to be constant. These moments where you take time out to look at the world racing by are moments I cherish, nobody knows you, you are sitting there without a care in the world, with no place to be and all day to get there. I bought my first bumper sticker in the garage, "Big Sky Montana". I put the remainder of the miles in and got to Billings, the last thirty miles on the straightest road imaginable cutting a path through an impossibly flat landscape. I found a place to stay and went out for a few beers and something to eat where I was served by yet another gorgeous waitress. At that stage it was over a year since I had a shag and little did I know my losing streak was set to continue every day for the rest of that year and well into the next one. I wrote in my diary "About 8 minutes with Princess Leia, that's all I need!"

Cody, Wyoming

The next day I set off to see the Little Big Horn battle site before looping South to Cody in Wyoming. This site is famous because its where Custer's last stand happened. It was the topic of at least five movies I saw growing up. Chaps in Ireland and I reckon probably England have a little giggle when they hear the words, "Little Big Horn" chiefly because across the pond, horn is another word for an erection. I can imagine the early settlers from Ireland and England as they rode through this land in their wagon trains having a little giggle to themselves "hee hee, Little Big Horn." On either side of the road as you approach the site are wheat fields stretching out to the horizon. The contrast of the blue sky with the yellow crops and rolling prairies below, took my breath away. The battle site is wonderfully preserved, in fairness the Americans know how to keep a National park looking

good. You can imagine the battle and how it played out when you stand on the hill where Custer fell. History isn't all that flattering to Custer and one of the first things you find out when you go to the site is that he's actually buried in Arlington cemetery in Washington DC. All that there is to remind you of where he fell is a little stone marker, with white writing on a black background, the monument is well done and not a bit tacky. I stood there looking at the marker with the long grass bending in the warm summers breeze taking the plaque in and out of view, it was a lovely moment. From there I crossed the Big Horn Mountains moving into the state of Wyoming. A sign as you cross the border says "Forever West" and the cowboy vibe is very much to the forefront in the state. Wyoming is also big, about the size of Britain, but with only half a million people living there, it's

absolutely empty. The road takes you up and over Mountains and as you're riding along you find yourself looking out over a vast plane below. The enormity of what I was looking at was very hard to take in. I was overcome with a feeling of just how lucky I was to be there. Later in the day, I was stopped on the road for about twenty minutes due to road works and talked with a Native American, who turned out to be an Inuit from Alaska. I asked him whether or not he was worried about getting burned in the heat of the sun to which he replied, "No I already got burnt once this year so I won't get burnt any more". This was one pink skinned Irishman who wished he shared that particular attribute.

I arrived in Cody late in the evening and had dinner on the sidewalk of the main street. As I sipped on my beer, just up the street the sun was setting as the gentlest of breezes blew into my face, the perfect end to a spell binding day. The next morning I'd breakfast just up the street from the motel and was served by the loveliest girl in the whole world. Yes, I'm sure with all these references to waitresses, I'm coming across as a sex starved nut job from Ireland, you'll get no argument from me. I reckon she gave me some extra scrambled eggs too.

It was now a week since I'd left Ireland and I was very excited because Yellowstone was on the docket for that day. It's a huge park that takes hours to drive through, but its an amazing place which draws over 3 million visitors every year. It was, believe it or not, the worlds first ever National Park. You can see everything from wild buffalo and wolves roaming the planes to geysers and large volcanic areas which steam with the heat from the earth's core. I was on a roll.

NOT DEAD YET

Red Lodge, Montana

As I left the park and cut up for Red Lodge Montana I rode the Beartooth Highway, which gets its name from one of the mountains which is visible on the route. It's one of the best motorcycle roads in the USA and it carves a path through an incredible series of twenty different mountains. Not surprisingly, its almost always jam packed with bikers. Along the way I stopped to help out a Canadian trio who had a puncture, in less than an hour they were back on their way with the tire fixed. Most of the motorcyclists I know observe a code where, if you pass a biker broke down by the side of the road, you always stop and help them if you can, you never know when you'll be the one that's stuck out there. I was after wandering in Montana for well over a thousand miles and it was time to start heading to somewhere closer to Los Angeles, so I made my way to Dillon, a full days ride away and still in the state of Montana. It was on days like that I realized just how big the USA is, every state is the size of a country in its own right, for example Texas is the size of France, and France is the largest country in the EU.

Dillon, Montana

The route took me back through another section of Yellowstone Park and there I saw a scene I know will stay with me forever. The road rose about a hundred yards above the plane. Halfway out to the horizon a river flowed and about a mile distant there was dense forest. A lone buffalo was treading his way down to the nearest bank of the river finding the best place to cross. He strode out into the water and maneuvered his way over and up the far bank of the river and continued his journey. It seemed like I was watching something from two hundred years earlier and the whole time it was unfolding, in my head I kept humming the soundtrack to Dances with Wolves. It was one of those days where you couldn't get a tune out of your head, but were really happy for that to be the case. A quick note, the conservation work that the USA government has done with buffalo has steadily grown their numbers to over 200,000 throughout the USA.

I continued on towards Dillon and stopped for gas taking time to hit the Men's to do a number 1. As I spent a

penny I looked at what I thought was a condom machine hung on the wall beside me, to my amazement it was something much more outlandish. On the dispenser on the far right was a huge sign saying "Rough Rider Condoms", with raised rubber studs for extra sensation, "fair enough" I thought to myself. In the middle was, "4 play" an erection ring which promised that if you made four purchases you would receive the entire series. Finally there was "Horney goat weed", a product to prolong sex with ingredients like Long Jack and Biopene. I started to wonder was it so long since I'd sex, the whole world had moved on to studded condoms, cock rings and performance enhancing pills? This was also Montana, not exactly known as an epicenter of sexual liberation and experimentation. It occupied my thoughts for a good part of the remainder of the day, "Just how far from the flock have you strayed Oisin!"

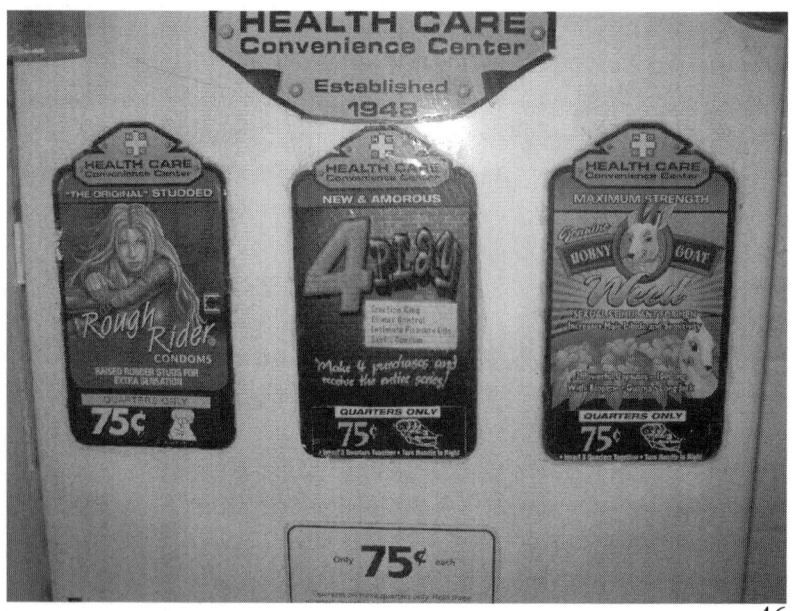

I knew when I started riding on the 9th day that I needed to put up some serious miles, I'd only four days to get to Los Angeles and even taking the most direct route it was well over a 1000 miles away, but I still had a lot of places I wanted to visit before then. With that in mind, I "Iron Butted" 558 miles the whole way to Wendover on the Nevada Utah border, riding mostly on highway 93. Along the way I met some great people who were really interested in not only me but also the trip and just loved the bike. A big barrel of man called Chris would have liked nothing better than to set off with me round the world and even offered to make a donation to the trip which I obviously declined but thanked him very much for the thought.

Wendover, Utah

The combination of being tired and roasting hot caused me to nearly fall asleep several times. If you start to dose in a car there's a good chance you could recover it as you roll out towards the verge of the highway, on a bike if you fall asleep, you're dead, plain and simple. Along the five hundred and fifty mile journey I rode in four different states, Montana, Idaho, Nevada and finally Utah and I'd a serious dose of monkey butt as I pulled into a place to stay.
Wendover is where the Bonneville Speedway is located. It was made famous by the film "The World's fastest Indian" with Anthony Hopkins and is one of the places in the world that everyone who is into speed should visit. I drove the bike down onto the flats and had a great time running the bike up to 80mph in various locations. One

of the great things about doing it in this location, is that you don't have the normal guides to tell you what speed you are going. On a road, apart from the odometer, the trees whizzing by or the white lines or other cars all tell you that, "Yep I'm moving fast" but in Bonneville because it's just a white salt surface under a blue sky, you've only the odometer and the wind in your face to guide you. The faster you go the more it feels like you are riding on a cloud. I think because I'm from Ireland where everything is green, I find this type of location more stimulating than most. Nothing grows there, there's no water, just heat, salt, and blue skies. For whatever reason the aridness really strikes a chord with me.

Later on I went into one of the Casino's for a buffet, I was starving. The whole place was full of either really old or grossly overweight people so I just had the main course and left. The last time I was in Wendover a teacher showed me one of only two places on earth, that you can see the curvature of the earth from land, and when it got dark, I went back to that location. As I sat there and quietly marveled at what I was looking at, namely the lights of the cars driving from Salt Lake City towards Reno as they drive over the flatness of the Salt flats, I got to wondering what each light represented. Each individual point of light was a person, or a family. They were all headed somewhere and all of them were blissfully unaware that they were being watched. It all makes you feel insignificant, and that as much as we'd like the world to revolve round us, the lights in the desert will be still there, whether or not we choose to look at them. I also started to think, "What if that teacher and I are the only two guys in the whole world who know where this place is?" It's not like it's marked and there isn't really even a place to pull in off the road to have a look at it. So, full

NOT DEAD YET

of the contentment which comes from "knowing things" which others don't, it was time to leave for Reno.

Reno, Nevada

The distance between Wendover and Reno is about four hundred miles but it feels like a thousand. The roads are impossibly straight and combined with the excruciating heat as you ride through the desert, it feels like you're in Purgatory. I stopped in a McDonald's in a small town along the way and a bum was making a nuisance of himself to get some food and money, which he got. He made everyone feel so uncomfortable the whole time he was there. As I studied him from a distance, I genuinely got the impression he was enjoying what he was doing, like he had it down to an art form. Further along the road I stopped for gas and something to drink. A van load of guys got out cussing and bitching about getting cleaned out in Reno and how they were "never going back to that shithole". A girl who I passed on the road about twenty miles earlier pulled in for gas and said hello as she went into the shop to buy some stuff. I couldn't help wonder where she was going, what her story was and why she was heading this way. Maybe she was headed to Reno to get work, maybe to put her life savings on the roulette wheel, on such things your mind mulls when you're

riding along. She looked a little bit lonely, just like me. I wanted to strike up a conversation to help pass the time and get some human interaction, but the moment passed. It was time to get going again. I got to Reno and for the first time since I got to the states I felt a little bit nervous about my surroundings. As with all Casino towns, there are lots of pawn shops, gun stores, and plac-

NOT DEAD YET

es where you buy liquor, a powerfully bad combination. I was meeting Mark O'Connor, who was from Ireland, he used to live just a couple of doors down from me and

had moved to Reno with Microsoft. He was the first person I'd been out with since leaving Ireland and I was delighted with not only the company but to find out what it was like to move from Ireland to the middle of Nevada. We went out for a serious steak and a couple of beers in a local Irish bar and got caught up on all the comings and goings from the road where we grew up.

Mammoth Lakes, California

I woke up the next morning and taking Mark's advice, I rolled up an amazing road to a place called Virginia City, an old western town. The road up was a real treat and after a couple of days getting scorched in the desert, a rain front moved in and soaked me, I couldn't complain. Taking Highway 395 south I eventually got to Mammoth Lakes in California where I stayed for the night, an easy ride to Los Angeles. The road I was planning to take would take me through Lake Tahoe and Yosemite National Park as it worked its way South through the Sierra Nevada Mountains. If the weather is good these are amazing places to visit, but so far all I was getting was pissing rain so I hadn't really taken in that much. When I was approaching Mammoth Lakes it was a Sunday and everyone was headed back to LA after the weekend. The road was mostly single lane and when you would get to the passing lanes, the whole convoy of cars you were stuck behind, would all turn into Mario Andretti's and start flooring it, at one stage I was doing 80mph and

was getting overtaken by all and sundry. As I got closer and closer to the centre of the weather front that had been drenching me, the temperature had dropped from 39degC in Nevada to 10degC as I stopped for the night. That night I went out for some grub and at the table next to me, there was a bunch of dicks from the film industry all shite-talking on about various films and such and such a director and this and that producer. They broke the poor waiter's heart. The menu was merely a guideline for them, and each and every one of them wanted a variation of what was displayed, with a different dressing or a custom dressing, oh to have a grenade handy. It took me back to Tok in Alaska where a year previously, I had gone out for something to eat. The choices were Dinner, did you want it or not? After dinner I rode around the town trying to find something to do but failed miserably and so headed back to my motel and watched TV for the rest of the night.

Los Angeles, California

On the 13th day of the trip I was bound for Los Angeles, I wasn't overly looking forward to driving into Los Angeles traffic but I reminded myself that I'd ridden through Guatemala City, Los Angeles wasn't going to be anything to be concerned about. I met a couple on a bike who rode with me as far as Bishop, just south east of Yosemite National Park. It was great to have some company.
The Sierra Nevada's dominated the views the whole way south, they are some of the most striking mountains anywhere in the world. The road to LA took me through an airplane graveyard in Mojave as I rode Highway 14

south into the desert where the heat became absolutely stifling. Leaving that behind I took the 401 into LA, a ten lane highway jam packed with cars. I found my way with very little trouble, it was my fourth time to LA so I knew the route pretty well. Later on that evening I met up with Joe and we got on with the very serious job of planning how the hell we were going to get this production made.

CHAPTER 5
CONFESSION AND HITTING THE BACK WALL

From a very young age, I had very big feet and had huge problems trying to find shoes that fit me. When I was growing up my mother would buy me shoes which were one or two sizes too big so I wouldn't outgrow them before they were worn out. The result was, I ended up walking around like Ronald McDonald with a big dopey looking pair of clogs on for the vast majority of my youth. Some of the slagging I'd get included, "So, are you paying road tax on those shoes." "They're fucking canal barges!", "Do those shoes come with indicators?", "Hey Big foot, ya big foot bollix ya" or the classic "Ya big shoe wearing bastard ya!" and so it went all the days of my youth. Right now I've a size 14 foot (size 15 US), and I told myself a long time ago that if my feet were to grow another inch I'd just start cutting my toes off.

It might be a good time to just write a little bit about the word "cunt". How did he go from shoe to cunt? It'll all make sense I promise.

Women hate that word. In Ireland however, and Scotland for that matter, it's never used to describe female nether regions, and when it is, I do think it's a particularly dirty word. In the USA, it is pretty much the worst word you can possibly say whereas in Scotland, it can even be a term of endearment "Awreet Cunt! Howya doin!" or "He's a funny cunt that boy!" When it's not used to describe a body part, I happen to think it's one of the best words ever invented. I love how explicit it is. If you were to say that someone is "making a cunt" out of something, your left in no doubt that they are doing a bad job. If you asked someone what a particular person is like and the answer came back, "He is a cunt." It is definitive, he's not nice. In Ireland it's increasingly used

NOT DEAD YET

in positive terms. I'll give you some examples. A difficult math(s) problem is described as a "Cunt of a problem!" A professional who needs a lot of data before making a decision, could be described flatteringly as "a Cunt for data!", similarly a person who just got a great deal on a new car, would be affectionately and favorably described as "a cute cunt!" In fact, if you just told a friend about a great deal on anything you just bought, were he or she to describe you as "a cute cunt" afterwards, you'd be pretty happy about that.

Back, to the shoes. One day, I went to confession in Ireland, a bi-monthly event. I think I was about eight years old. The confessional chamber was made of wood and about eight feet tall. It was a standalone unit and no matter what church you went into, was almost always made of wood and stood about a foot from the wall along one of the side isles of the church. It had three seated compartments which you walked into and all had a door which was closed behind you. The one in the middle was for the priest and the ones either side of him were for the sinners. You knew there was a priest in there because of the yellow light which shone through the purple curtain pulled across the top half of the priests door. The priest would open and close the shoot on your confessional chamber when he was ready to hear your confession.

A point worth mentioning is that people in Ireland always went to the same church, and I do mean always. The only time I'd ever been to a different church was when someone I knew was getting married or died in a different parish. Back then, people didn't move. In the twenty years growing up in Castle Close Clondalkin, I can only think of three families that left the cluster of eighty or so houses on our road.

Normally you would queue up for confession by sitting on one of the benches close to the confessional and wait your turn to go in. You would kneel down and let on you were praying lifting your head occasionally to watch people come out of the box and try and figure out how much of a sinner they were based on how long they would spend praying afterwards.

Depending on how sinful you were, you might get "Ten Hail Mary's" which was the typical sentence. If you were a complete bollix you'd get "Ten Hail Mary's, Ten Our Fathers' and Ten Glory be to the Fathers". As a by the by, devotion to Mary was far stronger in the Irish Catholic faith than someone not from Ireland might guess. The example of the typical sentence of ten Hail Mary's was the typical case, but there was also the Rosary which involved reciting 50 Hail Mary's, 5 Our Fathers and 5 Glory Be to the fathers. The rosary, then also had five different types of mysteries, so it was possible to get the moral equivalent of "life imprisonment" which would be to recite all five mysteries of the Rosary, a total of two hundred and fifty Hail Mary's, twenty five Our Father's, and twenty five Glory Be to the Father's. Your Rosary beads would be burning in your hands from all the handling after it. Each bead constituted a prayer, as you finished one prayer you moved on a bead. One lap of the beads constituted just one of the mysteries of the Rosary. Needless to say if you were bold enough to get the mysteries, there was a good chance you'd starve to death before you finished.

This particular night there was about twelve or so people queuing up to be absolved and we shuffled along the bench as the priest worked his way through the waiting people. Normally I'd go up with one of my brothers and we'd sit on the same bench being very giddy. All the benches were wooden so if someone farted, it sounded like someone beating a snare drum which would always result in a round of uncontrollable giggles, which would only subside when the shoot of the priest's confessional opened.

If you can imagine the scene, a large empty and dimly lit church with twelve or so souls queuing up for absolution in front of a large wooden confessional lit only by a light behind a purple curtain where the priest was sitting.

It was my turn to go in.

I thought about what I'd tell him, "Lying to my mother, using bad language"; there was no way I was going to tell him that I was having carnal thoughts about the paper girls arse. I got up off the bench and walked the ten or twelve steps on the cold granite floor in my oversized shoes. As I opened the door and stepped up to get into my side of the confessional, my shoe caught on the lip of the door, causing me to fall head first into the confessional. The whole unit tilted back eventually banging up against the rear wall with a thunderous bang. All the people who were queuing in the church came over and pulled the whole thing back down to a chorus of "Jesus Mary and Joseph!" The priest and an old lady who was in the other side of the confessional got out with red, shocked and angry faces.

"Sorry Father", I said meekly.

I was pretty sure he called me a cunt under his breath.

It mightn't sound like much now, but believe me, back in 1978, in Clondalkin Village in Dublin Ireland, this was the modern day equivalent of shagging a goat in the town square and yep, you guessed it, I got the five mysteries of the Rosary.

CHAPTER 6
TRIP PREP IN LOS ANGELES

I eventually made it to Los Angeles, booked into a hotel and gave Joe a buzz to come pick me up when he was ready. We'd a week to get a lot of stuff done and when we hooked up for beers and nacho's that night, we came up with a list of stuff we needed to take care of.

It broke down into a couple of categories. Firstly there was Mechanical, the modifications we needed to make to the bikes to make them as bullet proof as possible for what we knew would be an unbelievably testing journey. We'd over 45,000 miles ahead of us, any enhancements we could make now would no doubt pay us back many times over during the course of the following year. Also, what parts on the bike based on our research were likely to fail en route, if we could take some of them as spares, we could prevent ourselves getting stranded in a country that didn't have a BMW dealer.

Second was filming equipment, we still needed to buy some cameras and film gear, as well as fit the mounts we were going to use to get the action shots we'd need for the documentary. We also needed to figure out a microphone solution for how we could record reasonable noise free audio from the Helmet cams as we rode along.
Third was the huge task of figuring out exactly what we were going to bring other than the film gear. The fact that we were taking so much filming equipment meant that we had to cut out a lot of other stuff, for example our big production camera took up nearly one whole pannier which meant I'd no room for tools, we'd have to share a set. The same was true for puncture repair equipment, first aid kits, maps, guide books and a multitude of other bits and pieces.
The big test would be, could we carry everything we needed to film a documentary and all our other kit and

personal effects on just two bikes. Most people who are going on a journey like this struggle to find room for everything and they don't have to cope with carrying all the film gear, with spare tapes, memory cards, hard disks, cables, chargers, and of course computers so we could back up the film we would be taking every day. It didn't look doable.

We kicked off with the mechanical modifications. My bike already had a headlight shield, a wheel lock to prevent damaging the forks when I'd crash, a throttle position sensor cover and a set of extra saddle bags for carrying extra gear. To this we added an additional set of crash bars and a quick disconnect power outlet for hooking up power to our helmet cameras, as well as some camera mounts. We duplicated anything done to my bike on Joe's.

One of Joe's friends, Harry, helped us by manufacturing

the camera mounts which could be installed anywhere on the metal frame of the bike and swapped to different locations with ease. Harry was a great guy who had his own custom shop where he took on any manner of modification, believe it or not he made a VW Golf Motorcycle. All of Joe's friends made me feel right at home and it seemed like every night we were going out with a different bunch. It made me feel good about Joe as a prospective traveling and business partner, anyone with this many friends and people who like him, must be a great guy. We also went out with Joe's long term partner Jeanette, they had been going out for 16 years. It was only natural that she was apprehensive about him going on such a long trip, a year is a long time and its not like we were taking a low risk path.
Every day we'd make a list of what we had to do and then at the end of the day compare notes on how we were

doing, and then scrub through what was on the docket for tomorrow. The hardest thing about getting stuff done in LA was the traffic, you can spend hours sitting on the

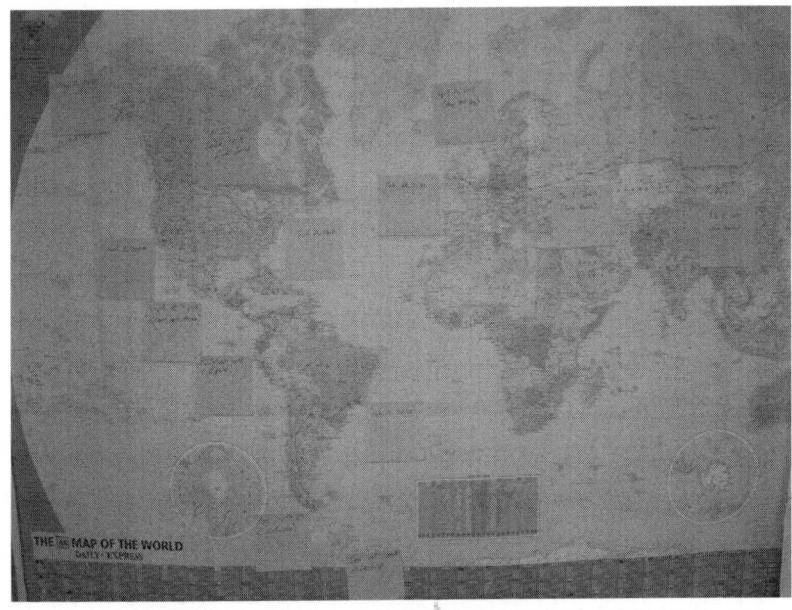

freeway waiting to get to where you want to go.
Time was quickly passing, our goal was to leave on the 1st of September, and as the day came closer and closer, Joe was concerned we weren't ready to go. This was the second full week I'd spent with him, and I was starting to get to know him a bit better. He'd worked as his own boss for years and hated feeling like he was being managed, which I think he felt I was doing by insisting that we leave on September 1st. He wanted to push the start date to the second, because Jean was an aerobics instructor and had a class that morning. She was going to come along with us for the first few days and help us shoot some drive by scenes and action footage. Even with

weeks of notice she wasn't able to rearrange it, it didn't pass my sniff test. I thought that Joe was using this as an excuse for something else. I bit my lip but made it clear that one way or another I was leaving on the 2nd and he could just catch up with me if it didn't suit.

I left him to have a day or two to sort out his company stuff and hung out by myself for the final two days. I managed to get myself into a negative mental spiral as I started thinking about all the things that happened. I felt I'd hauled my ass from Ireland to there and he wasn't ready even with all the notice he had. On top of that, Jean was coming along for the first few days but that had morphed into Jean coming along till we crossed into Mexico. I started to wonder whether or not he was committed to completing the project. I had flown to LA for a week in August already to prepare for the trip, and had now driven to his home city from Dublin, Ireland. I'd left my job and we'd spent a small fortune on equipment that he said we'd need. I was also staying in a hotel for the second time, if Joe had come to Ireland, I'd have sorted him out with a place to stay. I'd already sunk well over $25,000 dollars into the project (buying the bike, shipping it to North America, Pre trip flight to LA, 15 days hotel stay over two trips to LA, Camera equipment, Modifications to the bike, insurance for the bike and myself, rider gear) and over the course of the day I convinced myself that the whole project was a big mistake. Joe showed up at my hotel that afternoon we talked for over an hour, I flagged all my concerns and for the most part he was able to allay my fears. We patched things up, we were leaving on the second. I should have walked away at that point.

There was overwhelming data to say that we were completely in over our heads and it was never going to work. I was caught up in the idea of making our own "Long Way Round". I also couldn't bear the thought of going back home with my tail between my legs. I'd left my job, told all my friends and family that I was heading off filming a documentary, I just couldn't give up. The line items that were obviously broke at that point included: 1) We had a huge high quality camera, I didn't know how to use it and Joe wasn't overly familiar with using it either 2) We were filming in three formats - AVI (Helmet CAM), Tape (production camera - no clue what this format was but we hadn't taken any video with it and converted it to a common format for editing yet) and two different variants of HD1080p - 3) We were going to edit the film using Final Cut Pro, neither of us knew how to use it 4) We hadn't scoped out the length of time editing the project would take when we got back - it was likely to take 6 months for two amateurs working full time, if I'd known that at the start - I would never have even started. 5) Neither of us had any acting experience and thinking that we were going to be able to just plonk a video camera at each other and perform, was naive in the extreme. 6) We were still only getting to know each other. We didn't know how to diffuse arguments that arose between us and being men, we had difficultly communicating how we were feeling.

Stubbornness prevailed in the end and we agreed to continue.

As we worked through some of the technical details of filming, we had a shocking eye opener as to how much work it was dealing with the different types of problems that cropped up. It was way more difficult to integrate the file types from the various cameras than we thought. It was almost impossible to get a low vibration action shot from the HD cameras. No matter what we tried we couldn't get decent audio up to the helmet cameras without a serious amount of wind noise. Every attempt we made to reduce or filter out the noise further proved the point that we were complete amateurs. Our editing software, Final Cut Pro wasn't straight forward to use, both of us had been raised on Windows machines, so just trying to use the editing software and get used to the Mac at the same time was a challenge.

We talked about taking a week long editing course when we got back from the trip, realistically this was something we should have done from the start - at least that way we'd have known what sort of shots worked well and what didn't, we kept muddling on reassuring ourselves that things would work out.

CHAPTER 7
SOUTH WESTERN USA

We spent a few hours talking about what exactly we were trying to do and why, somewhere in all the running around over the last seven days, we'd lost sight of it a bit and it felt like things were starting to come together. We knocked out all the final packing, the bikes were in tip top shape, all the modifications were complete, the weights were balanced across each pannier and most importantly, we managed to fit everything we needed to take into the available space, without having to break out the KY jelly. The trip was about to start, and we were ready to go.

D-Day came and it was roasting. Standing around in my Alpine Stars All Weather Gore-Tex trousers had my arse feeling like it was cooked and ready for carving. All day from early morning till the sun went down, it never dropped below 35degC. Did you ever see the episode of Friends where Ross has the leather pants? It was the same sort of thing, by the end of the day my trousers felt like a big two legged condom had been rolled up on me. I thought I would be taking them off with a paint scraper by the end of the day.

Kingman, Arizona

We left Los Angeles a little later than planned, it always takes more time to pack than you'd think and we burned straight away for Barstow about two hours north east of Los Angeles. It's a good place to stop because it marks the end of LA traffic, a sensible place to pull over and take a break. I was so thirsty I felt like I had to peel the tongue off the roof of my mouth.

From there we rolled to Needles, where both of us discovered problems with our bikes. Joe's sump guard was

NOT DEAD YET

ready to fall off, two of the bolts were broken, and my final drive had a leak. First day, not three hundred miles driven and we'd both non trivial problems with the bikes. We weren't panicking as we knew we'd be able to get them sorted in Phoenix, Arizona. Joe had a talent for the mechanical stuff and we talked the problems over, obviously the final drive was the larger of the two problems. I wasn't sure if it was something that needed to be fixed immediately. When it came to anything mechanical with the bike, I trusted him completely. If he said it was ok to drive, well, that was a 20 times more informed opinion than mine. We said we'd monitor it closely and get it sorted in Phoenix and continued on.

Route 66 runs both parallel and at times is part of Interstate-40 and where they were separate roads, we took Route 66. With it being September, the tourist season had dried up and the road was completely empty. We

pulled into Kingman Arizona that night, with the first day done having covered over 350miles, it felt great to be finally on the road.

Prescott, Arizona

Our second day on the road was very straight forward. We cruised on Route 66 for the first half of the day, and for the second, rode down to see Joe's sister in Prescott, Arizona. On the way to her house, we drove through a swarm of bees. It was the first time it's ever happened to me and the best way I can describe it, is that it's like someone threw a bucket of marbles at your helmet as you drove by at 60mph. They were splattered all over my windshield and visor with about five of them hanging dead in my beard. Joe got a bunch right in the face as he'd been riding with his face shield up, one blowing up on his sunglasses. How we didn't get stung I'll never know, the 60mph probably had a lot to do with it though. That afternoon we'd more minor bike problems, my final drive was continuing to leak, my rear indicator stopped working and Joe's front bulb blew. The most used phrase in the previous 48hours was "BMW's man, fucking BMW's". We stopped in a cool cafe called the Road Kill Cafe for grub. I had visited the place the year before and it has the best apple pie you'll ever taste. You know it's good, when you're taking a nap later and you're still thinking about it.
Up to this point, with respect to filming we were probably averaging a D "Minus", the main issue being that any time we took the HD cameras out we both turned into orang-utans and couldn't seem to get a sentence out to

save our lives. I guess it was only natural, neither of us had any experience at this sort of thing. We told ourselves that this is the worst we'd be and we'd get better as we went.

Phoenix, Arizona

The following morning I went out to fill up the bike with Gas. When I came back I noticed a small pool of final drive oil on the ground, and given the oil reservoir only has 180ml worth of storage, this was a major problem. It had been dripping but we'd been topping it up and

getting by, but with this much of a pool forming in just a second or two, the drive could leak all the oil and tear itself apart at any time. After I inserted about two billion bucks in the swear jar, we burned straight down to Phoe-

nix to Victory BMW, where we got it repaired.
I has used these guys the year previous when I came through to get the bike all sorted for Latin America. The guys were great and took us in straight away. As the folks were working on my bike we decided to head off and find a place to stay. No sooner was Joe's key in the ignition than he had a EWS ignition ring failure and his bike wouldn't start, all of a sudden both of our bikes were on the operating table. The EWS ignition ring is a known weakness in the 2006 BMW, I wont bore you with the details, suffice to say its something that BMW should have recalled and fixed on the 2006 model years ago, the bike goes as dead as a dodo and you can't even jump start it. I'm certain the engineers working at BMW wanted to recall this problem as its talked about on all the motorcycle forums but no doubt the accountants at BMW got in the way, "Sure that would cost too much

money!" We ended up hanging out in BMW all day, the guys there were great to hang out with and let us film them changing out the seals and the EWS.

The worrying thing was that we were only three days into the trip and we both had a complete and utter show stoppers on the bikes. Make no mistake, had these issues happened in the Bolivian desert, they would have been identifying us by the age of the vulture crap on our bones. After the lads in Victory BMW had finished up the repairs, it was time for some grub. We chatted about the schedule, and even though it was only three days since we left LA, we were already two days behind our original schedule. I'd no confidence in the bikes, the 2006 BMW 1200 wasn't as reliable as the 1150, and we were both worried about whether or not they'd make it. To drown our sorrows we had a couple of 22 ounce Fosters in the Outback steakhouse.

Page, Arizona

The forecast for the following day was for storms north of Phoenix and the weather guys were spot on. About seventy miles south of Flagstaff we got pummeled by a doozie. We stopped in Flagstaff for gas and then rode off in the direction of Sunset Crater National Park where they filmed a piece of the movie Easy rider. It was overcast, and the fact that we were soaked through, meant we didn't really get anything out of it. From there we rode to see some Wupatki Indian ruins, which apparently date as far back as the 11th century. Thankfully, as the evening wore on the sun finally came out in time to treat us to a wonderful sunset as we headed for the town of Page in

Northern Arizona. As we rode north there was an orange hue floating above the distant hills to the west. On our right side, the moon was rising, reflecting the orange color as it rose above the terracotta cliffs that seem to be everywhere in this part of the world. Every now and then the moon would get covered by a cloud and the whole world would go completely dark. We were riding on highway 89 with only a set of cat's eyes to light our way. Several times I came over a hill with the full beams on and the cat's eyes in the centre of the road seemed to stretch off into infinity, cutting through the pitch black-

ness all around.

As you get closer to Page the road cuts its way through the gigantic shadows of mountains barely visible in the moonlight. With Joe riding behind me, my shadow was constantly thrown up onto the cliffs as we wound our

way through the hills north in the direction of Page. On account of it being Memorial Day weekend, all of Page's places to stay were sold out. We continued ten miles up the road to the Cowboy Inn where every room had its own name in a cowboy theme, my room was called "Rodeo Rider". I thought to myself "Jayzus, I'd love a ride!" I was knackered so I went to the room, turned off the light and went to sleep. The next morning we moved on in the direction of Zion Canyon. Zion Canyon is a little like the Grand Canyon, except you get to ride through the bottom of the canyon as opposed to looking at it from above. The canyon itself is over 3,000ft deep and runs for over 16 miles and along the way you pass through several tunnels and are constantly confronted with massive red cliffs as the road winds its way through.
We pulled over and tried to start filming what we were seeing. We didn't have a script to follow. What would

we say? Do we just film ourselves driving through the canyon? How much footage should we get? How much

of the final documentary would be about Zion? We had absolutely no clue what were doing so we settled for trying to film shots of us driving through the canyon and some stills of the rock formations and wild life.

At this stage, we were constantly experimenting with different camera types and angles. The big production camera took fantastic images but it was too much hassle to get the file from tape, put it onto your laptop, then compress it, then cut it together so you could make a quick video to upload to Youtube. It was also a major pain in the ass to constantly unpack it and set it up on the trip pod, take what might amount to ten seconds of footage and then pack it away again. The hand held HD cameras file size was way too big, and then the POV cams which were attached to the bikes were ok from a file size perspective but the audio coming from the microphones was terrible and the footage wasn't in HD. We tried some cheap HD cameras which we held in our hands as we rode through the canyon, the result was mediocre at best. All of these quality and integration problems had convinced us to spend a day on just film formats to see if we could consistently get an output which met our needs. We knew we had time and location on our sides while we were in the USA, but once we got to Mexico,

we would have to make do with what we had.
Ely, Nevada

The following day we wanted to see if we could make it

the whole way to Bonneville for the speed trials but by 6pm we were both wrecked and so pulled into Ely instead, leaving only a 130 mile jaunt up to Wendover the following morning. We went to Great Basin National Park along the way where you can get views of the desert from 10,000ft up and see some of the most ancient trees on Earth. We finished the day off sitting on a patio downing a couple of frosted Coors light's after a long hot day in the desert.

I had a dream that night where I woke up covered in spiders. I can't help wondering what part of evolution thought it would be useful for our survival, if every now and then we woke up roaring in utter terror! I went in for a shower the following morning and there was a teeny weeny little spider on the wall, I hit him with the equivalent of a lump hammer about 20 times "Die Satan's spawn! Die!"

NOT DEAD YET

Wendover, Utah

We spent the next two days in Bonneville, the idea was we'd take a day off and work on video formats and integration. Once we'd made a bit of progress, we went down to the salt flats to film some speed runs, running the bikes up to 100mph to see if we could film it. Simul-

taneously, we'd also get the footage on the POV cameras so when it would come time to make the production, we could cut the whole thing together and it might make a good scene. One of the problems we encountered was that there was a lot of rain the previous week so the salt was a lot softer than normal. It completely covered the

bikes in salt and made the surface less stable than you'd like. With all this in mind, I set off shitting bricks to do my runs. I ran it up to 100mph twice and while it was nerve wracking, it was absolutely exhilarating. While 100mph isn't that fast, to do it on soft salt is pretty radical, however there's lots of folks driving machines there during speed week well above 200mph, so it wasn't that studly. Once we were done we headed to the buffet, and nailed about 30,000 calories a piece. The grub was magic and in a day or two, I knew I'd be falling off the top of the crap of the century. Wendover is an ok town, but as is the usual story in towns where you have casinos, there's always at least as many pawn shops. The casinos are full of elderly people playing slots and by and large no one seems to be happy or smiling. The people who worked in the hotels weren't the sharpest tools in the shed, I guess it's hard to attract good staff into the desert.

The mad thing is that the town should be great. It should market itself to petrol heads and speed enthusiasts all over the world. The speedway is hardly mentioned in the town really, or at least you would never know walking around the town, that five miles out the road there's people riding machines on the ragged edge having the time of their life.

Mexican Hat, Utah

We made our way to Mexican hat, the closest town to Monument Valley. To get to the town, you have to take a winding dirt road down the side of a mountain with a cliff face on one side and a sheer drop always on the other, with no road barrier. It's easily one of the most thrilling roads in North America, albeit a short one. Once we got to the town we went out for some grub in a restaurant called Swinging Steaks. The "Chef" is a cowboy who has a grill which swings back and forward over the flames ten feet from the seating area. It was nice in a novelty sort of way. The next day we set off in the direction of Monument Valley, one of the world's most awesome spectacles. It was very noticeable there that almost all of the tourists were from Europe. It really roared at you, everywhere you looked and in all the voices you heard. There wasn't an American to be seen. Maybe it was just the time of the year.

Flagstaff, Arizona

From there we rolled back down to Flagstaff, our last crossing of Route 66. The following day we'd move on down to Phoenix and get any kit we were missing before heading into Mexico. I also planned to get an oil change

on the bike. The next time I'd see a quality BMW dealer would be Colombia, so I wanted the bike tip top before taking on Mexico and Central America.
I settled in to watch a bit of TV, it was Joe's last night with Jean so I left them to say goodbye to each other. The most noticeable thing about US TV (apart from all the ads) is that you can see almost every manner of violence and mutilation, but every swear word is completely dubbed and there's zero nudity, not even a little bit of it, not even one boob. Why gratuitous violence is deemed socially acceptable, but swear words and nudity are censored out is beyond me. "That guy just shot that guy in the head" said Timmy. Yes he did but he dropped and F-bomb while doing it, so turn off the TV.

Phoenix, Arizona

We collected the bikes from Victory BMW, who as always did a bang up job getting them ready. After a bunch of catching up with folks I know in Phoenix, we rode south, headed for Tombstone. Andy Flanagan, who'd been ferrying us around Phoenix helping us replace damaged or missing kit came along for the spin on his bike.
On the south side of Tucson we pulled into Pima Airfield, also knows as an Airplane Graveyard, the stats on the place are out the door. There are a total of 4700 planes of every variety, spread across 2500 acres of land. It started as a result of the cold war thawing, when Reagan and Gorbachov started to downsize their respective military arsenals. The Americans put their stuff here to decommission it, so the Soviets could use satellite photos

to check on the USA's implementation of arms reduction. B52 bombers, Stealth fighters, jumbo jets, helicopters, you name it, it's there and it's a great way to spend an afternoon. Joe was in his element, I think he would

gladly have spent days just walking around the place.

Tombstone, Arizona

That evening we ended up in Boot hill, Tombstone. I was there in 1997 and it was a good day out and was very authentic but the touristy folks have been up to mischief since then and it's been butchered. It looks all nice and pretty now. It's a cowboy graveyard, nice and pretty isn't something any of these places ever were. Tombstone itself was made famous by Wyatt Earp and Doc Holiday and the gunfight at the OK Corral which went down

in American Western folklore. The movies Wyatt Earp with Kevin Costner and Tombstone, with Kurt Russell

NOT DEAD YET

caused a major spike in tourist visits which also prompted them to rejuvenate Boot Hill. We talked about it that evening between gulps of beer and we reckoned that when it came to relics of the old West, they should just try and prevent it decaying any further. After all, it's supposed to look all roughed up. The powers that be shouldn't try and change it into something they think people want to see. It is what it is, that's the attraction.

We altered the plan a little and decided to stay an extra day in Tombstone and do some touristy stuff and try and get a bunch of it on film, then we'd cut down to Douglas on the Mexican border the day after. The main reason for the change of plan was that it was Mexican Independence Day, it didn't make sense to be crossing into the country on a national holiday. While myself Joe and Andy were out for Dinner, I got a text from home which had two XX's on the end of it. I asked Joe whether or not they did that stuff in the states, y'know sign off with various amounts of X's. In Ireland if you finish off an email to a girl who is a friend or a girl you like, you'll use a single X, if she's your girlfriend you'll use XXX. If she's a relation you might use XO to designate a kiss and a hug. It seems like the Americans didn't use this convention, so myself Andy and Joe went back and forward about the meaning of a single X, or XX or even XXX. It turned

out it all means very different things in the States versus Ireland and the UK, I'm sure its a tremendous comfort for you to know that bikers talk about such manly things on the road. The next day we combed up and down Tombstone and filmed as much as there was to be filmed - probably the most interesting place was the Birdcage Theatre. While it was surprisingly small, and didn't look like it could hold too many people, it was interesting to see how people had a good time back then. There's also a couple of pictures of Wyatt Earp's girlfriend, Josephine Sarah Marcus, who was an utter knockout even by todays standards.

USA / Mexico Border

Our biggest day since leaving LA was almost upon us, today we would cross into Mexico. We left Tombstone at about 8am and headed south east on Highway 80 for Douglas, a short run of about 50 miles. Along the way we passed an incredible open cast mine called the Lavender Pitt, close to the town of Bisbee. It was only closed in 1974.

We arrived at the border for about 9am and got our paperwork together for the border crossing. We went into the border office and there was a problem when one of the girls tried to process my application. She told me that I already had imported a bike, and couldn't import another without canceling the first one. The bike to which she was referring was the bike I did the Pan American bike trip on, the previous year. I forgot to clear the bike through customs when I left Mexico and went into Guatemala. Without the bike or the permit, there was no way they were issuing me with another. So for four hours with the aid of a fantastic border guard I tried to prove to them that I had left the country with the bike, and could they make an exception.

At about 1pm they said, "Ok, we've talked to a guy, Jose Antonio Casas (made me wish I'd a triple barrel name) and if you go to Nogales, which is south of Tucson he will be able to help you."

I could see Joe was pretty pissed off. We were going to have to burn another day on the border crossing at a minimum, and what If I wasn't allowed in at all? Would that mean the project would be over before it even started? As part of how we divvied up the responsibilities on the trip, it was my job to get us through the borders given I'd quite a bit of experience, and here I was flunking lunch at the first attempt. The second point was that I'd

been harping on about being so far behind schedule, and there I was causing us to lose another day. We rode West to Nogales, and passed through the American side of the border and arrived at the Mexican processing center. Nobody spoke any english, so all I got was "You need to go to KM 21 in Mexico." That's where the customs office was apparently. At this stage it was 4:30pm, so we had two options. Either we went into Mexico to KM 21, which sounded suspiciously like the sort of place they castrate Irishmen, and make yanks eat the resultant bratwurst, or we give up and try again tomorrow. We said "Fuck it, let's get a motel and try again tomorrow." We had two problems:
Would the aforementioned Jose Antonio Casas be working on Saturday (it was friday)? Only he knew what was going on. What if I got there and they told me to fuck off back in the general direction I came from. The only solution the border guys were offering was to ship the original bike back to Mexico and export it properly, "Fuck that!"

CHAPTER 8
LEDWIGES

NOT DEAD YET

I can hardly remember anything about growing up, it's like all my memories start at the age of 14. I can remember stuff from before then, but I have to try, and what I do remember is all reeking with stuff I'd rather forget. Well, what's all this got to do with motorcycling? When you're riding a motorcycle there is nowhere to hide. Your head is stuck in a helmet. There is no radio, just you, the view, the sound of the wind, the vibration of the bike and the world passing by so quickly at your side and yet so slowly ahead.

In these situations especially on the worlds open planes, thoughts and images come flooding back into your head in an uncontrollable manner. If you were in a car you could let down the window, change the radio station, put on a different CD, strike up a conversation with the person next to you, and maybe even make a phone call to a friend, anything to change the radio frequency in your head. In a helmet there is nowhere to run, you have to deal with each and every random thought as they torment, amuse and keep you company mile after mile.

> "Through The Force, things you will see.
> Other places.
> The future…the past…old friends long gone"
> Yoda.

Sometimes a hilarious memory will arrive and you find yourself tearing down the road at 70mph roaring laughing. A memory of something that happened to me 27 years ago is a good example.

At the time, Clondalkin, the village where I grew up had only a couple of shops which sold groceries. Was it

Smith's, Murphy's and Ledwidges? Something tells me not to try to think too hard about it. Anyway, my mother had long since used up a line of credit in Smith's, which back then was called "putting it on tick." If you wanted a loaf of bread but didn't have any money, you would say to the grocer, "Can I get that on tick?" which meant you'd pay him later.

Ledwidges was now the only place in the village where we could get something and pay later. I hated having to go into a shop and ask for stuff on tick, it was so embarrassing. The person behind the counter would always give you a message to give to your mother to call in and pay back some of the money which was owed. The fact that my mother owed money all over the village meant that she couldn't go out any more, although she didn't mind sending up yours truly to be the patsy. On this particular day my mother was sending me up to Ledwidges with a shopping list.

We didn't have a car, so I had to walk about a mile up to the shop and a mile back, with the back-leg the worst as you'd be dragging down a half dozen plastic bags of messages. Messages, yep that's what we called groceries back then, if you were gone to the shop for groceries you were gone for "messages."

I stood in our back room reading through the list, if I got it wrong there would be a right hand in the kisser waiting for me when I got back, I read it out to her to make sure I knew what I was getting myself in for. I scanned the list hoping to God that there wouldn't be a stone of spuds on it. Carrying down bags of messages which included 14 Lbs of potatoes would leave you feeling like an orangutan by the time you got home. Reading it out,

"Bread, milk, sugar, butter, Napisan, Napisan, me fuckin bollix, I'm not getting you fuckin Napisan!" I didn't know what Napisan was, but I reckoned it must have been small nappies (nappi-san get it?), so therefore must be women's sanitary towels. We had so many names for them when we were growing up, (Crash mats, Man hole covers, jam rags, maxi pads the list went on and on) I hadn't heard the name Napisan before but was certain it must mean crash mats, and it was bang out of order for me to be sent up for them, especially getting them on tick. That was "women's business". (Napisan as it turns out is actually used for starching shirt collars, something I was blissfully unaware of until I was in my mid-twenties. When I found out, I nearly died from the bout of laughter which ensued.)

My mother waved a fist at me at which point I skedaddled up the road before she followed through with her threat to "slit your throat in six places!"

There were two routes to the village from our house in Castle Park, one via the Watery Lane and the other through the main Castle Park Road. I would always walk up via Castle Park and come back down the Watery Lane to avoid meeting anyone who'd see me dragging all the bags of shopping behind me.

I got to the Ledwidges none the wiser that Napisan was for shirt collars and went about putting all the grocery items on the list in the basket, taking time to do several drive-through runs in the isle where the crash mats were stored. I was desperately hoping to see Napisan, and "I was in my hole" getting into a conversation with anyone who worked in the shop centered around, "Excuse me, do you have Napisan" With the basket full of everything but the Napisan, I did my last run through the crash mat isle. Not seeing Napisan, I picked up what I was certain must have been a good alternative, Vespre Ultra towels. I went up to the checkout and the girl helped me bag the items, taking care as they always did back then, to put the "Women's business" into a brown paper bag. The girl who put them into the bag looked at me with one of those looks which conveyed "Why the fuck is your Mother sending you up for these?"

I burned home with the bags of messages, down the watery lane, desperate not to meet any of the lads. If I'd been found walking down the street with this particular payload, I would have been teased about it till I was 52 years old.

I got home and unpacked the bag onto the dining room table where my mother was sitting drinking a cup of tea. I unpacked the bags per the list, reading it out as I unpacked the bags to avoid a smack in the head. As I retrieved the last item from the bag I said, "They had no Napisan so I got you these", handing her the big shiny yellow pack of Vespre ultra pads.

I'll never forget the look on her face as she was trying to draw a link between starching shirt collars and women's sanitary towels. Her face then settled to a look of, "What sort of a gobshite, am I rearing!"

NOT DEAD YET

CHAPTER 9
NORTHERN MEXICO

It's worth taking a moment to set the scene in Mexico at the time we were due to cross the border. Let me begin by saying that the Mexican people are wonderful. They are welcoming, humble and care deeply that you have a good impression of their country. It has cities to match anything in the USA and Europe like Guadalajara, Mexico City, Guanajuato, and Zacatecas but it also has terrible poverty.

To the south of the country is Guatemala and Central America, which is significantly poorer than Mexico, so the easiest way out of Mexico in search of economic prosperity, is to head north into the USA, illegally. The border is full of unscrupulous individuals ready to exploit these people who are merely trying to find a better life for themselves and their family. The demand for drugs is so high in the US and with so much of the supply now being funneled up from South America into Mexico, the President of Mexico had deployed the army into the border regions to root out the drug cartels who traffic the drugs. The cartels have too much to lose and so too have the gangs they are supplying in the USA, so they are not taking the government action lying down. Supplied with weapons from USA based gangs, in many of the border towns the escalation in violence was terrifying. The viciousness of the killings seemed to have no limit, in one example an entire bar full of people were lined up against a wall and shot by one of the drug cartels. The majority of the problem is thankfully limited to the border regions so we had said that as soon as we got south of the border, we wouldn't stop till we had a hundred miles behind us. Some of the stories we had been told included: When you go through the border you'll be spotted by a gangster, they will radio ahead to a buddy somewhere down the road, who'll have a truck ready. You'll be stopped, your bikes and all your possessions will be robbed from you and if you're lucky they may decide to not kill you. The police will stop you and you'll have to bribe them to get through or they'll lock you up and throw away the key. As soon as you arrive at the border, you'll be shot. The bikes will be robbed as soon as you leave them alone. You won't be able to get clean water, you won't be able to get clean gas and finally the food will poison you. Thankfully, I'd been through Mexico before on my previous trip and Joe had been down the Baja Peninsula in Western Mexico, so we took all these stories with a pinch of salt.

I'd a decision to make. If I went through to the customs guys and they said, "No you cannot enter into Mexico till you get the other bike back", the trip would be over there and then. I started playing with the idea in my head of just driving by customs, i.e. go through Mexico without the customs clearance forms for the bike. I had bike insurance, an international drivers license, all my own entry paperwork for Mexico, the only thing I would be missing is a blue document which allowed the bike to ride in Mexico as a temporary import. The way I saw it was, if I got stopped down the road I could just play the dumb tourist. "Oh I'm sorry, I'll go back and get it, aren't I a silly Gringo." At that point if I got turned back, I'd still have exactly the same shot as I currently had of getting through customs anyway. I decided to take a gamble. The customs guys are mostly trying to stop people bringing guns into the country, which like Ireland and Europe, are against the law in Mexico. The checkpoint where they take your customs papers is a little after the main customs office on the road out of Nogales. Could I get through the checkpoint without the permit? Maybe they won't check. What was the worst that could happen? Mentally I spent quite a bit of time weighing the odds and decided to go for it. I sat on the bike, queuing up

with Joe as we approached the checkpoint. As we got closer I was making a button on the motorcycle seat with my ass cheeks on account of nerves, if I was snared I was bollixed, but I kept telling myself "This trip is about getting to where we have to go, no matter what." They waved me through without checking and as we drove the road I was feeling like my balls were so big that I must clank when I walk. Like I said already, I had the insurance and a bunch of the other paperwork, so if stopped by the cops at some later point, they would mostly look for my license, passport, and insurance, almost never the customs documents. On top of that, the cops and army in Mexico are cool, they don't mess you around and as long as you're not doing something you shouldn't be, they leave you alone.

We pulled off the road after an hour and went into one of the convenience chains, Oxxo for something to drink. These are something like a 7-Eleven in the States or a

Centra / Spar in Europe and there are over 11,000 stores dotted throughout Latin America, they are everywhere! In them you can buy every drink that's available in North America and you'll almost always find them as part of a PEMEX, which is the State run gas station chain. There's

quite a lot of misinformation about Mexico, especially in the USA, centering on availability of water and quality of petrol etc. All of it is utterly false. The PEMEX chain which runs all the gas stations guarantees you can get 95+ octanes throughout the country. The prices are fixed by the government so no matter where you buy it, the price is the same and it's very good value, running at about 70 cents per liter. The gas stations are everywhere, with over 8,500 of them located on every road imaginable so you'll never have a problem getting gas, or have a problem with the quality, anyone who says different, has never been to Mexico.

Hermosillo, Mexico

We continued on for Hermosillo under a brilliant blue sky with huge white puffy clouds. The road down to

Hermosillo is mostly dual carriageway and is in great condition. There are two road types in Mexico, The Ruta Cuota, and The Ruta Libre. The Ruta Cuota are toll roads and are as modern as anything you'll find anywhere in the world. They have very few checkpoints and gas and food is readily available in food courts peppered along the route. The only downside is that they are heavily tolled, to stay on the toll roads all day is easily going to cost you $40-$50. The Ruta Libre are the free roads. They are much busier, and travel through all of the small towns and villages that dot the countryside and are far more challenging. As you go through the populated

areas they have small ramps called reductors which are not always well signposted or even marked and are an ever present hazard to motorcyclists. If you want to see the real Mexico, you need to take the Ruta Libre, but if you're stuck for time, get on the Ruta Cuota for a while and then get off later.

On the road we passed lots of giant cactuses, and while this area is considered part of the Sonoran desert, it's a green desert. You can't see any sand, the ground is covered with a multitude of green bushes so it doesn't look like a classic desert, if that makes any sense. We got to Hermosillo in the early evening and went for some food in a nearby restaurant, both buzzing that we were in Mexico.

That evening, we stood around chatting outside the motel rooms drinking some beers as a thunder storm rolled in. Our routine was always the same. We would get to where we were going, before we had a shower we'd each do a diary of the day in front of the camera while our memory was still fresh, then we'd download all the pictures and video we took for that day onto the hard drives and then back all of it up. We were being brutal on ourselves and stuck to this regime like clockwork. We both hit the scratcher early knowing we'd be up and out on the road much earlier the next day.

We added some rules of thumb to the trip to take account of the fact that we'd be arriving in towns which we didn't know, and speaking a language we didn't understand. The first was that we would always aim to get to the town we were staying about two hours before nightfall, it meant starting earlier so we weren't burning daylight in bed. Secondly, we'd always try and stay in a place which had internet so Joe could keep tabs on his business. Thirdly, when we got to towns, we'd always try and get off the street as quick as possible, and find a hotel quickly. That way if we did end up in the wrong end of a town, at least we weren't' going to be riding around multiple times drawing attention to ourselves. We were also in "Get the shot" mode. If we were stopped by the army or police, we would of course be filming it on our Helmet Cameras. No matter what happened, if it was

interesting, the other person would ask "Dude, did you get the shot?"

Cuauhtémoc

We left Hermosillo at 7am the following morning. We were making our way towards the Copper Canyon via Cuauhtémoc (don't try and say it if you're eating your breakfast). The road to Cuauhtémoc is called the Ruta Sierra or "The Mountain Road". We ended up riding about 350 miles, but because the route took us over the mountains, we were a full twelve hours on the road to get there. All day we were flung left and right as this huge ribbon of tarmac snaked its way through the mountains. We got stopped along the way for an inspection by the army which was painless enough, however my ass was twitching that the first words out of their mouths would be "Permit", to which I would have countered with "It's a long story, do you by any chance happen to know Jose Antonio Casas?" They wouldn't let us take any pictures, there was huge paranoia anywhere near the border in case the picture would make its way to the drug cartels. Further along the road Joe got a nasty sting, we reckoned it was an African attack fly, its only reason to live is to attack, apparently they were trained by Chuck Norris but escaped and since then have been wreaking havoc on motorcyclists. On a serious note Joe's finger was the color of a beetroot, we covered it with the various ointments we had in our first aid kits hoping that would take care of it. I had left the hotel without any water, I was certain it wouldn't be long before we got the opportunity to pick some up along the way, but because we were taking the boonie route over the mountains, four hours in stifling heat passed without a place to get a drink. My mouth was so dry my tongue felt like a brillo pad. When I eventually found a place I downed a liter of water, a Pepsi, a Gatorade, and 2 cans of 7up. Joe looked at me

like I was throwing it all into a black bucket, "Where you putting all that shit man!" That night I was lying on the bed as the thunder banged away outside, much like the previous night in Hermosillo. Once you cross the Mexican border, the ambient noise rises up about 20 decibels. Screaming dogs, cats, unbelievably loud cars and trucks, car alarms, people hanging outside your door for a chinwag, one thing was certain - peace and quiet was a thing of the past. The Mexican people up to this point had been fantastic, we hadn't encountered a single problem. We were also stunned at how green that part of Mexico was. As we got closer to the mountains the world became one massive ever green forest. On my previous trip I had gone down the Pacific coast of Mexico, we were now in the central spine of the country and it was covered in forests with mountains for as far as the eye could see. We both remarked "Wow, I never expected

Northern Mexico to look like this!"

Creel

We drove to the town of Creel the following day, which is the gateway to go and see the Copper Canyon, one of the premier tourist attractions in Northern Mexico. We reckoned that at that stage we'd been riding for four hundred miles in the mountains with wonderful bending twisting roads the whole way, we were having a ball. The weather had also been great, we had seen nothing but blue skies with great big columns of white clouds by day and ferocious storms by night. So far Mexico was exceeding our expectations by a long way. The whole countryside was ablaze with yellow flowers, for hundreds and hundreds of miles it was the dominant color by the side of the road. We stopped at one of the many shrines

you see to the Virgin Mary along the road, all of the candles had been lit by someone earlier in the day. On lots of the very dangerous bends there is a painting of the Madonna on the wall, I guess to prevent people crashing into it. On the face of it at least, Mary, the mother of Jesus appeared to be the most important figure of worship, much like Ireland. Creel itself is a very poor town. It was the first time we saw indigenous Mexican Indians, and they were poorer than church mice, your heart couldn't help but go out to them. I found myself getting very frustrated and sad that people had to live that way. While the Indians were very poor, they were selling something, that is to say they were trying to make a living by selling handcrafts, they weren't begging or looking for handouts. The Indians had been the big losers with all the border violence, tourist numbers had plummeted and as a result there was no one buying any of their goods. I just

couldn't say no to the Indian kids selling all the bracelets and necklaces and ended up buying a bag of stuff that I'd no room for on the bike, but it made the kids day and so made me feel pretty good. I remember having a couple of arguments with folks about giving charity, about whether it was a good thing to give money to kids who are begging. Well, the argument goes you shouldn't give it to them as it only encourages them to beg further. My cut would be, when it's a kid of about three years old, with a runny nose coughing and spluttering begging, surely it's the right thing to help the poor lad? What are

you going to do, walk by him and say "Sorry, I'm not going to give you anything" all the while thinking to yourself "by the way it's for your own good, now out of my way, I'm off to the buffet to stuff my face". If you believe in a God, maybe you're a Christian or a Muslim, maybe even a Buddhist, and you ask yourself the question, "If Jesus, Mohammed, or Buddha was standing right there, would they help the kid out?", of course they would. Anyway, my 2 cents is "if you can help, then help", especially if they are selling something, buy it - have one less beer that night - one less cookie the next day. Joe had a great perspective on this. When we were in Los Angeles driving around to collect some gear, he pointed to two people on the side of the road at a traffic stop. One was an American with a sign begging for money, the other was a Mexican selling oranges. Joe remarked that the Mexican was more American than the other guy because he was selling, he was fulfilling a need, he was working, and the other guy was a bum. Interestingly, my cousin who works for the UN told me straight out that any money that isn't 100% directed to the root cause of the poverty, is a waste. It's a complicated issue. oe and I were the only tourists in Creel, we hadn't seen anyone who looked like they were from anywhere else other than Mexico. We went out for a couple of beers that night and couldn't help remarking to each other "Where the hell is everyone?"

A buddy of mine in Ireland sent me on a news story from the Daily Telegraph in the UK. Five people had been killed at the same border post we had crossed only a few days earlier. Twice that day we passed large convoys of masked soldiers, every one of them was carrying a pump action shotgun or some other serious looking weapon. It wasn't hard to figure out why there were no tourists. We eventually got to Copper canyon which is a generic name applied to six different canyons each formed by a different river clustered together in the Sierra Madre mountains.

We arrived late in the evening so the light wasn't great from a filming perspective, but it was still awesome to behold. The main difference between it and the Grand Canyon is that when you look at it the dominant color is a copper green which is how the canyon got its name. There was not even one other tourist, just Joe and I. We tried to ride around it to see if we could get a better vantage point but didn't have much joy. This area, if they ever get the violence sorted out should become a major draw for motorcyclists, the last two days riding on the Ruta Sierra had been a wonderful experience. It wasn't the first time we arrived at a location and immediately started filming it. If felt like there was no room to enjoy it. As soon as you saw it, you had to break out the film gear, try and get the right shots, then maybe give a brief commentary on what you were looking at and pack everything back up. On some level it felt like filming it was preventing us from enjoying it as individuals, it was just work and it was really hard to strike a balance between the two.

We made our way back in the dark to Creel and went to bed knackered tired. The following morning I woke up to a punctured tyre, a screw had driven its way up into the rubber. We'd just gotten all the gear packed up and it was about 98DegF and then I saw the flat tyre. Let's just say a sentence like, "Ah for fucks sake!" was uttered more than once. We knuckled down fairly quickly and had the whole thing repaired in less than 20 minutes. The first of the day's catastrophes was over and done with and I was all smiles. We loaded up the bikes with good luck charms and protective beads that we bought from the

Indians in Creel and at the Copper Canyon. There was everything from Rosary Beads to little dolls and dodgy looking smiley faced characters, we were covering all the bases. There is an old saying, "There is no such thing as

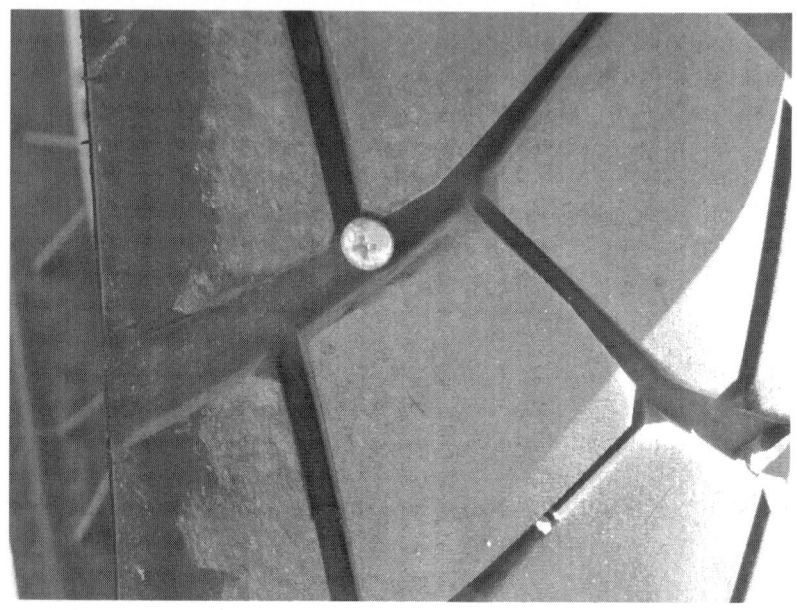

an atheist in a fox hole", referring to the fact that everyone in a battle believes in a God. Traveling around the world on a motorbike is fraught with danger from many different sources. I'm certain for instance that Rosary beads were the only reason the police let me out of a very dodgy situation in El Salvador a year previously. The officer held up the beads and looked at me and then waved me through, every little helps.

Hildalgo Del Parall

Later on, as we were riding towards Hildalgo Del Parall, Joe came to a sudden stop on a dangerous bend. I missed colliding into the back of him by inches. I was doing about 55mph, it would have been curtains for the two of us had I hit him. I drove down the road and circled back. I could see by the way he was shaking himself he'd been stung in the face (we were nicknaming all beasts of the air that sting as African Attack Flies). As I drove back a truck again just missed Joe as he came round the bend to unexpectedly find him parked close to the side of the road. There aren't any lay by's or hard shoulders in these parts so if your parked up, you're in harm's way. I pulled up to the start of the bend and sat there with my hazards on till Joe got back on the bike and pulled into a safer spot. It was the third time in about ten days that he'd been stung, this time beside the right eye and the little fucker had stung him a bunch of times, a sore bastard.

After putting a dose of cream on the affected area and spending some time talking about how lucky we were to be not injured, we went on our way. We stopped every hour or so and both talked at length that the section of road we've been riding since Hermosillo, "has got to be one of the top roads anywhere", all day again the road continued to snake through the most glorious Mexican countryside.

We got to Hildalgo a little after dark and started chatting about our schedule. Any time we talked about the schedule we'd end up arguing. Joe worked for himself, he did this was because he didn't like to be managed by anyone. I was anxious that we stayed on track with respect to time. I felt that the product has the best chance of being sold if it had some flow, it should be north to South and East to West. We also had to leave Ireland no later than mid May so that we would be out of Alaska before the

winter came. In order to get that done, we had to stay someway close to the schedule.

Up until that point, we did the work out on the road during the day filming etc. and then at night we spent our time downloading the video to portable hard drives and copying the data to backup disks. Most nights it was taking about two hours and depending on what time we'd arrive in a town sometimes it was 10:30pm before we had time to scratch ourselves. The durations were due to filming in HD, the file sizes were massive. The whole thing was starting to become hard work, and we continued to drift off schedule, falling a day behind schedule every three or four days. We came to an agreement of sorts. It was ok to be behind schedule, as long as we were ahead of schedule regarding the video content we were collecting. So if we were ten days behind schedule, but were getting gold footage, then who cared, we could make up the time later on. What was completely unacceptable would be to be behind on footage, and behind on time. If that was the case, we'd only be kidding ourselves, and the project was doomed to failure. That evening the clouds came in and there were ferocious bursts of lightning hitting the horizon all around the town. "This ain't like home!"

Durango

We headed south for Durango, the coolest sounding town ever. On the way we continued to get stopped and searched, it was happening daily at this stage and normally they'd search only one pannier. The further south we went the less we were searched but our paperwork was checked and examined by the army normally at least twice a day. The army guys were always friendly and more interested in the bikes and where we were going than in giving us a hard time. Durango was the first town we parked the bikes in the hotel lobby, which is always cool. We went out for a stroll and the town drunk came over to Joe and started chatting to him. Surprisingly he had perfect English. I was a bit struck by that. Here was a guy who'd gone to the trouble of learning another language and could speak it fluently, and had decided to take up the role of town drunk, it didn't jive in my head. The whole town was decked out with Mexican flags for the Independence day celebrations and it was lovely to walk around on a warm summers evening eating ice creams watching all the comings and goings in the town.

Zacatecas

From Durango we rode 220 miles to the city of Zacatecas, one of the most beautiful cities I've ever visited. I was stunned I had never heard of it because the town has been designated a Unesco World Heritage site because of all the baroque architecture. While there, we visited museums and old Franciscan churches, went to festivals and joined in on every manner of celebration imaginable. The entire city breathes life, energy and culture. We went up to the mirador which overlooks the city and it felt like we were standing over a model toy city. It's just one of long line of colonial gems dotted throughout Mexico, and was founded because of the silver in the mountains. While we were in the Franciscan church we bumped into

an English wedding party, the English bride was marrying a local diplomat. The grounds of the church were immaculately preserved and beside it was a museum where they were running an exhibition of the history of masks in Mexico. We were both blown away by the scale of the exhibition which had thousands of different masks, some dating back to before the Spanish arrived and if felt like we spent the whole day taking pictures of them.
That night we were out for a couple of beers when we noticed throngs of people walking around the city following troops of musicians. They would stop at random places, everyone would have a dance and a drink and then in unison they would all move on again. It's the Zacatecas version of a pub crawl I guess. I'd never been in a place like it, and in some ways I was delighted I hadn't heard of it before. If places like this become known, commercialism would follow and the whole

reason why the place is great in the first place would disappear.

After two incredible days in Zacatecas we rode the short journey south to the town of Guanajuato, it's the sort of place that every time you write the name, you find yourself checking the map to see if you spelled it right, and just looking up at it on the sentence above, it still doesn't look quite right, anyway it's an Indian name. The road conditions started to deteriorate big time on our way and we learned a good lesson about driving on roads which are colored in red on the map, don't go that way! Guanajuato is almost in the dead centre of Mexico. It's located in the mountains and was built to service the mining industry which was located there when the city was a major source of silver and gold. The whole town is built on hillsides and the streets are connected by a series of tunnels which travel underneath the city at every

manner of angle. The town is run down in places but is still very beautiful, and it looks and feels authentically Mexican. There was no pandering to chain restaurants or any form of brands, it's a million little shops and restaurants all glued together. There were hundreds of police officers and soldiers on the go, myself and Joe, still hadn't figured out what the hell was going on to warrant such a military presence. All we did know was they went mental if you tried to take a picture or a video of them. That evening, college bands started playing music all around the town and it seemed to kick off spontaneously. The singing was led by local students all dressed up in various outfits and they put on a great show. The whole town got involved to cheer them on. It's a great place. The only thing to taint the place was the poverty which at times

was pretty grim.

It seemed to me that if your old, an Indian, or a dog, and happen to find yourself in Mexico, well then you're pretty much fucked.

We passed an old lady sitting on a step in one of the very busy markets in the town. I stood at the top of the stairs looking down to where she was. Her pants were covered in dirt and the lines on her face were of a woman who had worked hard, I put her at over 80 years of age. She had four sweets and a bottle of water to her name and a little plastic cup which occasionally people were tossing a couple of pesos into as they passed. Every time she would take a sweet out of the bag and put it in her mouth, she would tie the bag up in a knot and put it back in her pocket, as if to keep it for tomorrow. After about two minutes she would take out the bag, have a look at the sweets and almost seemed to be pondering "will I have another?", she would undo the knot and take another sweet and savor it like it was her last.

Joe came back and we gave her a 50 peso note, you can buy about 50 tons of sweets with that in Guanajuato, she'd have enough sweets to wear out a teenagers jaw now. I couldn't help thinking that me and that old lady had one thing in common, namely if there's a packet of sweets with only two or three left, I always eat them now too. Tomorrow's tomorrow, but a sweet in the gob is a joy today.

CHAPTER 10
SOUTHERN MEXICO

NOT DEAD YET

We continued south in Mexico and made our way to Tula, a ruin site which pre dates the Aztecs near Mexico City. Its famous for several standing pillars which have faces carved on them, called the Toltec Warriors. Most of the ruins go back over 1500 years.

After a couple of hours wandering around the site we moved on towards Teotihuacán a much more visually stunning ruin site to the North of Mexico City. We

arrived too late to get in that evening so we got a hotel nearby and came back the next morning at opening time. The trend of almost no tourists anywhere continued unabated. Not only had Mexico to deal with the drug related violence at the border, H1N1 (Swine Flu) was scaring people away at a phenomenal rate. We nearly had the place to ourselves when we got there. It did start to pick up a bit later on, with some tour buses arriving from Mexico City.

Being something of a keen gardener, I really liked the ruins at Teotihuacán which were surrounded with beautiful wild flowers, it was a sea of daisies and buttercups. When I mentioned it to Joe he looked at me like I was a

pillow biter.

The ruin itself dates back to 100BC and was taken over many times by rival powers before the Spanish arrived. The name itself translates to "Place where the Gods were born", and at its peak the city had a population in excess of 150,000 people. From our perspective, the really great thing about the place was that they let you climb up to the top of the pyramids which gives you an amazing view of the "Avenue of the Dead" which runs through the centre of the site. To spice up the visits, a lot of the tour guides harp on the thousands of human sacrifices that apparently took place there.

Later in the evening we went for a beer with a Dutch girl called Ruchamah. She was killing time till her bus came to bring her back to Mexico City. She was a fine thing, very worldly and we seemed to hit it off. She was based in Antigua in Guatemala, which was on our route and we made plans to hook up for a beer there. I gave her a lift on the back of the bike to her bus and we said good

luck.

All the towns in this part of the world have Indian names, and you'd be amazed how hard it is to remember directions and signposts if you can't pronounce any of the towns to which you've got directions to. All day there was lots of "ehhh" and even more "Emm" with copious

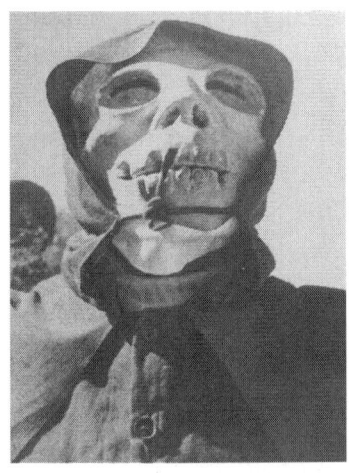

amounts of "Ahhh's".
At this stage we were getting mountains of footage but were slipping miles behind schedule. It was almost October 1st, we were nearly on the road a month but weren't even half way through Mexico. At this rate we wouldn't have any spare days in our budget were something to go wrong further down the line. The big constraint we had was we had to be out of Brazil by mid-February. That meant we had to get to Ushuaia for Christmas or close to the New Year. We had now only three months to get from where we were to the southern

tip of South America. It might seem like plenty of time, but when you consider we were trying to film the whole thing, I was starting to get worried. We also had to keep a week spare for Joe to go back and do some work in LA, I was convinced we had to pick up the pace. Joe didn't agree, and didn't buy into the notion that delaying today meant missing out on something in South America in order to get back to Ireland in time. I started to wonder if he ever intended on doing the Dublin to New York portion of the trip, after all he only intended initially to do the Pan American, what if he backed out halfway? There was nothing in writing to say he had to stay. Niggling thoughts had started to grow in my head, and most likely I was just being paranoid. Riding along along on the bike with your head stuck in a helmet never gives your brain a chance to reset, if you've something on your mind, it'll keep spinning till eventually it goes out of control.

Oaxaca

We made our way to Oaxaca (pronounced Waa Haa Ka). We stupidly (my fault) decided to go through Mexico City which was a terrible mistake. We got lost and I asked five different people for directions out of the city and got four different answers. The problem was that everyone tells you the way they would go to get out, and seeing as the city is a labyrinth, everyone has their own methods. What you really want is the dumb ass version, not the way you would go if you lived in the city. We resorted to the tried and trusted method of paying a taxi to lead us to an area where it would be easy to follow the way out of the city. The city has a population of 22 million and every last one of them seemed to be on the roads we were on that day and we'd to pull over several times to stop the bikes overheating. The traffic was appalling and in a guide book I read that Mexico City is a sprawling Octopus of twenty million souls, that is a perfect summary.

We eventually got to Oaxaca as night was falling. Joe stayed in the motel to do some work and I went in and around the town to take some pictures. I visited the top few tourist attractions including some fabulously ornate churches. The town centre had a lovely feel and they were hosting an open air opera concert. It was a wonderful finish to a bad day. I went back to the hotel bringing Joe a couple of beers as a peace offering. We'd been sparking and I wanted to sort things out.

San Cristobal de las Casas

The following morning we pushed into the Chaipus region of Mexico and stayed in the Hacienda Don Juan in San Cristobal de las Casas, about as close to the border with Guatemala as you can get. From there we planned to go slightly north to the Mayan ruins in Palenque, and then tour round the Yucatan peninsula before eventually crossing into Belize. The Hacienda is run by one of the world's greatest gentlemen, he couldn't do enough to make us feel at home. I stayed there the previous year and loved it and he'd extended the premises by about 50% since then. There was only four people staying in the hotel and you could see he was worried about business. That evening I got my first dose of the ringaskiddies, every fart was preceded by an arch in my left eye-

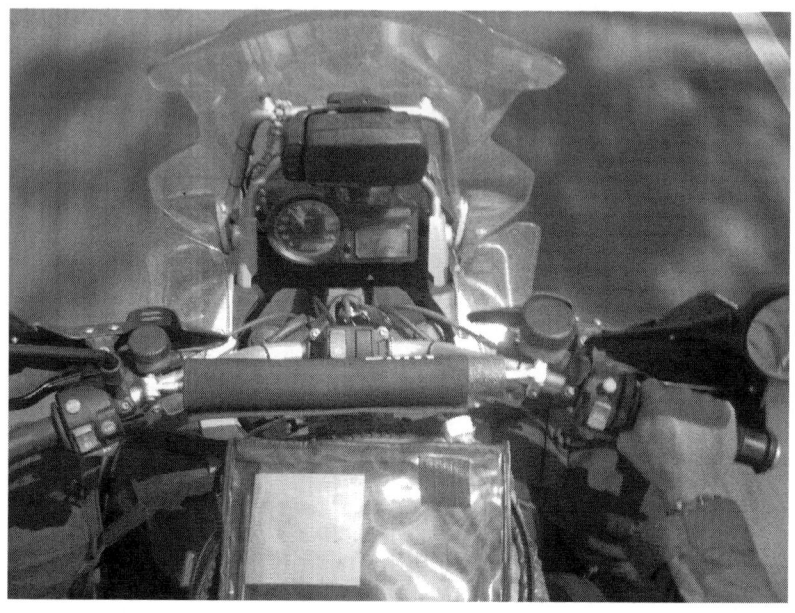

brow to check for valve integrity, thankfully it only lasted the one evening.
Everywhere you look in Mexico you're constantly reminded of how bizarre a place it is. You could have the most wonderful vista in front of you and then right in the middle of the field of view would be a landfill. In all of the ruin sites we´d visited so far you could see houses and shops from the ruin and there was always the ever present emaciated dogs, all mickey and ribs or eight teats scratching off the ground.
San Cristobal is full of Indians all selling various trinkets, clothing and food. I bought some chewing gum from a kid who was about four years old, after which I went home for a snooze. I headed out later to see a band

and have a couple of drinks and when I was heading to get a taxi back to the hotel, the same kid was still out selling stuff, I knew there was no way he'd taken a break. I bought the rest of his stuff off him and gave it to a bunch of kids hanging around on the church step. When I think about Mexico and go through my diary, I sometimes can't believe the contrast. There are so many good points peppered with the not so good. The good includes incredible scenery, really friendly and helpful people, wonderful culture, amazing history and vast amounts of awe inspiring architecture and archaeology. The bad things included the dogs, the old, the speed bumps, the checkpoints and the poverty in the Indian communities. All in all, I would still wholeheartedly recommend it though.

Palenque

We made the short hop from San Cristobal de las Casas to Palenque, a journey of about 140 miles or so. It took almost four hours due to a combination of check points, mountain roads, ball crushing reductors, and women, children and cattle on the road.

Palenque is located in the revolutionary part of Mexico, it wants its independence. It's also the part of Mexico which has large areas of jungle. The people in the town are Mayans and aren't in the least bit welcoming. Every wave was greeted with a blank stare, I remarked to Joe,

"Dude they don't like us." I suppose its not altogether surprising, the Mayans have been slaughtered in their millions by foreigners over the centuries, so just because we decided to ride down the road on our motorbikes waving at them, isn't going to change how they feel about the last couple of hundred years. We rode around to the ruins at first light and met up with the illustrious Victor Damas, one of the best tour guides this side of the River Shannon, a proper gentleman. The things this guy told us about Palenque, had us constantly saying, "No way!". It all sounded very far-fetched if it wasn't for the evidence he showed us, suffice to say there were Egyptians, Chinese and far eastern Indians all hanging around Palenque way before Columbus was a wink in his father's eye. So, it's all either part of some elaborate hoax perpetrated in the 16th century or it's the real deal, but no matter what the origin, the place is magnificent.

It was the first Mexican ruin we'd seen where there was no encroachment by anything man made. The whole place is surrounded with impenetrable jungle and the noise of the growler monkeys first thing in morning was like there was a pride of lions about to come tearing over the hill and make mincemeat out of you.

We stayed in a big hotel that night where we and a pair of newlyweds were the only guests. The whole H1N1 and drug violence were continuing to rear their ugly head everywhere we went. It was like the whole world went someplace else other than Mexico that summer, and not for the first time I felt very sorry for the folks completely dependent on tourism for their livelihood, they were hurting big time.

We were in a jungle area and the mosquitos were as thick

as thieves. I was going to bed every night with enough deet on me to stop a bull elephant charge and still managed to get eaten alive. It's the fact that you know the bastards are in the room, it gets you all itchy and aware that there's a fucker on the wall looking down at you cleaning his knife and fork, saying to himself, "Fat boy there looks like good eatin!"

Walking around that evening I was reminded why Tarzan could never be a woman, there are far too many creepy crawlies, lizards and snakes in the jungle.

Given the political problems in this region of Mexico we were getting stopped a lot more often and searched much more comprehensively. We were filming all of the searches with our helmet cams which were powered by the bike's canbus, as long as the bike had power the cameras had power too. While I was tossing out the contents of one of my panniers for the soldiers, I reminded Joe that his lights were still on forgetting that he was of course filming the whole thing, secretly of course! Joe looked at me like I was an ape, rightly so.

Puerto Angel

We left Palenque and made our way to Puerto Angel our first overtly beach town of the trip. There was a festival that night and the ability of those women to dance and move each arse cheek as if it had a mind of its own was a rare and wonderful talent.

We hit more and more camouflaged reductors as we continued up the Yucatan. The visible ones are easy, just slow down and over you go. Others you see too late and jam on the breaks and in the process of slowing down

get your underpants wedged up your arse at 40mph. The camouflaged ones you hit and get a 250kg whack in the balls as the bike is flung into your nether regions while your in the air holding the handle bars. Now if the word ramp conjures an image of a smooth gradient in your mind think again, think rather of the sort of thing you'd put on the road, if your intent was to keep shock absorber companies in business.

The roads were lined with Indian women and children walking to wherever they needed to get to. Several times we saw children as young as four and five years old walking along the road with no one looking after them. This was on a two lane road shared with big articulated Lorries with no hard shoulder, it seemed crazy.

We had our first route change conversation at this point. The original plan had been to go into Belize and then cut back into Mexico before going on into Guatemala. If you

NOT DEAD YET

remember I was in Mexico illegally, so in all likelihood once I left, I very much doubted whether I'd get back in with the bike, so once we got into Belize we'd have to push into Guatemala without returning to Mexico.
I looked at Tikal and suggested that it was the right place to head for after Belize. It would mean we would do the Yucatan first, then Belize, then Guatemala.

It was a change of plan but on the upside it would gain us some time back, but mostly it would mean I wouldn't get caught out on the customs angle. Joe made me sweat it, and reluctantly agreed to the route change. When you travel for extended periods with someone, they can become the outlet for all your frustrations and you can become fixated on issues that arise. I think this was the point at which we stopped being able to communicate with each other and the project was permanently and irretrievably doomed. I couldn't understand why the route change was an issue, of course it was the right thing to do, if I got hassle at the Mexican border things could have gotten nasty very quickly, what if I'd been arrested, I'd knowingly broke the law. I kept asking myself "What's his version of events? Why is this a problem? Is it because he wants the whole thing to fail? When you can't communicate with someone these questions go unanswered, the problems continue to brew and brew out of all proportion until they eventually sour the entire relationship. To be clear, any communication problem was at least 50% my problem, we were both to blame. I kept the head down and said to myself "Keep going, it'll work out."

The Yucatan peninsula is a feast for the eyes. The water in the ocean is a postcard turquoise blue and the beach sands a wonderful white. It was more beautiful than I could have imagined. We went for some grub on the strand in one of the towns we stayed, and had some freshly caught fish watching the sun go down. It was all very romantic except there weren't any women, although as Joe pointed out "Dude there's two lizards having sex on the wall". Like I said many times before, "This is Mexico, this is Mexico."

The humidity at this point on trip was like walking into a hot wet sponge, the only respite during the day was a cold shower or to jump into the ocean. The water tanks in the places we stayed were always stored on the top of the buildings where they were roasted by the heat of the sun during the day, invariably the cold shower was almost as hot as the warm.

Progresso

We moved on to the town of Progresso, just north of Merida, on the map, look to the left of Cancun. Two days earlier I was giving out about the Mayans and how they weren't the friendliest bunch, well the Mayan gods took their revenge that afternoon. While I was moving my stuff into the hotel I whacked my head of a low concrete ledge. I wasn't sure if it was just me but I was certain it was in the shape of an "M", as in M for Mayan. Who knows though, that little scar on the head might just become a talking point with Wonder Woman sometime soon. She'll gives me little kisses on my forehead and she'll say "El Fonzie, where did you get that scar?" I'll say "Saber tooth Tigers baby, they should never be given weapons."

While we were on the road I was keeping an eye on the

Department of foreign affairs website to make sure we weren't walking into any unknown situations. It made for depressing reading.

For Honduras it said the following: President Zelaya returned clandestinely to Honduras on 21 September. The situation in Honduras is tense and unpredictable and may deteriorate very quickly. A temporary curfew is currently in place with timings changing on a regular basis. As a reaction to this, neighboring countries (El Salvador, Guatemala and Nicaragua) may close land borders and stop air links at short notice. Anyone intending to travel to or through Honduras should contact his or her travel operator for further advice and to keep abreast of the situation by monitoring local media. For Guatemala it had the following cheery nuggets: There have been confirmed cases of (H1N1) (Swine Flu) in Guatemala. Screening equipment has been installed at airports to check incoming passengers. The World Health Organization (WHO) has raised its pandemic threat alert Phase to Level 6. You should also monitor local media reports for any developments and advice. You should be aware that public medical facilities in Guatemala are limited and health insurance is required. You should carry evidence of your insurance at all times and use private clinics where possible. There has been a reported outbreak of Dengue fever in the Department of Izabal, especially in and around the towns of Puerto Barrios and Livingston. There are confirmed cases of Classic dengue and Dengue Haemorrhagic. You are advised to take additional health precautions against mosquitoes and be advised that the authorities are publicly spraying a mixture of insecticide and diesel to combat the outbreak. We advise against

climbing the Tajumulco volcano in San Marcos or visiting the surrounding area due to recent unrest in local communities involved in land use disputes. Since 4 April 2009, there have been a series of earth tremors throughout the country measuring above 4 on the Richter scale. Please continue to monitor our travel advice before traveling to Guatemala. Since March 2009 there has been an increase in violence with co-ordinated attacks on buses, which has left several dead. While foreigners and tourists are not directly targeted, you should remain vigilant at all times in urban centers and crowded public areas.
We knew we'd need to stay on our toes. There were many more risks once we started to travel in Central America.

Chechen Itza

We continued our tour of the Yucatan and drove from Progresso on the northern tip of the Yucatan to Chechen Itza, another of the Mayan ruin sites in Mexico. This one, due to its proximity to Cancun had a lot more tourists and we didn't have as much access to the ruins as we were used to, but was still a great day out. Of particular interest is a field with large stone rings on the surrounding walls where its presumed some form of ball game was played. We bumped into a couple from the North of England back at the hotel, Grahame and Sue, who were taking a year out to do the Pan American highway, a nicer couple you couldn't hope to meet. The four of us went out to a Mexican restaurant close to where we were staying and tucked into a mixed buffet, which turned out to be a big mistake. The grub moved like a bob-sleigh team down a mountain as it cascaded from my mouth to

my arse in less than an hour.
We left the next morning after about four hours of crap-

ping and gingerly made our way to Tulum, a Mayan port near the border with Belize. I'd the biggest dose of ring sting since Tim Robbins in the Shawshank Redemption, but at least the worst appeared to be over, I was taking it very handy on the bike, any sudden bumps might crack the dyke.

The bikes were running smoothly, and really the only issue raising eyebrows was Joe's front tire, neither of us were sure he'd enough thread on it to make it to Panama and with some of the worst roads on the continent coming up over the next week or so, it would be a constant source of worry.

I was just about to turn 39 years old, it was the 7th of October and that night I wrote in my diary: "In 3 hours I'm 39 years old" and as is the case with all men who hit this particular milestone, today was a day to torture myself about what I've done in my life and more importantly what I hadn't done.

Tulum

We got to the ruins at Tulum, which look out from the top of a cliff over a white sandy beach with brilliant blue waters below. It is a classic picture postcard destination. On the downside, due to its close proximity to Cancún, it's packed with tourists and much like Chechen Itza, you can't really explore the ruins, everything is barricaded off. Given its location the prices had hiked up enormously too, everything was at least twice as expensive as what had come before.

Allow me a quick diversion: Two weeks previously when

we were on our way to Copper Canyon we stopped by the side of the road for a drink. While we were parked up, I took the opportunity to do a number 1. Note I was wearing motorcycle trousers so not only is there a zip but there's also a waterproof flap or sheath around the zip, so your John Thomas doesn't get cold or wet, the only price to pay being the inconvenience of having to push it out of the way while your spending a penny. Anyway, while doing up the zip, I caught about twenty ball hairs in my fly which were then ripped out in one fell swoop, not a big deal. It bled a bit and the people of Mexico heard rumor that night of Wolves crying in the mountains.

For the girls out there, ask your man to confirm that you can't lose a ball hair without taking the root with it. It's a sore bastard, if you lose twenty of them in one go, just multiply the pain accordingly.

Anyway about two days later a little small lump appeared. I'd describe it as the sort of thing the average fourteen year old would wake up with, after downing about five Easter eggs. He'd then burst the zit from the end of his nose onto the mirror, so being almost 40, I decided to try the same thing, it burst, bled a good bit and I hoped that would be that. Unfortunately, three days later the bump was back, this time about 50% bigger. A very much unwanted routine then started which cycled between bursting, bleeding, and growing over the course of the next few weeks. It was getting to the size that it could be confused with a third ball and the rate of growth was very disturbing. I guess the warm weather and inevitable sweaty nether regions especially on the bike, in the alpine stars all weather motorcycle trousers didn't do much to help the healing process.

The lump became lumpier and a lot less "burstable" or maybe it was burstable, but I wasn't prepared to use that much force in such close proximity to my crown jewels, if you know what I mean.

Well anyway, it was my birthday and I was thinking, "You never know, an angel might send me a fine woman looking for a shag and how am I going to explain this!" There's no way I could, so I resolved that it had to go.

I was going to try and lance it, however not having a syringe or a needle I said I'd use the end of a scissors. Now, if any of you are in any doubt, this is seriously hard-core stuff. Sticking a scissors into your scrotum is a sure fire way to make it into Hard-core monthly.

So, I got my fingers behind the lump (making sure there were two full balls and a series of tubes behind it) and pushed it as hard as I could towards the surface of the skin on my ball bag. I then jabbed the end of the scissors in it, well holy fucking fuck.

It was right about then, I realized it would have been a good idea to have the first aid kit to hand as my nut sack started spewing puss and blood. I ran into the bedroom clasping the balls and the wound with enough force to crush a coconut. I spilled the first aid kit out onto the ground and got a bandage that would have been big enough to pitch a tent with. Then, awkwardly with one hand I took the lid off a bottle of TCP and doused the wound, the memory of the stinging sensation will go with me to my grave.

I remember getting an email that night from a friend asking did I have any news. I replied, "No, same ol same ol."

The good news was that 24 hours later there were no lumps, just a big bandage around my nuts with another one of life's little lessons learned, namely, Angels never send women round to shag you on your birthday.

In the early afternoon we went out for some grub and beers with Grahame and Sue on a lovely beach under a thatch roof. It was magic stuff and as good a way to spend your birthday as any. I was desperate to get in swimming in the beautiful water but with the gash on my head, and hole in my scrotum albeit self-inflicted, I thought it wise to give it a miss. Knowing my look it would start bleeding and attract sharks, and while a shark attack isn't the worst way to go out, I really didn't want to be eaten balls first.

On the way back to the hotel we were stopped by the Mexican police. We were driving without helmets, none of us knew it was against the law, and the country was full of people driving without them, but these guys seemed determined to make a point. After a few remarks about taking the bikes, they let us go and we burned back to the hotel for a couple of Sol's at the bar.

The next day we were headed for Belize. We talked about how we'd change how we operate once we got into Central America, for example always filling up when the gas tank got to half empty (or is it half full?), which would help prevent us getting stranded in places we didn't want to be.

Neither of us had a clue what to expect in Belize, although neither of us expected it to be overly problematic, the border was about 240km from where we were, so all going well we'd be there for midday and hopefully through by about 2pm.

CHAPTER 11
SEX EDUCATION

NOT DEAD YET

I was 14 in 1984 and was close to holding the world record for the longest continuous boner in history. It wasn't unusual I don't think, but in Catholic Ireland back in those days, anything to do with Mickies (John Thomas, aka Penis) was considered to be the work of the devil so it wasn't the sort of thing you could ask your friends about. The closest I ever got to any sex education was an episode of Dynasty or Dallas, or every now and then some movie that was on RTE 1 and 2 had a quick flash of some girls boobs and that would tide you over with wanking material for a few weeks.

I had an older and younger brother with only three years separating the three of us. I often think maybe we'd have been better off having a sister, at least at some stage we might have got to ask the question, "Ma what's that?" The running joke when we were growing up was, when you asked "What's that" pointing at a girls vagina, the reply was "That's where God hit her with a hatchet". Anyway, my secondary school, run by Marist brothers must have come up for some kind of a review and was found, not surprisingly, to be desperately deficient in terms of sex education delivered to its students. I got a serious upgrade in my own sex education when some of the lads had robbed there Dad's porno mags and brought them down to the back field. It was there we first saw the weird and wondrous world of women's vaginas getting drilled by gargantuan pork swords.

Looking at the porno mags, we all walked away thinking that we'd worms for dicks compared to these guys, and that if we were ever to attempt shagging a girl we'd need a plank strapped to our back, to prevent us falling in. Some of the things we truly believed in back at that innocent age included, Shag a girl up the tradesman's entrance = boy, up the front bottom = a girl. Shag her once for one baby, twice for twins. A girl's period and having an orgasm were the same thing (if only). Girl's boobs were permanently full of milk. If you ever got the opportunity to "finger" a girl, the more fingers the better.

No doubt driven by the mother of a teenage girl who'd had the misfortune of being "heavy petted" by one of my peers (ref: more fingers the better), a group of almost a hundred teenage boys were all corralled into a double room in Moyle Park College. The room was full of the sort of teenage boys you'd expect in a very working class area, and a very large cohort of the lads came from poor backgrounds. Normally the odds of getting this group of lads not to descend into complete and total anarchy would be very long and things were starting to get rowdy when a 5ft 4inch Pakistani doctor walked in.

We were all told to behave by one of the Marist brothers and the doctor began to tell us all about puberty, sex, and a whole host of other topics. He covered penis length, saying that not to worry, "your lad (penis) is longer than you think", it always looks bigger to the other person looking at it. There was a palpable sense of relief, as up to that point we'd all seen porno mags stacked out with guys with John Thomas's like Clydesdale Stallions. He went on to discuss the female boob, it was new information to find out that you could only get milk out of it when she'd had a baby, it also made instant liars out of a few of the lads who said they they made a cup of tea with the milk from their birds tits. He talked about balls, and masturbation and how there was nothing wrong with it much to the chagrin of the watching Marist brothers.

Half the class nearly broke out into a celebratory wank. They had been wracked with guilt and fear about going straight to hell with every shuffle of the wrist.

He talked about shagging in detail. He then went onto a topic which no one in the room was prepared for, shagging a virgin.

Now, it was something which half the room claimed they had done, and seeing as the average age was 14 and it was 1984 in Catholic Ireland, most were surely lying. He got onto the subject of the hymen. The whole class hushed, you could hear the hearts beating, "What the fuck was a hymen?" The doctor went on to describe how if you were shagging a virgin and assuming she hadn't played sports or rode horses, that you may have to break through this hymen, a wall of muscular tissue, the first time you had sex. This breaking had to be done with the pork sword.

The whole room sat motionless with a stunned silence. One of the lads up the front of the room raised a nervous hand slowly to ask a question, "Eh Sir, scuse me Sir, em I've a question Sir. What if you can't break the hymen?" We all leaned forward, waiting with bated breath for the answer. The doctor replied, in fairness to him, not meaning to be funny, "Just bring her down to the doctor, and he'll break the hymen for you." The Marist brothers laughed first.

The school chats in the yard centered for weeks about women with hymens like trampolines ready to slingshot you back against the wall if pushed too hard against them.

CHAPTER 12
BELIZE

We left Tulum on the 10th of October under a cloudless blue sky, where everyone was Mexican and spoke Spanish. By the time we'd rode 240km down the coast we were in the middle of a tropical storm and everyone was speaking English with a heavy Jamaican accent. At least 50% of the population was Afro-Caribbean, I couldn't believe the world could change so much in such a short distance.

We arrived at the border and got through in less than two hours. The lines of traffic mirrored the border between Mexico and the USA, a massive line heading into Mexico and almost no one heading into Belize. People always follow the money, and migration always happens from poorer countries to richer ones. The average salary in Belize is only one third of what people earn in Mexico, about $10 a day.

I was anxious to leave Mexico mainly because our insurance had expired since the 2nd of October and this, on top of not having a customs immigration permit was making me feel like I was pushing my luck. The main road which runs through the country is paved but isn't lined, it's just a thin spool of tarmac making its way through the countryside. There are very few signposts but seeing as there's so few roads it's not that difficult to figure out where you're going.

Belize is truly a cultural melting pot and its 321,000 inhabitants are made up of Maya, Mestizo, Kriol, Garifuna, East Indian, Mennonite, Arab and Chinese. There is no place on earth like it. Probably the least strange thing that happened was a Jehovah's witness giving me a million dollar note with some religious stuff written on the back.

As the storm continued to move closer we made our way quickly to the town of Orange Walk and found a place to stay. We went out for some grub and were stunned at the amount of Chinese restaurants, Belize looked too poor to have so many. The town itself was in bad shape and it wasn't long before we'd seen everything worth seeing.

As I sat on my bed that night, I counted seventeen mosquito bites on one ankle, it was either seventeen individual mosquitos chowing down or one big fella at the buffet all night. If it was just one, he must have been a stone weight by the time he finished. The itch was excruciating, exacerbated by having to wear motorcycle boots all day.

We left the town of Orange walk and headed south through the centre of Belize. The fields we passed were full of Banana and Sugar plantations and when we

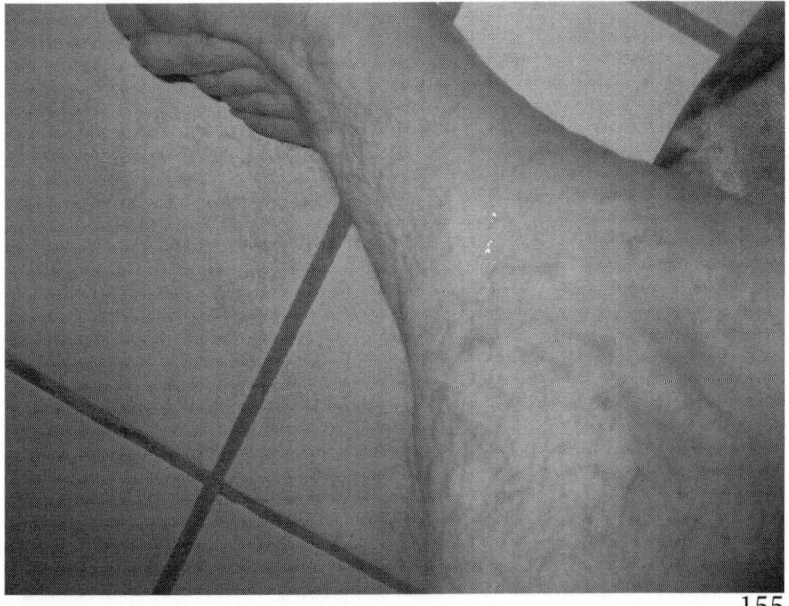

stopped in a shop, an old map labelled the country as British Honduras, Belize only got independence from Britain in 1981. Everyone was bilingual mixing up English and Spanish without any problem, and speaking Creole when they didn't want you to understand what they were saying. It's quite an empty country, only 320,000 people living in an area about the size of Ireland or Massachusetts in the USA. That's just 14 people per square km, compare that to New York where you've over 20,000 people crammed into the same space. It went some way to explaining why the infrastructure was so undeveloped, also because it was poor, no one owned cars anyway. Mostly we saw folks riding bikes or getting around on horse drawn carts.

Placencia

By the end of the day we were hurtling along an orange colored dirt road making our way to the coastal village of Placencia. The more southeast we drove, the more tropical the landscape became with lots of rain forest dominating the landscape. Similar to Mexico the heat and humidity were brutal.

Lots of the houses were built on stilts, no doubt to combat flooding and there was a lot of marshy land at the side of the roads. On the way we crossed some seriously rickety bridges which we couldn't believe were being used by articulated Lorries.
Most of the shops we went into were only half stocked and if you were for instance to buy flour, it's sold in plastic bags which the shop splits up from 50kg bags. The same is true for sugar and all the other bulk goods,

in many ways it felt like we stepped back in time twenty years. This part of the world caters almost exclusively to the American tourist market and as we were pumping up our tires four folks from Alabama passed us and stopped to say hello. It was a very strange moment, four folks from the South Eastern USA, talking to an Irishman and a Californian out in the middle of rural Belize.
Placencia lays claim to the narrowest street in the world, which is really just a concrete pavement big enough for a pram running between long rows of beach houses.
In search of somewhere to stay we got the bikes stuck on sea sand and it was a nightmare to pull them out. We eventually made it and booked into a lovely beach house

which had a restaurant and bar on the beach.
That evening I went for a walk around the town, the whole place was really relaxed and I passed the evening

watching a football match being played near the village square. When it was over, I headed back to the beach house bar on the beach and hung out with Joe for a while. I wrote in my diary "As I write, I'm looking directly at the beach and the sea is no more than 20 meters away. I'm sitting underneath a coconut tree wondering if one of them will fall out of the tree and hit me in the head. Joe just headed into the ocean, its dark, and he's had about five beers, hopefully he makes it back!" First thing the next morning I made the short walk to the beach. I was the only one there and I stood looking out at the incredible turquoise sea, breathing in the fresh air. Just then, two dolphins popped their heads up out of the water and played not five meters from the shore right in front of me, before heading off further down the beach. I said to myself "Usual story, something great happens and Hughes has no flipping camera!"

San Ignacio

We left Placencia and our first task of the day was to tackle a fairly serious dirt road as we made our way up towards Belmopan where we would turn left and head for the town of San Ignacio, about twelve miles from the Guatemalan border. First we dropped the air pressure in the tires which makes riding on dirt and sand a whole lot easier and then once the dirt was over we'd pump them back up again, it would be impossible to do a trip like this without a portable compressor.
We stopped a bunch of times to get something to drink, the humidity had us both soaked with sweat. We also passed by two towns called Listowel (name of a town

in County Kerry in Ireland), and also Spanish Point which is in County Clare, There must have been a lot of Irish there at one point. Joe got great mileage out of a town called Middlesex, "Dude - that town is called Middle-sex!" I told him that it's named after a town in England, I can't think why all the time I was growing up, I never once had a little giggle about it.

When we got to San Ignacio we crossed the Hawksworth Bridge, it turns out we shouldn't have, we had gone down a one way system, no wonder everyone was roaring and shouting at us. We got chatting to a really cool guy who worked in the local garage who gave us a lot of good advice on where to stay and on getting to the Guatemalan border.

There was a lot of Mennonites in the town, we saw several families riding around on pony and traps. The Mennonites are similar to the Amish in Pennsylvania, quite how Prussian protestants found their way to Belize is a story that dates back to Anti German sentiment post World War I, when they moved from Alberta in Canada down south into Mexico and onto Belize. I passed one of the girls who was wearing a one piece dress and a hat like they used to wear on little house on the prairie. The outfits leave only the face and hands bare, she was a timid little thing, about 21 years old and no more than 5ft tall. I said Hi, and she gave me a shy smile back, I reckon she liked me, but not in the way I'd like no doubt, she probably thought "Now look at the size of that fucker, If I brought him home we wouldn't need the horse to drag the plough, we could just strap it onto him!"

We checked into a hotel that had amazing panoramic views of the rainforest and we both had balconies that faced out onto magnificent views of the Belize countryside. As I was having a shower I noticed I'd officially re-entered the three ball spiral. I know somewhere down the line, whether it was to a doctor or maybe even if I was to lucky one night, it would all start with "I can explain, it's not what it looks like, it's a long story." I had a couple of beers with a bartender called Oscar and the manageress of the bar. We had a good conversation and

I learned a bunch more about Belize. The work week for Oscar was thirteen days on then two days off and most people choose to work their days off. On a Sunday they work from 6am to 10pm, but get an extra $35 for doing it. I nearly choked on my Margarita. Oscar told me that Irish missionary priests helped educate them when they were growing up, Father Ryan no less, the same name as

the priest who gave me my first communion, confirmed me, and also married me. He also told me that each of them had an Irish pen pal when they were kids.
We got onto some bigger subjects, for instance why Belize is so multicultural. Apparently it ended up with a lot of ex-military refugees from the various wars which have happened during Central America's torrid past. He also said that there was very little racism in Belize, everyone was so used to there being lots of variety all the time that it wasn't a problem. Even though Belize is such a small country I couldn't get over how much the culture within its borders had changed in only a hundred miles, in Placencia, it would be done when it's done, no hurry, no panic whereas in San Ignacio it was the exact opposite. Before we left for Guatemala, I checked out the ruins at Cathal Pech, a Mayan trading site at the meeting of two rivers. I was the only person there so I had the run of the

place to myself, it felt like I was in an Indiana Jones movie. It was one of the most magical places I've ever been, and in the two hours I spent there it wasn't until the very end that someone else showed up.

I was sad to be leaving Belize, I'd a great time there and would go back in a heartbeat.

We drove to the border with Guatemala and paid forty bucks a piece to get out of Belize, they didn't seem to mind that our insurance was up and that our entrance permits were also out of date, you'd be amazed how far a couple of Andrew Jackson's ($20's) will take you.

NOT DEAD YET

CHAPTER 13
GUATEMALA

Once we'd stamped out of Belize, it was time to stamp into Guatemala, things had been easy so far. First, you had to photocopy your passport, license and vehicle title which we had done before we got there. You then get an entry stamp into Guatemala in your passport. You then need a photocopy of this stamp in your passport, before you can import the bike. Of course, there weren't any photocopiers at the border; the nearest one was in the town just over the bridge, in Guatemala.

I set off across the bridge on foot while Joe looked after the bikes and when I was halfway, the heavens began to open for our regular afternoon dousing. I quickened my pace and shoved the documents up my jumper to stop them getting wet. No sooner had I opened my mouth to a guy in a shop to get two photocopies when lightning struck and the power to the whole village went off. I couldn't believe it. I asked the shopkeeper how long did

it normally take to came back on and he told me about twenty minutes, so I sat in out of the rain in his shop and waited.

In an area about the size of a small room in Ireland, this guy was running a shop and his missus was minding their five kids. The kids were too cute for words and I ended up buying them a heap of lollypops, it was an excuse for me to get one too. After a while and a lot of rain, the power came back on and I set off back across the bridge towards the border with the paper work and got the bikes imported. I was a bit worried that seeing as I'd fucked up the permits leaving Mexico last time, that maybe I did the same when leaving Guatemala and I wouldn't be let in, but there were no problems. We had just entered our fourth country, and the first thing we had to negotiate was a twenty mile stretch of gooey dirt road. We hammered through it on our way to Tikal stopping off to take pictures of a gorgeous lake on the way.

Tikal

When we arrived at the entrance to Tikal and looked at the poster, we recognized it from somewhere. Then it came to us, it was used in the first Star Wars movie. It's the bit where the Millennium Falcon lands at the rebel base, just before they blow up the death star. If none of this part makes any sense to you, you were probably born sometime in the eighties.

We checked into a hostel in Tikal Park and went straight over to one of the ruin sites. The ruins cover over 13 square kilometers and believe it or not, are only 20% excavated. It is one of the world's greatest treasures and

is completely unspoiled. We signed ourselves up for the guided tour the following day, this place was pure gold from a documentary perspective. Tikal is situated in part of a massive rain forest, the second biggest forest in the America's and this part of the world is called the earths 5th lung. The feeling it gives you, is like being in the movie Jurassic park, you walk out of a jungle trail and standing right there in front of you is a massive pyramid or temple. It is utterly breathtaking. We set off in the direction of one of the bigger ruin sites just as the

jungle mist was lifting.

The feeling that we were walking on 2000 year old trails towards the various ruin sites, just added to the sense of excitement. The place we were headed to first, was to get an early morning view of where they shot the scene in the first Star Wars movie. Even though it was still early in the morning we were lathered in sweat by the time we got to the top of the first pyramid. Incidentally that's one of the great things about this location, you can actually climb the pyramids and walk in and around them, at Chechen Itza and Tulum you had to follow and path. The view out over the jungle from the top of the Star Wars pyramid was like looking out onto a green sea under a blue sky. The noises coming up from the jungle were chaotic as millions of varying size creatures got on with the job of finding something to eat and drink, and something to shag. By the sound of things, they were having much better luck than me. If you haven't heard a growler monkey before, well just imagine Lions sitting up in very high trees doing the whole roaring and growling routine from altitude. As we walked along we saw a spider monkey moving through the tree tops, colorful bush turkeys, an animal that looked like a Meer cat, fire ants, and all sorts of birds. At one stage we were filming the monkeys going through the tree tops when several very large and colorful birds flew through the field of view. It all helped cement the fact that we were in a really special place in our heads.

I won't try and explain the history, I'd only make a balls of it, suffice to say the city is Mayan, it dates back to around 1000 BC, and it's visually stunning. One ritual worth mentioning is that the King used to cut himself

NOT DEAD YET

deliberately as part of a ritual, sometimes in the wrist,

sometimes in the stomach and occasionally the Penis and spread the blood to fertilize the ground. I couldn't help wonder if one of the Kings came along and at his coronation said, "My first law that I will enact as King of this great nation is that forthwith, there shall be no spreading of blood from the Royal Penis, unless it's someone else's other than mine!"

After many hours walking around in one of the planet's most awe inspiring locations it was time to get on the road again. We both could have stayed there a week but when it would come time to cut the production together, Tikal would get no more than a few minutes, we'd already seen plenty and had overstayed.

Guatemala's road conditions were awful. The potholes were so big you could throw a coin in, and make a wish. The Chicken buses were a constant threat as was the number of landslides we encountered as we drove along. Anywhere that had money had a guard with a pump

action shot gun standing outside. I was taken to the toilet at one gas station by a guy who was carrying a huge shotgun, if he had said to me "get in there and grab your ankles big boy", there was nothing I could have done about it.

Coban

We were headed for Coban, about 170 miles south of Tikal. After about forty miles we stopped to get some cash from an ATM and gas up. Somehow as we were leaving we ended up taking different roads, I turned right to go over the mountains, and Joe turned left. I stopped and went back and searched around for about a half hour but I had no luck finding him. I genuinely believe that we both thought that the other person had enough of the documentary, and had given up and driven away.
We left Tikal too late to try and get to Coban and I ended up riding the last ninety minutes in complete darkness. Somewhere very near the top of a world list

of things not to do, right up there with "don't tickle the great white shark" and "don't bite the tigers tail" is "don't ride in Central America after dark." The road conditions are atrocious with mega pot holes, herds of farm animals and people regularly walking on the road. The turnoffs are poorly signposted and there are hidden ramps for slowing traffic which can easily cause you to lose control of the motorcycle, the stats say that your 20 times more likely to die in a road traffic accident in Guatemala than Ireland and most importantly, it's when the bad guys come out to play. There are over 6,500 homicides a year in the country. I guess the summary is that there are just too many variables, one of them is going to get you, and your best way to avoid danger is to be able to see it first, traveling at night is too dangerous.

I came to a river where the bridge was out and I had to take a detour. That brought me to a makeshift ferry across a river which looked about as seaworthy as an Anvil and was completely overcrowded.

As dusk approached the road filled up with people walking back to their villages. The potholes seemed to get more and more frequent, I hit one so hard I was almost afraid to go and check the front spokes.

The women in these parts carry everything on their head, and the small kids do likewise. I saw a woman sitting at a food counter eating her dinner and the whole time had a bowl full of something or other resting on her head, never once having to take it off and she never spilled any of it. When I got to Coban it was well after dark and I struggled to find a place to stay. As if on cue, a motorcyclist pulled up alongside and asked me was I looking for directions, "you bet" I said. He took me to a great place, and the weight of the world lifted. These chance meetings happen so often on a trip like this, it really gives you a positive outlook on the world in general. The bottom line is that most people are great and will help you if they have the opportunity. I checked in and had an awful throat on me for a drink after all the hiking through the ruins earlier in the day. I went to a restaurant bar which was full of locals who eyed me a little suspiciously I thought. I sat down and ordered two sprites and a beer. I lowered both sprites off the head before relaxing with the beer. A guy was playing Spanish guitar in the restaurant and started playing the Spanish version of "My Way" and after the first verse the whole place was singing along, it was an amazing moment. Not long after, the power went in the building and I was taken back to my room by candle light. I was out for the count in about two seconds flat once I'd killed four cockroaches, one with a set of antlers on him the size of a Moose Bull. Guatemala's history is a tale of woe and misfortune like no other country. Things started going downhill when Spanish Conquistadors fought a massive battle in a valley near Quetzaltenango where less than 300 Spanish horsemen defeated over 30,000 Indians. The decisive factor was the horses, which up until the Spanish came, were not native to the Americas. Also, again in a nod to the Spanish version of history, the leader of the Spanish invaders, Pedro De Alvarado is supposed to have defeated the leader of the K'iche (Indians) Tecun Uman in hand to hand combat. It all sounds like a load of shite to me, I think it's more likely that the Spanish were just more cunning and pitched tribe against tribe and let them all kill each other while they sat back and claimed the spoils.

Over half the population of current day Guatemala remains Native American, the highest percentage in Central America. The country was ravaged by a civil war which only ended in 1996, the root of the conflict being the fact that over 70% of the land is owned by less than 5% of the population. This leaves the Indians scratching a living off the side of the road where they tend what little cattle and horses they have. Whenever you have this much injustice, civil war is an inevitability. Over 150,000 people were killed with a further 50,000 "disappeared" by the right wing government. The recent presidents of

the country were all USA backed, and to a man they've all been implicated in Genocidal type activities against the indigenous communities, the most hated of the lot being former General, Rios Montt. The other pox bottle responsible for horrific crimes was Alfonso Portillo, currently in Mexico where he is wanted for embezzling money out of Guatemala and war crimes. The more you read the history of the country the more you realize that from the moment the Spanish showed up in 1523, the place has been in decline. It's only when you see the ancient metropolis at Tikal and compare it to what you see as your ride through the country, you realize how far the country has fallen.

The police aren't trusted and for the most part keep a

very low profile. The Rough Guide to Central America handbook references daily public lynching's where people take justice into their own hands. The daily newspapers are filled with gore, and if you watched the news you wouldn't have the courage to go outside the door.

Having said all the above, since we'd been in the country we'd been treated with great hospitality and had found the Guatemalans to be wonderful hosts.

Antigua

I left Coban and headed south for Antigua, my aim to bypass Guatemala City via a north westerly route. I spent lots of time trying to find the road which was clearly marked on my map but after ninety minutes of searching I couldn't find either the road or anyone who knew where it was. Most people just shook their head and said, "There's no road there my friend." So that left the horrible thought of driving through Guatemala City to get to Antigua. There was nothing else to do but get on with it, so off I set. Along the way I drove like a lunatic, you have to, just to survive on these roads. I call it driving "defensively aggressive" now there's an oxymoron for you, the simple theme is that your best chance to avoid danger is to put it behind you, accelerate past it, so where possible your always looking at open road. At least three times, trucks and buses overtaking on the wrong side of the road came within a whisker of killing me.

Eventually, I got to Guatemala City and got lost within twenty minutes. The absence of road signs combined with a sign saying veer to the right but there being three roads which it could refer to, meant I was pulled in, getting directions almost every ten minutes.

Guatemala City has the worst ozone pollution in the entire world and certain parts of the city were a fog of un-combusted blue and black diesel fumes. I was choking as I was driving along and doing my best not to puke, I can't imagine what it must be like to live there every day. One of the guys I asked for directions from, while I was stuck in a never ending queue of traffic, had a pump action shotgun right beside him, these people don't mess around. Eventually and over an hour of being

lost, I found my way out of the city and onto the road to Antigua.

Antigua is a UNESCO world heritage site, and is a massive draw for people making their way through Central America. After taking a completely different road to get to Antigua and picking a hotel completely at random, l was stunned to find Joe was there waiting for me. I took it was a good omen for the trip and the project. We went out for some grub and stopped in a Native American cooperative shop which sold arts and crafts made by

local Indian communities. One of the galleries was very disturbing. It chronicled the abuse of the local people by businessmen, Westerners and the Catholic Church. It was very powerful stuff but I couldn't imagine that anyone would buy it and hang it on their wall at home. Antigua is a lovely place, an example of what Guatemala could be like if it can get its act together. It has wonderful cobble stone streets and all the buildings in the area have to conform to strict building standards with no on street advertising. The town is a magnet for indigenous communities to sell their various wares and it has a bustling market which has to be seen to be believed. In terms of great towns in Central America, most people would include this place in their top three or four places to visit.

The views in the town are dominated by a massive volcano, "Volcán de Agua" which I think most tourists look up at and think of Pompeii in Italy.

We met Cath from Australia, who was touring Guatemala while her boyfriend toured India on a motorcycle. I also met Deet, a 71 year old lady from the USA who had been living there for years. She gave me some great tips about where to go and what's good to do in Guatemala.

I spent the day just wandering and soaking up the town. There's an Irish bar called Riley's which isn't owned by Irish people and has the most expensive gargle in town. It got under my skin a bit that people trading under an Irish name were charging over four bucks a bottle of beer in a place where fifty yards down the road you can get it for $2, but the place is always jam packed and is a good place to meet folks.

I continued to wander and noticed that the Indian women brought there babies with them when they were selling their bits and bobs. They wrap them up in a blanket

weave, which is attached to their body and walk around the streets with them and suckle them as they are out working. When I think back to Ireland with hundreds of thousands of women constantly checking the volume on their intercoms in the sitting room to make sure the snapper is ok, it seemed too stark a contrast to digest. We saw girls as young as fourteen breastfeeding children. On my meanderings I'd been hit on by three gay guys, not a big deal, I've no problem with the whole gay thing. But as usual, I didn't get so much as a smile from any of the women, again no major problem with that either, I was on a barren run stretching back to the cretaceous period so I was getting used to it. As an aside, let's just for a second, actually a Nano second, imagine I was gay. Now, with what's left of my self- esteem and pride, let me run through the three lads who tried it on with me. The first was a four foot Indian guy who proclaimed himself gay and looking for new friends. The second was a guy dressed in a yellow spandex t-shift and matching cycling shorts with a bright purple hat, and the third guy was from the States, a bit of a Gene Wilder look alike. So, this is the part that irks me just a tad. What is it about the way I look that makes a four foot tall Indian think that my ass is in play for a bit of pillow biting. Fair enough if Brad Pitt came up to you and said "Dude, any chance I could smoke your pole?" to which I'd answer "Eh, no thanks Brad, I'm fine, flattered and all that but y'know, I don't putt from the rough." Then he'd say "OK dude, any chance you could head back to my place and give Angelina a couple of lengths of your pork sword?" Wake up Oisin! Wake up!

The following morning we headed off to Lake Atitlan,

one of the sites that was in the running to become one of the seven natural wonders of the world. The list had been whittled down to 21, it didn't look like Atitlan would make the cut but still had a shot. Atitlan is located

about two hours west of Antigua and on the way we encountered a massive mudslide which had shutdown half of the road. The hazards of driving in this country were innumerable; there were masses of overloaded trucks and buses, landslides, animals and people in the middle of the road, lunatic overtaking and even a massive disorderly funeral procession.

The plan was to loop round the lake and then head back home the way we came. Atitlan is the deepest lake in Central America and has three Volcano's on its banks, Pedro and Atitlan being the largest of the three. It is renowned as one of the most beautiful lakes in the world, Aldous Huxley famously wrote of it, "Lake Como, it seems to me, touches on the limit of permissibly picturesque, but Atitlan is Como with additional embellishments of several immense volcanoes. It really is too much of a good thing." Well said old boy, well said. Once you get off the main road and start riding on the loop around the Volcano the road conditions start to deteriorate at a very quick rate.

One 3km section as you travel down the side of Vulcan Pedro was a complete wash out with two foot deep undulations created by water runoff from the Volcano. These things are far harder to go downhill on, than they are up hill, it's much harder to control your speed for a start.

While we were negotiating our way, a Chicken bus came along, it almost hit me, and actually hit Joe's rear pannier

pushing him off the bike. Without a doubt, the Chicken buses are the biggest risk to a motorcyclist in these parts of the world, these guys don't give a toss. It was no surprise later when we saw a chicken bus stopped by the side of the road, having just crashed into a car.

Atitlan has many small villages dotted around it which I suppose in many ways represent the "Real" Guatemala. They're populated mostly with Indians and everyone dresses in traditional outfits. The views from the towns were all either dominated by the lake or a Volcano.

The big thing which Atitlan has, for me, is the clouds. Chiefly as a result of its altitude, every time you look at

the lake you get a different view depending on whether or not the clouds show up. We stopped three or four times and white puffy clouds were moving at a tremendous rate over the landscape, it was like one of those fast forwarded storm scenes you often see in documentaries. We got our last pictures of the lake and volcanoes as the sun was setting and had to drive two hours in the dark through the Guatemalan countryside in the pissing rain to get back to Antigua.

When I think of the diversity we encountered that day, it was almost overwhelming. Mudslides, Volcanoes, Lakes, Dirt Roads, Indigenous villages, funerals, overloaded buses and trucks before finishing off with a couple of bottles of beer in Reds bar, it was an incredible day.

I had breakfast in the same Cafe in Antigua two mornings in a row. It's a quiet little place and I always sat in the same seat with a view out the door to the square. Just outside the door on the left hand side selling papers, the same lady sat anxiously eying prospective customers. As people walked by, they all glanced down to catch the day's headlines. The same homeless man appeared right on queue to try and bum a free paper, and for the third straight day the lady told him to go away. A little further out on the street the same horse and buggy took tourists around the square and the people sitting on the park benches were all bathed in warm sunshine from a sky with many white clouds. A fresh cool breeze came blowing in the door, trying its best to turn the page of my book as a girl walked by the door crying into a mobile phone. The music in the Cafe was similar to the last two days, if not the same. It was always a ballad sung over Spanish guitar, the song always seemed to be a lament, in a country with a history like Guatemala's that's not surprising. Even though I didn't understand the words the feeling in the songs was intense, similar to way Irish music used to sound before the rise and fall of the Celtic Tiger.

The lady who ran the cafe said the word "Tranquilo" to me. It's not hard to guess what it means in English, but it actually means much more in Guatemala. Not only does it mean tranquil, relaxed and peaceful but it also means safe, and infers that while you are in this place you don't need to worry, and that's the feeling that Antigua gives a person. Every traveller negotiating their way through Central America always has personal safety worries at the forefront of their mind and the word Antigua has become a byword for safe haven in what is a harsh land. A year previous, I was in Guatemala and really didn't like it, I'd even go so far as to say, I hated it. This time round, I'm pretty sure if I had stayed another day I might never have left. I couldn't get over how much my feelings had changed about the country and especially Antigua.

We had the hardest part of our trip coming up, as we

would soon cross into El Salvador and Honduras. The travel advice was shocking, I said to Joe, "If we can get through these next two countries unscathed, I think we'll be over the worst of it." On my last night in Antigua I went out on the lash and like an idiot, I broke one of my golden rules, namely stay away from the top shelf. For most of the night I drank Mojitos. Even writing this I'm getting the shiver you get when you were absolutely locked the night before as you think of the demon drink that got you the hangover. The words "never again" were uttered many times. I walked home to the hotel to find myself locked out and after spending about forty minutes trying to get in, thankfully a very sleepy looking hotel worker opened up. I walked by him and at the tidy hour of 4am, I got into bed so drunk I had to catch the bed before trying to get into it.

Joe woke me up at 7am and then again at 8am, when he knocked me up the first time I thought I dreamed the whole thing and went back to sleep, no such luck.

Still drunk and swallowing regularly to prevent myself from puking all over the place, I packed up the bike and we headed off in the direction of El Salvador.

As I drove I was muttering away to myself something along the lines of, "What the fuck were you thinking you gobshite! Never again, I swear to fuck, never again, Oh Jayzus please don't puke inside the helmet, you're a gobshite Hughes, a fucking gobshite!"

NOT DEAD YET

CHAPTER 14
EL SALVADOR

As we approached the border with El Salvador, we stopped for gas and shared some Gatorade with two guys carrying pump action shot guns, lovely fellows. After that it was a journey of a little over 100km to the border. Along the way we rode through stunning green countryside, the trees in many places arched over the road from both sides and much like in Colombia the year previously, it was like riding in a forest tunnel for large parts of the journey. It took us two and a half hours to get through the border, which is the moral equivalent of light speed for Central America. The only delay was caused due to the customs guys being on lunch. Can you believe it, no one can either go in or out of the country legally for that hour? To speed things up a bit, but mainly because I was still rotten with drink we got a fixer to do the running for us, it was ten bucks well spent. Once through we headed down the Ruta 2, the coast

NOT DEAD YET

road in El Salvador. Eventually we made our way to the town of La Libertad where we stayed in a lovely place. The bikes were minded by a gentle spoken Salvadorian carrying a gun big enough to blow the head clean off a hippopotamus.

Along the way we saw a bus hit a cow but for the most part we enjoyed the road as it wound its way along the coast. We headed off down to the seaside for a fish supper and watched the locals play with their kids as a beautiful sunset lit up the beach.

Our first day in El Salvador was over and done.
We were hearing nothing but bad news on the Honduras front. There was a coup only a few weeks earlier and the whole country was very unstable. The border was going to be a fuck story before any of this stuff was going on, so we were very worried about the leg of the trip coming

up.
I wrote in my diary that night, "I'm off to bed, thank god for Solpadine, (pain killers from Ireland) I'd take two of these ahead of a shag from Sharon Stone the way I feel at the moment. Am I hallucinating or is there a lizard running across the roof, Frodo Lives but Hell awaits "
The following morning I cruised around La Libertad.

This is the place where the folks who live in the city head out to the beach. The main tourist zone is well kept and easy on the eye, but when I went onto the back streets you start to get a picture of what life is like here on a day to day basis, chaotic, crammed and unbelievably noisy. Over a third of the population in El Salvador live on less than a dollar a day and when you open your eyes and look round the poverty is overwhelming. People dry maize on the side of the road by putting a thin layer of it on the tarmac and I guess the sun takes care of the rest. The amount of cattle on the road is mind boggling, every available blade of grass by the side of the road seemed like it was being gnawed on by someone's cow, a real problem for motorcyclists especially at dusk or after dark. They can just take a mind to chew on the grass on the other side of the road and off it'll wander without checking if something is coming or not.

The chicken buses are ubiquitous and so is the blue black exhaust that they leave behind. If people don't get the bus they cram onto the back of Lorries, or wedge themselves tightly into the backs of trucks or vans. We'd seen so many people hanging off the back of vans, the road fatalities don't bear thinking about. The equivalent of getting up off your seat to let an elderly lady sit down on a bus is "No, you cram onto the bus love, and I'll hang off the back"

Perquin

We left Libertad and headed South East towards the Honduran Border. At the town of San Miguel we turned north headed for Perquin where we planned to stay for two nights. As we continued north the trend of people scratching a living off the side of the road continued, normally taking the shape of a barefooted teen tending half a dozen head of cattle making sure they don't wander out under a bus.

For most of our journey to Perquin we were flanked by Volcano's which had been ever present since we got into the southern region of Guatemala. We stopped for gas and shared some food with some locals who could all speak English and were a good laugh.

Perquin was a stronghold of the leftist rebel group FMLN in the El Salvadorian Civil war. The closer we got to the town the more graffiti we saw with those letters, normally accompanied by a red star on walls, lamp posts and even the road. We crossed a bridge that has so much graffiti on it that it was almost entirely red. In the river below the bridge several kids were swimming, they seemed to be only noise for miles around, it was a wonderfully peaceful moment, it almost belied the past atrocities and bombings which had happened in the area. The chief reason we were there was to see the Civil war museum in Perquin.

We stayed in a fantastic place for $20 bucks a night, it was called the Perkin Lenca hotel, and it's situated about 1.5km outside of the town of Perquin, if you end up

coming this way, this is the place to stay. That night I wrote in my diary: "I missed home all day today. I had to cure myself, I bought myself a small packet of homemade cookies and sat at the back of the restaurant in the Perkin Lenca eating them and sipping a nice cup of tea. I thought to myself this is exactly what I'd be doing if I was in Ireland right now."

That night I was sitting out on the veranda under a completely black sky listening to the vast array of noises which were coming up from the jungle, it was like the animals were all on drugs and going ape shit. It gets dark awful early there, about 5:30pm, so you end up winding your daily clock back, getting up around 7am and hitting the hay around 9pm so you can maximize the day light. There is absolutely nothing to do after dark, nothing. Once you've eaten people sit around and have a chat,

then go to bed.

The next morning I met Anita, a grandmother from Delaware whose son owns the hotel. She was wonderful to talk to and told us many things I never knew about the Civil War and the terrible things that happened in this

locality. After the conversation it was clear that we'd be staying an extra night or two, we never realized this part of the world had such a huge story to tell.

The hotel is perched in what would have been FMLN (Guerrillas) territory during the Civil war, and we set off for a museum a couple of hundred yards outside the town centre. You're not allowed to take pictures in the building itself, but outside is fine. Our guide was a guerrilla in the war fighting with the FMLN against the government forces and was injured in the process. He showed us shrapnel wounds in his head which had impacted his nervous system; he had a limp and couldn't open or close his right hand. Inside we walked through a flow of the causes of the Civil war followed by pictures of the war and lots of displays of guns and weapons used by both sides in the conflict. The pictures were disturbing and even though our guide only spoke Spanish, it was obvious he was visibly shaken as he recounted some of

the stories. We passed into their radio broadcast centre which used egg cartons as sound proofing and from there out into the yard. The yard had amongst other things, helicopter wreckage, a bomb crater from a 500 pound bomb, machine gun turrets and even an undetonated mine which was fenced off.

We were the only tourists in the town as you'd expect and had the run of the whole place to ourselves. We then moved on to the Guerrilla camp which was amazing. We walked through a hole in the fence which was surround-

ed by bullets on strings. Our guide was a young man, no more than 18 whose father had also fought in the conflict. He proudly pointed to a picture of his father in full guerrilla gear in one of the display areas. The camp was full of underground layers where the rebels would go when the bases were being attacked by helicopters or being bombed. There were paths cut through the jungle

NOT DEAD YET

which included a rope crossing and makeshift bridges. I was as graceful as a bull in a china shop with all the camera gear I was carrying trying to navigate my way round. We saw homemade tents, machine gun nests, mortars, RPG's, just about everything you'd expect in a guerrilla camp.

One of the most moving parts of the trip was an area where they kept records of solidarity that they had received from countries all over the world, there was even one in Irish. It was easy to tell that they treasured these greatly. I got the feeling that in the darker days of the war, these messages of support helped them to keep going.

That evening I was sitting out on the veranda looking off into the jungle, in the distance the mist was passing along the tree tops. Just then, a wasp about the size of a cuckoo flew into Joe's room, one of those ones that have arms for catching flies and small elephants on the wing. A crisp "What the fuck is that man!!" followed from Joe as it chased him out of his room. The weather then did the whole jungle thing and started to piss rain. The whole world stops when this happens, and you know it's getting close to time for some grub. That night we met two girls, one from Japan and the other Taiwanese who were staying in the same hotel, both were great fun. One was volunteering in the Perquin area to help build up the tourism industry and the other was her friend who was over visiting her for a holiday. Both were just out of college and they found everything hilarious, I think I used to be like that once. When exactly is it that we stop finding stuff funny and build up a layer of a cynicism around us. It was like a breath of fresh air talking to them. I walked back to my room and looked out into the jungle, it was like looking at a black canvas, nothing was visible.

I was messing outside on the veranda with the computer when the hotel dog came over. She was about 6 months old and just wanted to play the whole time, however her idea of playing was to bite the ankle off you. So I thought to myself, how can I get this maggot to piss off without kicking her. Hmm, I've just the job. I went in and sprayed my ankles with deet, two sniffs and she was gone like a scalded cat, "Lovely!"

The following morning we set off in the direction of El Mozote, the scene of one of the worst massacres of the Salvadorian Civil war. Over a thousand villagers including women and children were rounded up into a church and killed by Government troops, the youngest was only two days old. There is a girl who tends the area around the shrine who tells you in detail how the people were

NOT DEAD YET

killed. I don't have a lot of Spanish but I understood enough that I was shocked to the core. The shrine is understated and there are colorful murals of children playing under moonlight and sunshine.

The thing I really liked about the place is that it tries to be "that day" as it should have been, all those years ago. There's a silhouette of a family under a tree, and in my mind's eye I could see them sitting under the tree passing a warm summer's day. It doesn't try to shock you or fill you with horror as some memorials do, it's so simple and so quiet, that even the noise from the sweeping of the leaves seems an intrusion. We left saying nothing to each other and I felt like it was an hour before I even blinked.

That afternoon we made our way to the Honduras border for a dry run, we wanted to check out was it possible to do a temporary bike import there, and if so would

they be open on Saturday. It all looked good but there's an old saying, "Todays today, and tomorrows tomorrow", so we would have to see how things panned out.

NOT DEAD YET

CHAPTER 15
HONDURAS

We left Perquin later than expected. The day before we'd given the cleaning lady our clothes to wash and dry but by the time it came to leave they had just been washed, so we packed them away wet.

Cofradia

We knew we'd a tough run ahead, we had to cross the border with Honduras and find our way north to Cofradia, just west of the town, San Pedro Sula in Honduras. We'd did a reconnaissance run the day before on the border crossing and we knew it would be dirt road for the guts of fifty miles, but having ridden the first 20km to the border and managed it no problem we were fairly confident we wouldn't have any problems. We got to the border around 8:30am on the 25th of October. We had almost burned two months getting to our fifth country and had only two months to get the whole way to Ushuaia.
There was no way it was going to happen without cutting out vast tracts of South America, there simply wasn't enough days to get everything done. I had talked with Joe about riding the whole way down the Ruta 40, it would add a hard-core component with lots of wilderness shots. We had overloaded on Colonial cities so if we missed a few in South America the production wouldn't suffer. The thought didn't appeal to him. Joe also started to talk about the fact that it was going to take six months to edit the production, something which hadn't come up previously. I had thought it might take two months. By this stage we were barely communicating and as far as I was concerned, it was all over bar the shouting. It

NOT DEAD YET

was nobody's fault, it was simply too hard for two people to complete the project the way we wanted to do it. If you compare it to the Long Way Round they had a team of fixers to help them through borders, they had two producers to keep the production on track, and also two camera men. They had also undertaken a 115 day journey, we had signed ourselves up for almost a year, and this was two guys who didn't really know each other. The project was too ambitious and had we planned it out better, the only conclusion we could have drawn was that it was doomed to failure. I was worn out from it, and I knew the hard chat was coming up, I just wasn't sure when it would happen.

We'd chosen that border crossing into Honduras because the crossing on the Pan-American Highway is notoriously difficult to get across due to lots of undesirables hanging around trying to extort money from you. A year

previously it had taken me more than six hours and over two hundred dollars in bribes to get through. This border couldn't have been more different. The border guard just entered our name in a ledger with our passport data, and in another put our motorcycle information, and that was it. We asked him about either stamping out of El Salvador or Stamping into Honduras. He just said, "Tourista, No problemo!" We stood their looking at each other, what would this mean if we were stopped by the cops? We wouldn't have a permit for driving in Honduras. Similarly would we be able to stamp out of Honduras never having stamped in? We both felt driving up the road that, while we'd saved ourselves the pain of having to cross one of the worst borders in the world, we merely saved up the hassle for when it was time to leave Honduras. On top of that, Honduras had an on-going curfew as a result of the recent coup d'état and had a very unstable political situation, we couldn't help thinking that we might now be trapped in a country with no paperwork, we might just be fucked!

The next 40km was on terrible dirt road, but at least it wasn't sandy so the main thing I was worried about was damage to the bike. Some of the potholes, ruts and divots were nearly a foot deep putting the shocks and suspension under ferocious pressure.

We came to the first checkpoint of the day, manned by two soldiers. The first thing the lead soldier did was to shake my hand, he was a really friendly fellow. I told him where we were coming from, and where we were going and he waved us on. The good news was he never asked for a permit or any paperwork so it was happy days, maybe things had been improved in the last year.

When we were in Phoenix, Andy Flanagan introduced me to a guy called John Tindle, also a biker. We told him we were headed to Argentina on the bikes and he happened to mention that his girlfriend had a good friend in Honduras. Out of that chance meeting, we were now headed up to see Marcia in Cofradia, Honduras.

She worked in a hostel called the Piscina Gringa and we'd about four hours riding ahead of us to get there. Once we finished with the dirt road we were hitting construction zone after construction zone. One in particular had us filtering up alongside over a mile of traffic. When we came to a full stop the guy who was manning the stop sign said it would be another twenty minutes. We'd a long ride ahead so I motioned to the guy to let me through, hinting that the bike was small, and we'd squeeze up the side of the oncoming traffic. It turned out to be a big mistake as we both had to gun the bikes into the ditch to avoid oncoming trucks.

We continued north and made it to Cofradia in the early afternoon. We got directions to the hostel and went down an atrocious track which skirted between some really run down houses. I was beginning to think we'd made a big mistake by going there but when we found the hostel and went inside it was like we had walked into a different world.

The hostel was a great spot and they gave us a great welcome. We walked in and instantly had two beers plonked in front of us and our dry throats were a thing of the past. As it turned out there was a lot of Americans doing volunteer work in the area and later on that evening there was a large group of us sitting around talking and drinking beer, it was a great night.

Ben Udy, one of the guys who set up the Spanish school went on to become a good friend of mine and sent me constant notes of encouragement as I battled through Mongolia and Far Eastern Russia many months later.
I was anxious to get going as fast as possible so we could

get out of Honduras before things really kicked off with the political situation. Even if the political situation hadn't been melting down, the country has the highest murder rate in the world, at a shocking 85 murders per hundred thousand people per year, that compares with 4.7 in the USA and less than 1 in Ireland, so its not exactly a place you'd be going for your summer holidays. The next morning I was up and ready to go early, Joe was a bit ponderous and wasn't in the mood to leave. I said, "ok I'll catch you later." I only ever saw him once more and that was sitting outside a restaurant with some folks in Granada, Nicaragua. We both saw each other, he looked down, I looked the other way and I've never seen him since. I posted him back the large production camera when I got back to Ireland and sent him an email to apologize for the whole thing going pear shaped but he never replied. Like I said earlier, once we had stopped communicating in Mexico, it was only ever going to go one way.

I left Cofradia and went south in the direction Lake Yojoa. Along the way I came across some truly mental driving with trucks and buses overtaking when there was clearly oncoming traffic, it was crazy stuff. I was certain someone was going to end up dead right in front of me, on several occasions. Fear for my life on the road was keeping the inevitable depression at bay which would come when I had time to think about the implications of the project failing.

I checked into a hotel on the lake, had a shower and headed out to a seat on a pier. It's a pretty place to hang out. I sat looking at the water with the mountains in the distance and thought about everything that happened. I blamed myself. Joe was gone, the project was over, and all of my plans were in ashes.

I sat trying to figure out what I was going to do. Would I head back up north to the USA? My motorcycle permit issue in Mexico meant that I had to go south. There was no where I could ship the bike from in Honduras or

NOT DEAD YET

Nicaragua. I could probably do it from San Jose in Costa Rica, if not there, then definitely in Panama City.
I resigned myself to continue on till that point and make a final decision about returning home when I got there.
I had to get my clothes sorted out, the same stuff was still wet since Perquin and now smelt like rotten fish. I cajoled the cleaning lady to wash and dry them for me and a couple of hours later I had them back. For the rest of the day I hung out and watched the sun setting behind some mountains on the far side of the lake. It was gorgeous.
A woman and a kid showed up and broke up the moment, for thirty minutes straight the kid moaned and moaned and moaned. After about 20 minutes I was thinking to myself, "Missus will you ever throw that fucker into the lake and give us all peace!"
On the way back to the hotel I detoured out of the hotel

grounds to pick up some tooth paste. In the distance I could see three extremely dodgy looking hombres walking towards me. Instinct told me there was going to be trouble and I wasn't surprised when they started throwing shapes at me. I was scanning their hands to see if any of them had knives or any other weapons. As I passed them I was certain they were going to make a grab for my bag or attack me, so instead of walking around them, I walked right through them, not something I guessed they were expecting, "Permisso, por favor, permisso." I continued on down the road as they hurled abuse after me, the usual stuff "Hey Gringo..." blah blah. I knew that I had to walk back past them to get back to the hotel, so I went into a roadside cafe and waited for a truck to pull up. I said to him that there were bandits up the road and could he give me a lift to the front of the hotel which he did. The three guys, who had been joined by a fourth were looking on gesturing. I got to the hotel, went into the room and locked up for the night thinking to myself, "Honduras, I ain't ever coming back here!"
The room I stayed in was right on the lake so the noise of Bats, crickets, toads, frogs and every other creature that makes noise in a lake at night, was like a brass band playing outside the window. I did my best to get to sleep and not think about the project going tits up.

Choluteca

I left the lake the next morning early leaving for Choluteca, a jumping off point for the border with Nicaragua the following day. Along the way I drove through the capital Tegucigalpa which wasn't too bad as it turned out. The Honduran countryside is beautiful with lots of mountains and tree lined roads, so it's very easy on the eye as you're driving through, at times it even felt like driving through Canada. The whole day my mind was on the border crossing and how I was going to manage to get through without any inbound stamps or permits.

I got to the border and was immediately set upon on all sides by squadrons of assholes trying to be the one to help you across the border. They were joined by money changers all shouting "cambio cambio cambio" in my ear. Not unexpectedly, not having the right permit turned into a major deal. I had thought of just burning through but looking down to the bridge I could see that there was a military checkpoint, so that was ruled out.
As I pulled up to Customs and Immigration on the

Honduran side, I kept asking myself "How the fuck, do I explain this?" In Immigration they were looking for an entry stamp. I did my best to explain but failed miserably. I made it clear though that I just wanted to leave Honduras, normally the customs folks don't mind too much once your not staying. I stood there for about thirty minutes with a huge queue growing behind me till they stamped my passport for exit and gave me a little yellow ticket about the size of a raffle ticket. I wondered would this ticket get me through the military checkpoint. I went around to the customs and tried my best to explain what happened. I got a fixer who spoke English to explain, but all the customs guys on the other side of the window would do, was shake their heads or wave their fingers in a dismissive way. You know, that way that makes you want to reach in and break their fingers for them. After about 25 minutes of doing my best with the customs guys, I gave up. Armed to the arsehole with my little yellow ticket I said fuck it, chance your arm, maybe the yellow ticket is all the army will check for.

In these situations the result is always more important than the process, you can have a shower later, I always say. I got stopped as expected, the soldier asked for the ticket. I gave it to him and he waved me through.

I drove over the bridge roaring, "Yip-fucking-eee!!!!!" At any second I was expecting to hear the sound of gunshots going off. I literally ran around the Nicaraguan side of the border so I'd get the fuck out of there before any benny from the Honduran side showed up looking for me. I was through like a fart through a G-string and burned up the road.

Obviously I do not recommend this particular border technique. The elation at getting through the border was the first moment I'd felt good since parting with Joe.

CHAPTER 16
NICARAGUA

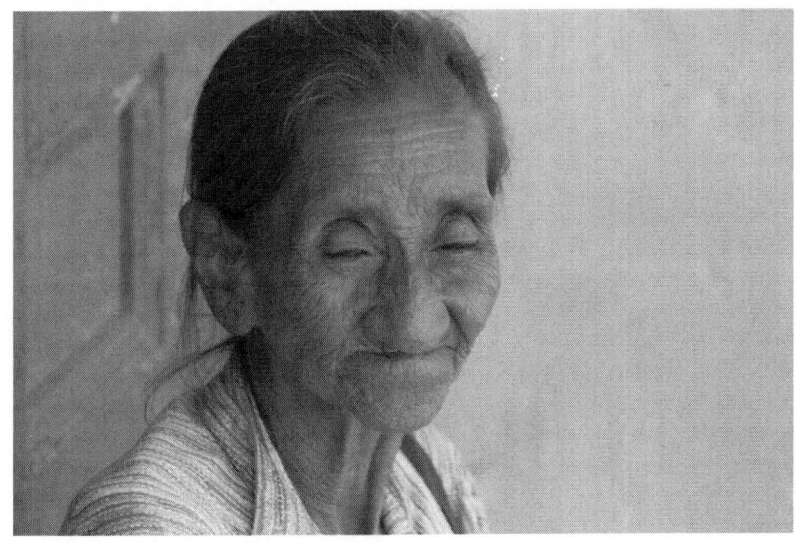

NOT DEAD YET

I had nothing but blue skies as I rode south for the city of Granada. The first blip I had all day was when I was stopped by the cops. They told me that I didn't slow quick enough when the officer raised his hand for me to stop, which was pure horse shit, I knew I had just rode into a shakedown. Some quick tips for you to always

adhere to, when you are stopped by the police in the second and third world. Firstly, be very polite. Secondly, be very apologetic, if you broke the law, you certainly didn't mean to and it absolutely won't happen again, you're very sorry. Thirdly, if your there doing something really cool, make sure you tell the officer, he's human too, and is likely to be interested in it. Fourthly never offer a bribe, make it clear that you're paying an on the spot fine and that all you have is $10, and would that be enough? I got through the first one with little enough hassle but was stunned to be stopped a second time only fifty miles further on down the road. The same thing happened to me in Peru a year earlier, they phone ahead to the their buddies down the road and give them a sucker alert. These next set of cops were making vague threats about arresting me and impounding the bike but having been through the routine many times before, I went along with it, eventually coughing up the ten bucks and going on my merry way. Now, there are people who will flat refuse to pay the bribe and sit there until the situation resolves itself. I'm not sure this is the way to go. The officer has nothing to do and all day to do it, he'll be there all day anyway. It's no problem to him for you to stay there and wait for hour on end, so you may win the victory and not have to pay the bribe, but your reward may be having to arrive in your destination well after dark, thus adding to the danger you put yourself in. So you had to pay a few bribes, big deal, its not like you didn't know

Central America was a dodgy place before you left. On my way to Grenada I was stopped a total of five times by cops and three out of the five times, the cops were really dodgy. The year previously I had no problems so something had changed there.

I set up a tour of Granada and the surrounding areas with none other than the right honorable gentleman, Juan Bosco Ruiz, a native of Granada who I nicknamed Che Guevara. We hiked up to the summit of Vulcan Mombachu which overlooks Granada. I'm a fat bastard so hiking anywhere other than to a fish and chip shop is an ordeal, I was sweating bullets after only twenty minutes. When we got to the top the whole crater was full of cloud so while it was a pain in the arse that you couldn't see anything, the hike was good exercise. If you believe that cobblers you don't know the big fella, I was sick as a parrot.

We hiked back down and while I was waiting on Juan

Bosco to finish chatting up every piece of skirt on the mountain, a poor starving dog came up to me. It could barely walk. I went in and bought it five packets of biscuits, three of which were packets of Oreo cookies, I can testify to their fattening properties. I also gave the woman who worked in the station some money to feed the dog for the next week or so. It would have been awesome to take him with me. After that we headed out on Lake Managua and sailed around the islands.

When we pulled up to one, a monkey jumped onto the boat, robbed a bag of cheese and sat at the back of the boat eating it. I'm not sure if it was a male or a female monkey and it had really unusual looking junk. It wandered around the boat sitting on all the seats and for some reason I was acutely aware that he seemed to rubbing its nether regions over everything he came in contact with. My initial excitement of having a monkey so close to me was tempered with my instructions to

Jaun, "Don't let that fucker sit on my bag!"

That night I met a fellow biker, Igor, he was up over 200,000km on his round the world adventure. We'd a great chat over a few beers about all the various places he'd been. The following morning I bumped into him again, he was just about to leave for San Jose in Costa Rica and while we yapped away, we booked his flight from Panama to Colombia.

I'd a good look round his bike. It was an 1150 GS and he had a ferocious heap of stuff packed on there, but the bike had taken him through Mongolia and Africa and around the world without any problems. I had a similar experience on my 1150, I think BMW may have broken the mold with that model. I would have loved to ride south for a while with Igor but he was in a big rush, his trip was coming to an end and he was on his home stretch. I still wasn't sure what the hell I was up to.

Granada is a lovely town, the streets are made to wander around in and all the touristy buildings are well maintained. When you look through the doors of the buildings as you pass, nearly all have a courtyard with lots of tall plants growing round some form of water feature. There are only two problems with the place. First is that its wall to wall angry beggars. An angry beggar is a guy who shouts at you looking for money. If you're having some breakfast somewhere, they'll start shouting in the

door at you, "Hey you give me a dollar" For the guys who shout at me, I normally reserve the middle finger. It was noticeably worse than the previous year and I talked about it with the owner of O Shea's Irish bar. His view of it is that the place was full of occupational beggars, people who get their "poor mouth" on early in the morning and go and do an eight hour shift of begging, finish up and then head off home that night. The second problem is that you can't sit down anywhere without being mobbed by street sellers. Everyone seemed to be selling ceramics. I wondered was there a rush on ceramics a couple of years ago that made everyone get into selling them. Even if I weren't on a bike I wouldn't buy a ceramic anything. The other thing they were flogging was hammocks, again I can't imagine anyone buying a ham-

mock and bringing it home with them in their luggage. During the heat of the day everyone runs for the shade and the nearest rocking chair, which is what I ended up being perched on for the remainder of the evening.
I left Granada in the pissing rain and got to the border with Costa Rica about an hour later. Everyone crosses this way, if you look at the map of Nicaragua you can see that Lake Managua funnels you down to the border town of Penos Blanca. I was a little late getting there, even though 8am may seem early, the reality is that lots

of tour buses also show up at this time so you find yourself behind long lines of folks all stamping in and out of the country. The recurring theme of large tail backs of container traffic continued, and when I was within about 40ft of the first checkpoint to leave Nicaragua, I was surrounded by a hoard of fixers and money changers. This particular area was much quieter the last time I went through so no doubt word is spreading that you can make a killing off the folks who are trying to make their way south. I hired a guy to be a fixer who turned out to be a complete wanker. The story was always the same, they make it seem more difficult than it is, keep you moving, keep telling you that to speed up the next part of the process would take another five dollars. When we'd moved around three times I told him to fuck off without giving him any money and working it out on my own, I was through the Nicaragua side in under an hour. All day it rained and with the incessant humidity, your body doesn't have a clue what's going on. You're getting wet from the outside with the rain, meanwhile to cope with the humidity your body is pumping sweat like a whore's bastard on the inside. You're clothes are stuck in the middle smelling like a horses arse. The humidity sends massive pillars of clouds into the sky which creates the rain and thunder storms that invariably show up later in the day. About ten feet away, rainwater coming off the roof was hitting the drain so hard that it sounded like a bull pissing into a bucket.

The Costa Rican customs guy was another in a long line of dismissive civil serpents. I wondered if they go and try to recruit specific personality types, I could imagine the ad; "Are you a prick? Were you fed with a sling shot as a child? Do you sniff bicycle saddles in your spare time? Do you shake your head and index fingers to the left and right uncontrollably without reason? If you've answered yes to any of these questions, well then, we've the job for you. Come work as a customs officer and become all you can be!

As I was waiting around for one of the customs guys to come and look at the bike to verify the VIN number, a kid had squished two cans of coke around each shoe and was walking around scraping them off the tarmac. He was having a rare oul time, and just beyond him, two girls of about four and five were having a screaming match, they had put their fingers in their ears and were screaming like Banshee's. I thought to myself, "where's a witch when you need one, we could boil these kids down and make flying potion."

CHAPTER 17
COSTA RICA AND PANAMA

NOT DEAD YET

Finally, three hours after arriving I was done. I was in the eight country of the trip. The first town of note you hit as you make your way south is Liberia. It's then that you realize Costa Rica isn't really Central America. At the corner of one of the cross streets, there was a Papa john's pizza, a Burger King, a McDonalds and a host of other chain restaurants, I hadn't seen anything like it since Phoenix, Arizona. I stopped for the night in a town called Tileran close to Lake Arenal. It's a grid town and is pretty boring. The women wore seriously tight jeans there, and most seemed to walk around sucking lollipops.

With so little going on I had an early night and set off early in the direction of Lake Arenal, a lake made famous by the Arenal Volcano perched on its shores. I stopped off on the way to fill up with petrol and top up the back tire with air, it had a slow leak since northern Mexico and it was high time to get that fucker changed.

The road started off cutting a path through luscious green countryside and then out of nowhere on a distant shore stood the volcano with smoke steaming out of the top of it. The early morning light really set the whole thing off. I'll never get tired looking at volcanoes. There's something about them when the smoke is coming out that says, "ticking time bomb." I spent over an hour looping around the lake after which it was time to head for San Jose, I was going to see if I could pick up a tire. The last time I was in San Jose, I got so lost it took me three hours to make my way out of it, that day was no different. It's like they used up all the signposts in the northern part of the country and ran out in San Jose.

I gave up on the tire pretty quickly and eventually I found my way to the road south but by this stage it was 3pm and I'd been on the road for almost eight hours, so I found a place to stay and hit the scratcher. I'm glad to report that miniskirts with white high heels were very much en vogue in that part of the world, I was rubbernecking all day.

That evening I stayed close to a mountain range south of San Jose where the air currents of the Atlantic and the Pacific meet, the sky was like a big movie theatre.

The Costa Ricans are a friendly bunch, very helpful and most have a little English so it makes it a very easy country to travel in. I was on the road for 7am headed south for San Isidro over the mountains. I was in great spirits, and it was a glorious day for riding a bike. The route took me up, over and down the mountain range which runs along the central spine of Costa Rica and with it being a Sunday, the roads were almost empty. I'd the hammer down the whole way. I continued south in the direction of San Vito and with the empty roads I made good time and was able to keep going for the border. As you cross from San Vito to Sabalito and on into Panama you get to a brutal stretch of dirt road which eventually brings you to the Costa Rican Customs station. There was no one there. I was starting to worry because it was the weekend. In a couple of days I was due to ship my bike to Colombia and in order for that to go smoothly, I really couldn't afford any more paperwork problems.

After waiting around for about an hour I said I'd stroll down to the Panama side, maybe they'd know what was going on. About twenty yards from the border a guy came out of a hut with a mouthful of tortilla's doing the Spanish version of ,"Where the heck do you think you're going!" It turned out he was the Costa Rican customs guy and he was a gentleman. He stamped me out there and then.

I went down to the Panama border, immigration looked busy so I went straight for customs. They told me to go and get some insurance, I already had some but they

said I needed it supplied by a company from Panama. I didn't mind as I knew it wouldn't be too expensive and so went off looking for someone official looking who sold motorcycle insurance. Then one of the most bizarre moments of the trip happened. A guy pulled up in a 4x4. One of the guys from the customs place was driving. He had three other passengers and told me to get in, that he'd take me to get insurance. I did what I was told and looked around the jeep and the other passengers all looked as confused as I was. We went down into the town and pulled of the main street down a lane to the

front of a fairly run down house. I said to myself, "That's it I'm fucked, I've just been kidnapped or am about to be robbed." Just then, a girl came out and took my paperwork and money and gave me the insurance forms. What had happened was the girl had just had a baby and was working from home. The guys at the border station were bringing the business to her. Now if that doesn't bring a new definition to the words "working from home" nothing does! Of course it would never work at a busy border crossing but up here in the mountains between Costa Rica and Panama, I guess anything goes. The only sour note of the border crossing was in immigration. There was about seven or eight Native American folks ahead of me in the queue, but the guy called me through first, despite me motioning that he should deal the Indians first and stamped me ahead of them. I felt bad mainly because it was the first time since Guatemala that I'd seen any Indian folks and I didn't like getting preferential treatment. I get the feeling they get a raw deal no matter where they go.

David

I rode down towards the pacific coast of Panama and stayed in a town called David. It had hardly stopped raining since I left Granada, and in the tropics when it rains, it belts down. If there were this sort of rain back

in Noah's day, it would only have taken 30 days to flood the earth. At this stage it was 82 days since I left home, Jules Vern was around the world at this stage and I'd just entered the ninth country of the trip. I lay in bed the following morning trying to figure out if I should get the bike serviced in Panama City or go to Bogota and get it done there. The big thing playing on my mind was the slow puncture in my back tyre and where it was once losing 5psi a day, it was now losing 20psi, so things were becoming a bit more urgent. It was Monday November 2nd, and I was due to fly out to Bogota on the 4th. I had to try and pick up some tools, I had left all the tools with Joe and there was no way I'd be able to get through Colombia without them. I checked my Spanish phrase book and there were no worlds to do with tools. I went around and asked a few locals where I could buy some, describing tools by making a screwdriver action with my hands, or a spanner action. They kept sending me to this place called Romero. It was a clothing store, I couldn't figure out what about the actions I was doing led people to believe I wanted to get some clothes.

Panama City

I gave up and hit the road, it was 9:45am and I told myself if I wanted to ship the bike with Girag Freight I probably had to be there no later than 3pm. It was 437km away so I'd a long ride ahead. From the moment my arse touched the seat of the bike to the moment I arrived in Tocumen airport just south of Panama City, I was pissed on mercilessly, by the time I was done, there wasn't a dry millimeter on my body anywhere. This was the rainy season and all it did in Panama was rain. Annually they get about 75 inches of rain, about double what Ireland gets, the majority of which is compressed into this time of year. The landscape is very green with lots of tropical forest, whether or not there's anything else to it, I couldn't perceive through the clouds and rain.

I crossed the "Bridge of the America's" which crosses the outlet to Pacific Ocean from the Panama Canal, it's a spectacular structure. On the right hand side hundreds of feet below the bridge I could see lots of smaller boats and further out to sea the massive silhouettes of Giant Cargo ships. To the left there was a huge ship coming out

of the canal and in the distance a plane was flying over the bridge, I don't think I've ever seen a busier view. I continued through Panama City, and on out to Tocumen airport where, having done this once before, I quickly found Girag. I was packed up and had the bike shipped in less than an hour, these guys really know their business. Most of them could speak English and the office girls were real cheeky and chirpy, a Latin American version of Scousers I think. I asked them does it ever

NOT DEAD YET

stop raining, they said "Yes, in January!" I stripped off outside the offices taking off my enduro suit and boots and changing into a tracksuit which would do me till I got a shower in the hotel. The girls in the office were all banging on the window wolf whistling, although I did a lot of miles that day so they were only looking out at an arse with a serious dose of Monkey Butt.

I took a taxi back to Panama and went looking for a hotel. The first place I tried was $179s a night, the second $159 bucks, eventually I found a place for $33. It didn't have air conditioning or even a ceiling fan so I spent the night drowning in my own sweat. The way the women dress in Panama is a treat, the standard get up in the city amongst the younger women at least, is skin tight jeans and a vest top. With all the rain it turns the place into a city wide wet T-shirt competition.

I took the opportunity to get some laundry done and

then went for a haircut and a beard trim after which I planned to head off and see the sites that Panama City had to offer. My hair was cut by a mixture of a male hairdresser (not barber) and a woman over 50. There were no major surprises till I asked them to shave off the beard. Did they do this with a razor, or an Electric trimmer? Nope, not a bit of it, they used a Wilkinson sword blade, y'know the ones you used to fit to a razor before disposables became the fashion. The lady undid the wrapper and showed it to me, I said to myself, "What the fuck is she going to do with that? Maybe tidy up my neck?" Nope, the bitch shaved me dry!

After that I flagged down a taxi, and negotiated with him a $10 an hour charge to take me around to see the sites in the city.

We started off with the Panama Canal, specifically the locks at Mira Flores. This place isn't as spectacular as you'd think. The locks on the Great lakes in North America at Sault St Marie actually handle more cargo freight than the Panama Canal and Suez Canal combined, so if its action you're after, that's the place to go.

After that my taxi driver misunderstood me when I said "Take me to the old town", by which I meant take me to the old colonial area of Panama City. Where he took me to was the most run down, decrepit, drug infested, violent shithole I've ever been to in my life. We tried out a couple of other spots but the teeming rain meant it was all turning into a damp squib. I cut the tour short and headed for a couple of cups of coffee and spent the afternoon watching people walk by in the pissing rain.

The logistics of the following day ahead were mind boggling
-Get to the airport, and fly to Colombia
-Get to Girag in Bogota, get the shipping documents stamped and head to customs (different buildings)
-Get to Customs and clear the bike, hopefully in one day
-Get back to Girag and pick up the bike, hopefully the back tyre wasn't completely flat
-Get to BMW and beg them to take the bike in (tires, oil, service all need to be done)
-Find a place to stay and more important than anything else, get some clothes washed!

Oh, and do it all in Spanish!

CHAPTER 18
THE WOMEN YOU WONT MEET

Now, why would I bother to include this chapter at all? The reason is, I know out there somewhere, is a lug who thinks that all his women issues will be sorted when he gets on the road. He'll be beating women off him with a shitty stick once he starts to get to foreign lands. All I can say is that it didn't happen that way for me, maybe others tell a different tale, but I'll refer you back to the sex education chapter, most guys lie when it comes to women.

So, what are the reasons you won't meet any women while you're on your big adventure? The first reason you won't meet women on a bike trip is that you'll look like shit most of the time. Your hair will look as greasy as a rat's ass from wearing the helmet. Your face will be redder than a baboon's arse due to the elements battering up against your face all day. You'll be filthy a lot of the time, and when not filthy with mud and dirt, you'll stink of sweat so bad you'll be burning your clothes halfway through the trip.

The second reason is that if you travel in different countries, in all likelihood you won't be able to speak the language. There is no girl going to engage in any horizontal jogging if you can't have a conversation with her first. It's hard at the best of times to chat up a girl, even in your native tongue, what makes you think because they can't understand you, you'll have a shot.

The third reason is that you won't even meet them. As you'll be traveling with a bike you'll have to stay in places where there is secure parking. If you end up in a touristy town, all the fine looking women will be up the road in a hostel with no parking going surfing. Are you planning to pack a surf board? If you were going to hook up, it would likely be with someone you'd meet in a hostel who was also traveling, but you'll be elsewhere, so too fucking bad.

The fourth reason is that most of the time when you get to a town you'll be knackered tired. You are on a big trip with a large number of miles to do every day and everyone always underestimates the amount of miles they have to do each and the effect it has on them physically.

The fifth reason is that you'll have ring burn quite a bit. No matter which country you go to, once it's off the beaten track, one way or another you will get a dose of ring sting. No man is capable of chatting up a bird while clenching his arse cheeks together to prevent a detonation. I'm certain if you did have the opportunity to score, God will work out a way that it happens on a night when your arse is doing its best impression of the M25 Motorway.

The sixth and most important reason is that you will spend a long time on your own feeling lonely. What will happen, should you end up bumping into the bird of your dreams is that you'll run your mouth way too hard about the trip, the bike, and everything you've seen. You'll also have a horn on you so large that you'll be foaming at the mouth, desperate for a shag. We all know women only shag guys who look like they don't need or want a shag. That girl will have gotten up and walked away in under an hour.

The seventh reason is that most women don't think riding a bike round the world is that cool. Say if you were a guy, and just for a day every girl in the world thought like a guy, and also liked motorcycles, well then you would have the sheets sucked up your arse by all and sundry. You would have the women form an orderly queue while you iced the end of you knob to shag the next bit in a long line of talent that was about to come into your teepee. However, it is mostly guys think riding round the world on a bike is cool. Any of the girls who think its cool are already getting nailed by a better looking guy than you.

The next reason is the competition is fierce. In most towns you'll travel through it will be full of hounds. When you get to the good towns, they'll be full of women. However they'll also be full of six-pack toting Latin demigods or some fucker with 19inch Bi-ceps, long hair and a guitar swinging off his back. You won't stand a chance.

The ninth reason is that you'll be thinking of a girl at home, and you'll miss her. You'll also be feeling a bit vulnerable and needy. Chicks can spot that shit a mile away. They'll flag your ass as being weak and run a mile. I wish it wasn't true, and maybe it isn't, but it's my experience. It may of course, also be down to the fact that I'm a fat bastard with a mouth like a sewer, I'll leave that to you to decide.

CHAPTER 19
COLOMBIA

NOT DEAD YET

With the day I had coming, I was sure things were going to fuck up somewhere along the line. I flew with Air Copa from Panama City, and got to Bogota around 11:30am. The first thing I did was look for a Taxi driver who spoke English. I found one, a lunatic called John Freddy Lopez who spoke about as much English as Manuel in Fawlty towers, but he was all that was around. I told him the deal, Girag Freight HQ then customs, then Girag again, and then BMW, then a hotel and I agreed a price for the lot with him up front. Then I told him, it should take maybe five hours, but if we were done in two hours I would still pay him the full amount, about $60. With this bonus structure in place he turned into Mario Andretti as we whizzed around Bogota. By about 2pm, I had my bike and the whole shooting match was done and dusted. The people in customs and Girag were first class and I really get the sense that they make an extra

242

special effort for tourists. To get the bike out of Girag's terminal, I'd to drive it into the office area and down a flight of stairs which is a great way to start any days riding.

We then burned off for BMW with me following John Freddy's Taxi on the bike. They took me in, took the bike off me and were as friendly as anyone could hope for. Once done, we went off in the Taxi to find a hotel. It wasn't long before we found one and I was standing in the lobby with all my bags and baggage with a big happy head on me. The enduro suit had been strapped to the back of the bike during transit, it was soaking wet and smelt like a kipper's arse. The stink of the thing was turning everyone's nose up, but John Freddy came to the rescue and made me out to be an Indiana Jones adventurer type who was riding all over the world. Instead of being Jeremiah the gypsy, I was Indiana the intrepid! The hotel laundry took all the gear, even the enduro suit and boots and agreed to wash them all for me, what absolute superstars!

So that was it, the bike would be with BMW till the Friday morning which gave me a full day to go off exploring in Bogota. I was blown away by the reception I was getting, things seemed to be much more friendly than the last time I was in the city, the Colombians were

the nicest people you could hope to meet and I couldn't wait to get out and about in the countryside again. I spent quite a bit of time mulling what route I would take through South America. At this stage I was still doing a bit of filming, and part of me still held onto an idea that I might be able to cobble a YouTube based documentary out of the footage I had. Plan A was to do Colombia,

Venezuela, Ecuador, Peru, Bolivia, Chile, Argentina, Paraguay, Uruguay and Brazil returning to Ireland in February. Plan B was to cut south directly to Ecuador, find a nice place to hole up for a while and try and figure out what to do next. Plan C was to cut home early. The problem with plan C was that I had nothing to go back to in Ireland, it was winter and there was a brutal recession so it would be miserable. I postponed the decision for another day.

The population of Colombia is about 45million people, with about seven million souls crammed into the capital Bogotá. It's about three times the size of Germany, so to travel the length and breadth of it was going to take a long time. I was also planning to head to Venezuela, which would mean I'd end up riding through 6 of the 10 most violent countries in the world on the trip. The news was all bad regarding Venezuela, so I popped off a note to my buddy who lives there hoping he'd allay my fears. He came back with, "My friend the situation in the borders is tough. At Cucuta the border is closed because of the murder of two Venezuelan national guards, I think you should cross in Maicao." I put it to the back of my mind and headed off into Bogota to see the sites.

I started with the Mirador which overlooks the city. It's a cable car ride to the mountain top and from there you can see all of Bogotá. It's a nice view but to get the most out it you would need to be there on a windy day as the smog develops quickly. From there I headed to the National Museum, which was cool enough without blowing my mind away, but it's as good a way as any to spend a couple of hours in Bogotá. After that, I went to the Zona Rosa, the sexy area of Bogota, with all the shopping malls and fine looking women. I'm not sure why I went there, I hate shopping at the best of times. On the upside it did give me the opportunity to chow down on a bunch of Colombian empanada's, a parcel of pastry stuffed with various types of meat, not unlike a Cornish pastie, lovely stuff! I was warned at least five times to make sure I took taxis and to protect my bag at all times. The level of concern people have for tourists in Bogota would make you blush, but after a while it starts to make you more than a little paranoid. As I sat outside the grub stall near the Zona Rosa there were endless lines of yellow taxi's and motorcycles passing. Most of the women were wearing high heel boots and miniskirts with leggings. Any jeans

or trousers that the women were wearing were so tight they looked like they would need to be surgically removed from the skin.

Bogota is quite cold, a bit like "Ireland cold" in October.

It was the first time I'd worn a coat since Canada and at night I heaped the covers on the bed. Incidentally, being the sort of guy who is warm in bed is very attractive to women, in fact it's one of the chief reasons us fat dudes get girls back in Ireland. The women need someone to keep them warm, it's also the chief reason why we wouldn't get a kick in a stampede when the sun shines or in warmer countries. So that's it on Bogota, it's not a nice city to look at, the architecture is a bit "Soviet" looking, and the good bits are only "ok"; but the Colombians, wow, it's like being at your grannies. Before I left the next day I headed off to get insurance for the bike, a bit trickier than it sounds so I recruited the right honorable John Freddy to give me a dig out. I got it sorted in about an hour or so and then headed off to collect the bike from BMW. On the way I got multiple warnings about driving at night through the mountains especially on the road to Medellin. Guerrillas were still very much in operation in that part of the world. It was pushing on for 11am in the day at this stage, I was getting nervous as to whether I'd make it or not.

La Dorada

I got to BMW and the bike was shining like a new penny, the lads did a great job. I drove it out onto the street and started changing into my enduro suit and packing the bike up to head off to Medellin (Home of Pablo Escobar). Later in the day I realized my camera had been stolen, it was a good one too, a Canon SLR. It was in the Taxi in my hold all when I went inside for the bike, I was sure it was John Freddy who whipped it. It put me

NOT DEAD YET

in an instant downer, it was just another problem, there was nothing I could do about it. The project had failed anyway so the SLR was no major loss. As I made my way through Bogotá traffic my minded started to think about the journey ahead, 434km in five hours, should be doable right? Was it fuck!

After three hours I'd only done 120km chiefly due to the traffic in Bogotá and the roads winding and twisting through the mountains. All in all I only made it half way, stopping in a small town called La Dorada for the night. As was becoming a reasonably regular occurrence, I'd parked in the hotel lobby where I was staying. It was easy getting in but when it came time to leave the next morning, the way out was blocked by a car, no one knew

who owned it. There was also a small motorcycle on the

path. The women who owned the place muscled the bike onto the road scratching the fuck out of the car in the process and then waved me out. I knew it was going to be tight and sure enough I got stuck. I could feel all the passers by saying "Look at the gringo, the big gobshite!" A couple of guys gave me a dig-out and we bounced the bike round onto the path. I drove off scarlet, waving to the lads as I left. It was about 160 miles to go to Medellin and the going was slow due to mountain roads and endless small villages and army checkpoints. There is an army presence on every bridge you come to but these are just young lads so it's not a big deal. When they stop you it's all about the bike, where you're from and mostly well natured general chit chat, at least as well natured as it can be when one person is holding a big bastard of a gun.

Every time you stop at a garage for gas you're surrounded by folks. I think Colombia must have one of the highest proportions of motorcyclists in the world, most driving 125CC's and when they see the big 1200 they all come over for a gawk and a chat. I was getting treated like royalty.

Medellin

The scenery along the way was a mixture of yawning canyons and gigantic green mountains topped with wispy clouds. Riding along through these vistas made me feel lucky to be alive and so grateful that I was getting the chance to travel in these circumstances. It was mid-afternoon when I arrived in Medellin, a city of 2.4million people. In the last quarter of the 20th century, Medellín became the headquarters of the infamous Pablo Escobar, the leader of a vast criminal organization, who became the seventh richest man in the world because of the drugs trade, according to a 1989 Forbes

Magazine's report. Because he and his associates based their business in Medellín, his organization was named the "Medellín Cartel" by the American media. He was killed by police forces on December 2, 1993.

I passed a Burger King and seeing as I hadn't had any fast food since Liberia in Costa Rica, I said to myself, time for a treat big man. I went in and stood behind a seriously hot girl in the Queue. She turned around and I smiled, she smiled back at me. I waited for my order, got it and sat down. I had only taken two bites out of my double whopper and I'm sure I had a heap of mayon-

naise/ketchup all over my mouth when the fine thing sat down opposite me. I said to myself "10/1 on, this one is a whore." Why did I think that? Well, seriously hot birds just don't sit down opposite the big fella without wanting something, and I was sure she'd enough ketchup. She could speak perfect English and we did the whole "where are you from "and "what brings you to Colombia" routine. In my head I was thinking, "Any minute now, c'mon baby, any minute here comes the punch line." So are you looking for company while you are in Medellin? I knew where this was going but said I'd play along. Sure I said, always! Then she, in a roundabout way said that the damage would be $400 and went on to describe how it was such a good deal because it included kissing. I thought to myself, "For $400 bucks darling it would want to include a whole lot more than kissing!" She went onto describe how the second day would cost $300 and the third day $200 or I could have the whole four days for a $1000. I asked her, did I look like I was 21 or that I'd a sack of Viagra strapped to my back! I wouldn't be able to shag anyone for four straight days. I told her I was grand and not looking for any action. Then I asked her was it normal to try and pick up lads at Burger King. She said no, she was on her lunch break. I roared laughing.

That night and for most of the following morning it lashed rain with lots of thunder and lightning illuminating the night sky. I was staying on the 14th floor of the Holiday Inn with a wonderful view of the city, I have to say it was a real treat to watch.

The next day lots of little things happened. First thing in the morning the cleaning lady came into the room and asked if I wanted any laundry done, I said absolutely. I'd had an on-going battle keeping stuff clean for a while and getting ahead would be great. I kept all the moldy stuff in a blue bag to keep it separated from the clean stuff, but of course the woman emptied it out on the floor to count each item. I'd say her liver nearly liquified instantly with the stink from the stuff in there, I was so embarrassed. She bagged it up and then came in with a sheet for me to sign. All my gear had gone for individual laundering as opposed to being just dumped in a washing machine, fuck it anyway. It would cost more than the gear cost to buy to get it cleaned! I neither had the heart nor the Spanish to take back the gear from yer one, especially after her having to sift through all that dirty clobber.

About twenty minutes later the minibar girl came in. Every day I said to myself, "Oisin stay away from the mini bar!" which consisted of a fridge full of beer and a bowl of assorted goodies, crisps, chocolates, jellies, and believe it or not condoms. I'd been in Medellin a little over two days and twice, despite my best intentions I'd emptied the mini bar of goodies and of course, the condoms had been left unopened. I could almost hear the cleaner the first day scoffing to herself, "Hrumph, had a bit of party did we, all by yourself by the looks of things!" (Condoms untouched) and the same the second day. I was dying to play a prank and leave a half dozen empty boxes of condoms around the place with a couple of empty tubes of KY Jelly, just to freak her out.

Later I went off to the shops to buy some toiletries. I picked up some stuff and as I was at the checkout, a woman started packing her stuff onto the conveyor belt behind me. I wasn't paying attention but the checkout girl and a very officious bagger girl, mistakenly packed a huge bag of Maxi pads into my bag. They had them bagged and billed for before either me or the woman who wanted them copped it. I was too busy checking out the hot bagger girl to notice. I'd paid for it by credit card so to undo the transaction would have meant me, the bagger girl, the lady, the checkout girl and an ever growing queue of people all standing around looking at a seriously large bag of crash mats for a very long time. To sort it out I just gave the bag of crash mats to the lady as a gift and said "No problemo!" You should have seen her face. Never let it be said that Irish men never made a contribution to the menstruating women of Latin America.

I did another round of sightseeing but didn't really see much to catch the eye, the most noteworthy thing being the old intelligence building. The taxi driver motioned it's where they used to inject people to get information from them, with Colombia's past I'd no problem believing it. The only other thing of note was the amount of homeless people on the street.

The City is built in a cleft between the mountains, so no matter where you look, the city is extending up into the mountains. As I was walking around I was having a bit of a lonely spell so I got a coffee and sat out on the street to watch the world go by. Just then, a girl walked right by me and began kick-starting a motorbike, she was wearing white leggings, it may as well have been Raquel Welsh kick starting a bike in a blue bikini. I would have paid her a hundred bucks just to stay kick-starting that bike for five more minutes, easily the highlight of my day.

I then hailed a taxi to take me to the grave of Pablo

Escobar. The taxi driver was stunned I wanted to go there and he didn't seem too sure where it was. In fact, most of the taxi drivers seemed clueless about where stuff was, everyone needed an address, much like New York I suppose. This is where Ireland stands out, most of the Taxi drivers work by landmarks, for example a pub. So you might say I'd like to go to Moyle Park College in Clondalkin, it's near the Steering wheel pub, and that's all he'd need to get you there.

That night I watched the movie Love Actually, and I was totally homesick after it. When I think of home, I think

of having a drop of tea, yapping with friends and family and that's it, that's what I miss. I couldn't help thinking that the world must be full of lonely people. I had to get out of the room to clear my head so I went to a bar which was part of the hotel complex. As I got close, I saw there was a girl singing a U2 song under a Guinness sign. Irelands reach is long, no doubt about it, it was a great moment but did nothing to cure my homesick blues. As the night wore on, torrential rain moved in and I sat drinking a couple of beers on the window sill looking out at it. I ordered some blood sausage but it looked way too much like a cooked dick for me to eat it. I went back up to my room and sat propped up against a wall looking out on the city from the 14th floor as rain poured down, it was a particularly comforting moment for some reason.

Caucasia

I left Medellin around 9am with the aim of driving for about seven hours and see where that would take me. With the fifth-largest area in Latin America in terms of size, Colombia is one-ninth the size of the United States, and is approximately the same size as the United Kingdom, France, and Germany combined, there was no point rushing anywhere, it was going to take days and days to travel around it. Getting out of Medellin was easy enough and the Ruta 25 quickly takes you up into the mountains. There are some terrific views but if you want to get off and take a picture you're taking your life in your hands. With so much traffic on the road and almost no places to pull in, or hard shoulders for that matter, it's very risky to stop. It wasn't long before I was in countryside which looked exactly like Ireland and much the same as Ireland, it was pissing rain and foggy. Things cleared up and I bumped into a police convoy of motorcycles. The police ride two up in Colombia, one driving with the guy on the back carrying some form of machine gun. Where they were off to and for what rea-

son, I've no idea, but I was struck how fun it is to have police in front of you with the sirens going and how shit it is to have them behind you!
I got stopped several times by the army but every time it was just for a chat. We'd exchange the usual pleasantries like, how are you, where are you going, nice bike, have a nice trip and that was normally it. They seemed so young, I was 39 although I only looked 38 and a half, but these guys didn't look a day over 18 or 19. I was stopping talking to other motorcyclists all day. Any time I'd come to a red light I'd be joined by about eight or nine other bikers and every one of them would burn off as soon as they got a green, as if proving a point and to prove a

point back, about 200 yards down the road I'd burn by them beeping the horn and waving. I eventually stopped in Caucasia, about 300km north of Medellin.

Cartagena

The following day the plan was to cut up for Cartagena, about a six hour ride away and from there loop around Northern Colombia into Venezuela, which was never out of the news for all the wrong reasons. Cartagena is a city on the North West coast of Colombia. It was where the Spanish used to funnel the gold that they were taking out of South America back to Spain. For that reason, it was regularly attacked by British pirates, including Sir Francis Drake. As a result of all the attacks the Spanish commissioned the building of a massive fortress, the outline of which extends to almost 11km. It took 208 years to complete. Charles III of Spain is quoted as saying when he looked out his window with a spyglass from Madrid in Spain; "For the price were paying for those Castles, we should be able to see them from here!" The city is divided into the new and old regions, the old being the region contained within the fortifications and it's renowned as being one of the most beautiful cities in all of Latin America. I was there a year previously and had a good time, the city was great if a little seedy, but overall it was a positive experience and I would have been quick to recommend the place. I was looking forward to getting there.

I left Caucasia heading north and everything was pretty run of the mill for the early part of the day. Any time you'd stop, lots of people would come round the bike taking pictures and asking you the usual run of questions, how many CC's, how fast can it go, and where are you going. There are two roads to Cartagena once you get to Sincelejo in North western Colombia, one is the Ruta 25, and the other is a secondary road which is a shorter route, the guys at a garage told me to go that way. About eighty miles south of Cartagena I was stopped by a bunch of cops, a lot more than normal, but as always, they were very friendly. I couldn't help wonder how come there was so many in one place. Well the answer was, no one was minding the chickens further down the road. About ten miles later I hit my first bunch of teenagers holding a rope across the road. It wasn't too much of a big deal, they didn't have too much conviction about them and dropped the rope when I drove the bike at one of the guys holding one end. As I passed them I couldn't help but notice the amount of rent boys. I told myself, "You're not at home now Oisin, to each their own", and

NOT DEAD YET

continued on up the road. A couple of hundred meters later I encountered a much more serious bunch of lads holding a chain across the road. I repeated what had worked before and aimed the bike at one of the guys holding the chain and popped the bike forward directly at them. If I went through the middle they would have just clothesline me off the bike. It worked again. Later on I got two dousing's by people throwing stuff from the side of the road, things were just heating up. A couple of hundred yards down the road I could see a large gathering of people; I thought it was too risky to chance on my own so I waited for a truck to come along. My thinking was I could use the truck as a battering ram. He would get me through if I stayed right behind him, it worked like a charm. This was a serious crowd I had just driven through, if I was on my own, I would have been in serious trouble.

Still later at a toll booth another bunch of kids all covered in sewerage and holding buckets of shit and piss were trying to extort money from passing traffic. I scooted round the side of them and rallied down the road. Every mile started to feel like it was taking an hour, I never wanted to get off the road so bad in my entire life. In sixty miles I counted ten of these situations, it felt like the whole world was going mental. A lot of the guys had died maroon hair and when I looked at them, there were lots of crazy looking lunatics, it felt like I was on the set of the movie Total Recall. I lashed the bike out of it to get to Cartagena so I could get off the road. I must have broken every rule of the road but I eventually got to a place to stay where, as I was unpacking the bike, a bunch of whores kept roaring at me, "Blo job ten dollars amigo". It was surreal. All of these women had faces like a bulldog licking piss off a nettle, no doubt their target market was the blind and deaf.

Later on in the day I tried to get out into Cartagena City from the hotel I was staying in. I couldn't even get down the street because there were gangs of kids who'd covered themselves in sewerage and they were throwing it over people unless they gave them money. On the other end of the street they were doing it with paint and to make the scene absolutely out of control, there were three or four whores all continuing to roar at me to take the opportunity to get a blojob from them for ten dollars, "Good price." The only way out was to take a taxi to an area where there were police. I'll travel a long way before I encounter as manic a situation as that again. I kept asking myself, "How badly off do you have to be, to cover yourself in sewerage and carry around a bucket of shit and piss with you all day?" Some of them were just kids but some were teenagers, talk about the recession biting!

I eventually got out of the street and got to an area where I was standing for about ten seconds when a guy covered in blood walked right towards me, "Man, what's fucking next!"

I was just about to go pack up the bike and get the fuck out of the city when I went through the walls of the city and walked out into a Carnival. In ten minutes the world had gone from utterly shite to party time. There was at least two thousand dancers in a parade that extended off as far as the eye could see and the celebrations ran well into the night. I met two Aussies, Tim and Triona who hadn't been inside the wall and couldn't believe how different things were this side of the city walls. Aussies are great, they all drink beer and all have easy names to pronounce. I'm sure my mother was doing LSD when she gave me the name Oisin, if she only knew how many times I've had to repeat how you say it. If I ever have a snapper I'll call him Tim. Every fucker knows how to pronounce it or if it's a girl, Ann, easy!

We sat around having a couple of drinks watching the parade go by, these people really knew how to have a good time and it was spectacular to watch. Everyone

eventually made their way to the main square where a salsa band was playing and the whole place went mental spraying one and all with suds and foam. The setup thankfully was well marshaled. It was like they gave all the cops the morning off allowing the scum bags to run riot, and then in the evening moved everyone in and the scumbags went home, I couldn't believe the transformation.

Later on I headed back to where I was staying and got

searched a couple of times for drugs. There was a serious crack down on in the city it appeared (note, not such a crackdown on shit throwers!) One of the women police officers who searched me was a knockout, she was the sort of girl who, if you knew she was coming around the corner you'd be fixing your hair before she saw you. I got back to the hotel and was eaten alive by Mosquitoes even though I had spent a good thirty minutes killing the ones I could see. As usual, I was using completely disproportionate force to kill them but the satisfaction was so good. The next morning I got up early in search of some breakfast before the nut jobs woke and hit the street. The bakeries in Cartagena are incredible, they're really cheap and have a huge variety of buns and rolls with every manner of topping imaginable, I wolfed at least a half dozen down between the bakery and packing up my bike to leave.

Agua Chica

I left Cartagena early purely to give myself a chance to get a hundred miles done before the bottom feeders would be blocking the road. As you leave Cartagena and head north-west towards Santa Marta you cross a land bridge over 30km long. On either side of the road, people have built shanty towns and make a living selling fish to the passing cars and trucks. At Cienga I cut south. I had planned to go North West but had enough of the bullshit on the road and thought to myself if I cut south and use the mountains there won't be any hassle. By 11am I'd two hundred trouble free miles done, so it was time to pull in and get some nose bag. While I was there I met two young fellas who had a pet Martika (what they called it) monkey, they've the cutest little face you've ever seen. The guys reckoned they make great pets too. If I had to characterize the roads which aren't in the mountains of Colombia, my abiding memory of them is green tunnels with white points of light all over the road.
I rode another 140 miles or so to Aguachica. In this town, while they speak Spanish it's the pure cockney version of it. It all meant that whatever smattering of Spanish I'd picked up, well, I may as well have been speaking Punjab, and no one had a notion what I was saying. This was all stuff which I'd said a thousand times before "Pepsi por favor", always met with roars of good natured laughing. I went to a restaurant and thought I ordered chicken, rice and spuds, and I got a stew, WTF!
I was continuing to keep tabs on the situation in Vene-

zuela as I was traveling. That morning this is what it said: We advise against all travel to within 80 kms (50 miles) of the Colombian border in the states of Zulia, Tachira and Apure. Terrorist and illegal armed groups are active in these states and there is a risk of kidnapping. The incidence of street crime in Venezuela is high. Armed muggings and "express kidnappings" are a regular occurrence. You should exercise caution at all times, especially when arriving in, and traveling around Venezuela.

I woke up at six the following morning with every intention of shooting towards the Venezuelan border; the plan was to stay in the town right beside it that night. I was up only about five minutes when I hit my head off the frame of the door, they're all six foot door frames, I'm 6ft 4 so If I didn't duck, I'd a good chance of scalping myself. I whacked my head off one just managing to hold the roar in, but inside I was cursing like a sailor at a prize fight. On the way out of the shower I slipped and went on my ear, I was saying to myself imagine you'd knocked yourself out and the maid walked in, you lying there in the nip looking the right fucking idiot. As I tried to pack up I kept dropping everything and I looked at my watch to see how much time I was losing arsing around the room and noticed it was Friday the 13th, a bad day for the Hughes kid to be doing a Mr Magoo impression. I said to myself, "Fuck this for a game of soldiers" and walked down to reception and booked myself in for another night. I then went back up the stairs and after stabbing my toe off the corner of the bed got back into the cot. I was afraid to look at my little toe thinking it might be somewhere across the room.

After about two hours I got back up and had breakfast.

Once again it wasn't what I thought I ordered. I got stew again but this time with eggs and yuka. (It's a root vegetable, bit like a parsnip) I think they couldn't understand my accent and just said to themselves, "What does he look like he wants to eat, hmm, yuka, that'll do." After that I went up the town to see the sights, which were limited enough, an old church and a town where almost all the traffic was motorbikes.

San Gil

First thing the following morning I met four Colombian bikers who were headed in the same direction as me and they invited me to accompany them; they were a great bunch of guys and we spent the morning and afternoon riding through mountains and Canyons north of the town of San Gil which is a couple of hours north

of Bogota. The lads even bought me lunch. I've been waxing on about the Colombians and how friendly they are, if you ever make it down this way, it will blow your mind. The rest of the day was just like a typical bunch of lads out on a weekend ride out back in Ireland, we rode the bikes, stopped to take pictures, stopped for gas and a soda, had a laugh, rode the bikes and stopped again for some grub. Anyone who has a bike and ever went for a ride at the weekend knows exactly what I'm talking about, it was great. I was supposed to head to Venezuela but the border situation was mental, I'd fifty more days on my Colombian visa and insurance so I planned to swing to southern Colombia for a while and see if it quietened down and then maybe go back, but the warnings were so strongly worded I was almost certain I'd pass on it.

The on-going battle with mosquitos continued. Is there anything itchier than mosquito bites on the knuckles? I woke up the next morning knackered. There was a mangy hound howling outside my window all night and I knew there was mosquito's feasting on me so I was scratching and shuffling around the bed into the wee hours. On top of that I had a serious dose of the Ringas-kiddies (aka the Trotsky's, the cream buns, ring burn). For 12 hours I didn't let the bog out of my site. I'd been getting six seconds notice before detonation, sorry to labour the point but at one stage I thought I was going to take off and fly to Tokyo. When I was certain my innards were a vacuum I left San Gil and headed towards La Dorada again, which completed a 2000 mile loop of Northern Colombia.

I got to La Dorada and booked into the same place I

stayed about eight days earlier. The owner and about half a dozen others came running out to me asking in Spanish, " How are you, where did you go, are you enjoying Colombia" and even gave me a bottle of water. It didn't

stop at the usual pleasantries, it went onto where was I going on the whole trip, where was I from, what's the political situation in Ireland, all of it in Spanish! As a quick reminder, this conversation was happening to a guy whose Spanish was so bad that only two nights earlier he ordered chicken and rice and got a stew! They racked me with friendly questions for over an hour, and didn't take the, "No entiende" (don't understand) for an answer. They just kept rephrasing till I got it, Jesus I'd some throat on me after it.

Now you might find yourself saying, "Hrumph, can you believe he stayed in the exact same place, whatever happened to experiencing new things!" Well let me say first of all it was Colombia I was traveling in, not the west coast of Kerry and after my experience with the shit throwers on the road, a familiar place to stay was

just what the doctor ordered. I sat out by a small pool adjoining the hotel that night and was tortured by a girl walking around in a thong bikini loosely covered with a sash. I nearly poured the beer into my ear three times. On top of that there was a gaggle of women sitting in the pool singing. If I was a ship and these were mermaids on a rock, there would have been a man overboard pretty quickly. Reading this back to myself I know I must sound like a sex maniac, but in my defense it was so long since my last shag, I was beginning to wonder if my lad even worked anymore.

I got up the next morning in no real humor to go out on the bike, I was starting to get a little road weary. With no real draw in a town you're always better to move on, hoping that the next place might have a bit more going for it. More often than not it's actually the road linking two places that holds the attraction for the motorcyclist and for me, that was certainly the case. As I left La Dorada heading west in the direction of Manizales, the road slowly twisted and turned its way up the mountainside until I was way above the clouds and then brought me skirting through mountain villages which were built on the mountain peaks.

Above the clouds it was freezing and I was delighted to feel cold again after spending the last few days cooking in my own juices, the sensation of cold hands was a great feeling. Coming from Ireland, it's like you're made for the cold, I am anyway. I wondered would I still be still saying that if I ever made it to Siberia! There were many occasions where there were sheer drops on either side, one mistake and it was game over. All they'd find is the bike and the enduro suit. The vultures were savage and they'd have you picked to the bone in an afternoon. Since Mexico, they'd been an ever present on the roads. Sometimes the smell of something dead wafts up under the helmet and there's always a pack of vultures standing by to tear it apart.

I stopped for grub in a mountaintop restaurant, the woman who served me had an arse the size of a mini cooper. She'd had a really hearty laugh and all I had to do was order food in my Dublin accent to set her off. One thing you get with every meal is a soup. It varies greatly in quality but the common denominator is a bowl of broth with a heap of spuds and normally a lump of mutton dropped into the middle of it. The stuff that morning was like something Stalin was serving in the Gulags, in fairness though, more often than not, it was very good. There was an old lady sitting just outside the restaurant bumming change, so I told the girl that I'd buy her breakfast. She sat a couple of tables down from me where they served her a huge feed and she nearly licked the pattern off the plates. This was the main coffee growing region in Colombia. I'm a pretty big fan of coffee but the Colombians have a really sweet tooth so if you order a black coffee they'll throw about two pounds of sugar into it for you. If you order just a black coffee with no sugar or milk you'll get a cup that while very tasty, will have your heart jumping out of your mouth with the amount of caffeine in it.

Manizales

I headed off in the direction of the town of Manizales, not knowing that this was the day when everything would go pear shaped. It started with my helmet camera. I hadn't noticed but the video it was taking was about 15deg off centre so all the sexy mountaintop video I'd been taking over the previous couple of days turned out crap. I also contracted a mega dose of ring burn. It took me down for five days and left my arse looking like the Japanese flag. Paradise during those five days would have been a dry fart. I'd been taking lots of Imodium to little avail, "how long does it take to kick in?!!" On the fifth day I was so hungry, I was convinced that my tank was crap free so I went into a restaurant and ordered

breakfast. A stern looking woman told me to sit down and went off to fetch me some grub. Lots of these places didn't have a menu. Breakfast was breakfast, you took what you got. I sat in the chair biting my nails wondering how far off the next rectal detonation was. The lady was hovering around, looking at me occasionally with a face that said, "Don't you fucking dare spit that nail on my clean floor." I put it in my back pocket still wondering if there was any grub coming. Did I have to order it separately? Like most days I'd little clue what was going on. When it arrived, I hungrily ate up and instantly flagged a taxi to take me back to the hotel. Only a few minutes into the Taxi ride, the signal had come from my stomach, two minutes to detonation. I clenched my arse cheeks so hard together, I didn't know which cheek

was my left and which was my right. While managing to keep a smile on the outside, inside I was saying, "Oh holy Jesus will you drive the car, drive the car faster you bastard, oh my god I'm gonna blow out an O-ring, oh Jesus hold on Ois, just hold on." I got into the hotel and burned up the stairs running from the knees down. I almost kicked in the hotel door then burst into the bog and got the tweeds down just in the nick of time, and there I sat for an hour doing a good impressions of an

AK-47 into the toilet. Eventually the sickness passed but I'd lost the heart and motivation to continue with any filming. I was done. The dream was finally dead, although in reality it was never more than a fools dream, it had been over since Honduras but a small part of me had been keeping up the pretense.

I spent the next day walking around the town. There was lots of interesting statues, the best was the Bolivar Serpent. The town is built on a mountain ridge, if you walk north to south its easy going, if you walk east to west your either walking up, or down a very steep hill. The town also seemed to have a great sense of family or at least that was my impression. That evening, the whole town was out for a stroll and a coffee and ice cream. Everyone seemed completely carefree as they ambled through the streets. The Colombians are a proud bunch, they love their country and they really care that you are having a good time and you like it too, and they greatly approve of positive remarks that you make about it. They appreciate small talk and politeness. How are you, hello, are you enjoying your stay, the weather is nice.

It was my second time in the country and at no time did I see any corruption. I'd been stopped a hundred times by the Police and the Army and they were always cordial and helpful. The only downside to the country, the same as all the other countries in Latin America, is the poverty. Every now and then I'd see an elderly person out begging with a face etched way beyond their years and I'd think to myself "Old lady what have you seen. Why are you alone? Who is looking after you? Where is your son or husband to protect you?"

I saw tens of colorful statues which lined the road, each

face of the statues seemed to be telling a different story. The whole town had tin roofs and when it rained the sound was wonderful. There was also lots of really cool graffiti around the town. I finally left Manizales the following morning and drove south west towards the city of Cali passing through it and making my way south to Ipiales over the course of two days. I had finally made

it to the border with Ecuador. I got to the checkpoints and stamped out of Colombia. I then went to customs and gave back the vehicle import documentation. I went back to the bike, put the key in the ignition to start it up and head down to the Ecuador side of the border, but the bike was as dead as a fucking door nail. I kept asking myself, "hold on, the bike has been running perfect. It must be something small." I checked round the bike for

anything loose but couldn't find anything. I was thinking maybe I was having a Mr Magoo moment so I ended up checking everything about twenty times, the same way you would if you looking for your car keys in the morning. The whole time I checking the stuff on the bike I had about twenty money changers all chiming in their two cents, to which I wanted to respond with machine gun fire.

No matter what I did, nothing worked. The bike was dead. It was only then I noticed the EWS warning on the display, "Oh you complete and utter bastard!" The bigger problem was that at this stage I was in no man's land, between borders! I was out of Colombia and not yet in Ecuador. My exit from Colombia hadn't yet been processed so when I tried to reimport the bike it caused all sorts of hassle. I'd just checked out of Colombia so they wanted to know why I was checking in so quickly, I tried

NOT DEAD YET

to tell them drawing lots of blank stares but managed to explain myself with the aid of a helpful border guard. I jumped in a taxi and headed back to Ipiales leaving the bike behind in no man's land. The taxi driver drove me to a guy who he told to bring his truck down to the border area. Starting to beam that we were making progress, my optimism soon faded when the truck arrived at the border crossing. The bike was fully three feet longer than the load area of the truck, "Ah for fucks sake, what sort of poxy truck do you call that!" The guys truck didn't look like it could haul a bag of apples not to mind a bike but I was grateful that he tried. With the bike still stuck in no man's land, I went back to Ipiales to see if I could sort something else out. The only thing I took a bit of comfort from was that, I was sure it wouldn't get stolen with the amount of guards in the area. I had no clue what to do. I put a couple of shout outs on motorcycle web-

sites to see if anyone had any ideas and I tried talking to BMW in Bogota. To compound the problem, any of the parts which might fix the problem were eight hours away in the city of Cali. It was BMW in Bogota who eventually came through for me. They organized a truck to come and collect the bike out of no man's land. A guy showed up where I was staying on a Suzuki 100, and told me to jump on. Isn't it crazy that I just did it? I wasn't even sure if he was the guy who I was supposed to be meeting. This was also Colombia, where people go missing all the time. Two minutes later we were flying down the road back to no man's land. There were massive tail backs at customs, thankfully the truck that BMW had organized had already gone ahead into no man's land. The crack we had booting along on that little Suzuki, a hefty 6ft 4inch lump from Clondalkin riding bitch behind a Colombian lad filtering though masses of traffic, I'll never forget it. The truck followed the Suzuki down to where the bike was and pulled up alongside the bike pulling out a plank of wood. I thought to myself there is no way the bike will make it up that ramp without it breaking, but I was out of options. We rustled up about ten onlookers and ran the bike up the ramp and to the surprise of all, it made it without the plank snapping. I doubt I'll ever be able to properly relay how stressed out I was running up that ramp with the bike, my sweet Jesus, I'm still not over it. Next thing one of the customs girls came running out to me to say that there was a problem with the customs paperwork so I ran in to get that sorted. I then jumped in the truck with the lads and drove to their office in Ipiales to make sure the bike got through all the checkpoints and made it to their warehouse ok. I sat there with the lads filling out the paperwork and I thought it was pretty fitting, the day had started and finished with filling in forms.

Cali

They then took the bike to the BMW dealer in Cali, and I planned to follow them up in a taxi. With a lot of luck I thought I might have the bike back by within 24hours. I arranged for a taxi to pick me up at 6am, it would be a ten hour drive to Cali so if I got there at four it would give me a shot of getting the bike back. I thought we might be able to get there in eight hours so when the guy came back to me and said that he couldn't leave till eight, I said ok, half glad of a few hours extra in bed after what was a really shit day. The guy showed up at 7:50, all good so far. The first thing he asked me for was money for Gas, not uncommon on a long run, these guys don't have a pot to piss in, and they don't own the cars, they merely drive them. I gave him $25 to come off the total when we'd get to Cali. This is the point at which things started to turn to shit. He drove down some gravel back roads to a beat up yard, where he beckoned to a guy who came running out of a tarpaulin hut. He started filling him up

with black market gasoline from Ecuador. In Ecuador, gas is half the price of Colombia so gasoline smuggling is commonplace. They have a signal which is to hold up an empty two liter bottle of soft drink with a pipe on the end, if you swing it up and down in the air that means you've got Ecuadorian gasoline for sale. Things were taking a while so I stepped out of the car and as I was walking around I noticed the guys tires were as bald as Madonna's bush, there was no way they would make it to Cali. I called him to look at them and he got a spare and put it in the trunk. I said, "Fuck it Ois, you're in this now, stick with it." I got back in the car and as soon as he tried to start the car it was as dead as a dodo. I said, "Fuck this, there's no way this bucket of bolts will make it" I said to the guy, "Look I'm going to get another Taxi" and gave him ten bucks for his troubles. I flagged down another Taxi who ended up charging me a lot more, but would only take me to the town of Pasto, I'd have to get another one there. The way I looked at it, that was closer to Cali than where I was, it was time to take it one mile at a time. When I got to Pasto the guy had rang a buddy of his to take me the rest of the journey. At this stage I had the eight ball firmly in my mouth and these Colombian Taxi drivers were screwing me to the wall money wise, but I'd no choice, the day was getting older and I had to try and get to BMW before they closed at six. By the time we got there, I was ten hours in the back of a taxi. The whole way the lads were playing Salsa music or whatever goes for Colombian elevator music, if I never hear a Salsa beat again, it'll be still too short a time. Along the road every manner of hold up happened, massive funerals, construction, landslides, check points, the end result being I got to Cali way too late on the Friday evening. I was stuck there for the weekend, BMW was closed on the Saturday and Sunday. If the truck didn't make it on the Friday either, the earliest I'd be out of Cali was Tuesday. We arrived in Cali a little after sunset and the taxi guy brought me to a touristy hotel. I went in, put the gear in a room full of mosquito's and headed down to the restaurant. I sat down and without ever ordering grub, the waitress put grub in front of me, soup, rice, chips, round steak and a drink of baboon piss. I didn't even try to argue, I was too fucked. There happened to be an advertising campaign running about Colombia at that moment, and it finished with the lines "The only risk in traveling to Colombia is that you'll never leave" or words to that effect. "This isn't what I had in mind!!!" With no choice but to hang out I decided to make the most of it and go exploring in Cali. It is a town with a serious pulse and a noise level way higher than any city I had yet visited in Latin America. From my Diary: "Every

now and then a siren goes off outside the hotel and when there's no siren there's the grinding noise of articulated air brakes. The fan in the room is on its last legs and is groaning in protest about being run on the ragged edge,

it looks likely to come out of its creaking bracket at any second, no doubt decapitating me in the process. There's a child roaring crying outside in the lobby because the twenty other kids who are playing chasing outside won't play with him. The guy in the room next door is trying to drill a hole out the back of his girlfriend and every now and then I hear the high pitched whirring noise of mosquito's in my ear. Peace and quiet is in short supply."
I broke out the lonely planet to see what the town had to offer. All I'd heard was that it was one of the plastic

surgery capitals of the world with lots of the local chicas all having various parts of their anatomy altered. It had a population of almost two million people and was one of Colombia's most prosperous cities. Since Medellin's role in drug trafficking was killed off in the early 1990's Cali had stepped in to fill the void. The city is surrounded by a huge fertile plane and thousands of African slaves were brought there to harvest the sugar cane crops which grow in abundance in that region. The legacy of it is that Cali is the most Creole city in Colombia and is also known as Colombia's biggest party town, with Cuban style salsa music blaring from every second bar.

The first place on my list was the Plaza de Caicedo, which wasn't particularly memorable. I crossed the river into a more touristy area which was full of restaurants and along the river the town was making a huge effort for Christmas, with decorations streaming in all directions. As it was Sunday it was quieter than normal and as the shop traders were opening I couldn't help but get the feeling that the whole town had a massive hang over. There were lots of homeless people sleeping in any bit of shade that was available and the usual crop of street traders all selling the same junk that's available in every town south of Tucson. It's a nice enough place, the outskirts are rough as fuck but other than that it's not a bad city, not a place to bring the kids though.

Ipiales

First thing Monday morning I was off to BMW to see first of all did they get my bike, and if so, had they fixed it. The good news was they had, it turned out the problem was the EWS, the same problem Joe had encountered all those miles ago in Phoenix. Lots of Coulda Shoulda Woulda's followed in my head, but fuck it, I told myself "what's done is done".

I burned out of Cali as fast as was possible, my aim being

to get as close to the border with Ecuador as possible. It was 10am when I finally got going and by 5pm I was back in Ipiales, where I checked into the same hotel I

originally stayed in. I left Ipiales in Colombia at 6:45am and had stamped out of Colombia by 6:55am, everything was going according to plan so far.

CHAPTER 20
ECUADOR AND PERU

I lit off in the direction of Ecuador and was almost the first person at their border checkpoint. I got stamped through immigration in a heartbeat and the customs guy had me done and dusted by 7:30am where after I was burning down the Pan American highway in the direction of Quito. I was so glad to be finally putting some miles up on the road

Baños

When I eventually got into Ecuador it was November 24th. The route from Colombia into Ecuador takes you up over the Andes which made the early going freezing. I crossed the equator and it was only 12deg C, albeit at a very high altitude, but even for that high up it was unseasonably cold.
I got stopped at a half a dozen checkpoints as I made my way south, there were Military, Police, Customs and some crowd dressed in grey with lots of guns, the latter meticulously searching the bike for drugs. I was thinking to myself, "I thought the drugs always went north?" but I wasn't about to get into a debate with a bunch of armed soldiers, I was just happy they weren't asking me to grab my ankles.
Ecuador is very cheap to travel in. A 500ml bottle of water is 22cents, a bottle of diet coke 40cents, a gallon of gas about $1.70 and a really nice hotel will run you about $15 bucks, if you give someone a dollar tip, they'll faint. The countryside is wonderful, be-speckled with Volcanoes, canyons and rivers. I got off the bike when I reached the equator and did the whole Beavis and Butthead routine as I straddled the equator line, "My crack

is the equator! My crack is the equator!"
When I got to Quito I got lost, again. When I'm going through a city, I'll often stop for directions, and in Quito I stopped at least twenty times. The people would always say just keep going straight "directo directo" but two

minutes later, as sure as shit smells, I would come to a T-section which they never mentioned. You can either go left or right and whenever the odds are 50/50, you get it wrong 90% of the time. (Ref: 50/50/90 Rule) The trend continued in Quito, every time I picked the right or the left it was the wrong way. I even started to say to myself "Ok Ois, you think it's right, so go left, that'll be the right way ", nope still got it wrong. I eventually found my way out and made it to Banos. The roads around Banos are like a labyrinth; you can drive for a hundred miles around the various mountains and still have only gone ten miles as the crow flies, if you're planning on going to Ecuador, I can't recommend this place enough. Banos itself is an adventure tourist Mecca. It has everything. The town itself is set right in the middle of the Andes and irrespective of whether you look North, South, East or West, you are looking at gigantic mountains. The town is full of restaurants and places to stay and has a host of companies running adventure tours where you can go canyoning, white water rafting, bungee jumping, bridge jumping or mountain climbing. The people in the town are friendly and very helpful with most having a smattering of English, German and even French. You could be forgiven for thinking you were in the Alps. There is also a great market where indigenous Indians sell every manner of jewelry and bits and bobs. All of them are hand made by local Indian communities, you can even see them getting made behind the counter and as with everything in Ecuador, the price is very cheap. I took a few days out to figure out what I was going to do. I had to spend a day or two "mourning" the failure of the project. Some people would say just move on, put it behind you, pick yourself up and get back on the horse. For the most part I would agree with that, but I do think it's important to spend some time analyzing where things went wrong and given the opportunity again, what would you do different. I was also beginning to think that there was something wrong with me. On my last trip I had said goodbye to Geoff only a couple of days into the trip, and now I had done the same to Joe, was it all down to a fundamental character flaw on my part? I also had to figure out where I was going to go

now, I didn't want to just recreate the trip I had taken the previous year by following the Pan Am South.
I'm a firm believer that the biggest part of emotion is motion. For me at least, if I can keep moving I can normally stay in a positive frame of mind. I need to feel that I'm making progress to a worthwhile goal. I can't just "amble", I have to have a destination. For that reason, just hanging out in South America was never going to be an option. I started mulling several options, "What about doing the Ruta 40 in Argentina?" Over the course of three days, walking mile after mile around Banos I finally had a plan for what to do next and I was also happy with the narrative I'd created in my head for why the project failed. The project failed because we took on too much. We hardly knew each other yet we had signed ourselves up to traveling and working together for a full year. Traveling the world on a motorcycle is a big chal-

lenge, when you throw having to film it on top of that, it starts to test the bounds of possibility. Joe was also trying to keep his company going in Los Angeles. We underestimated the amount of work involved in integrating the various video formats, the time to edit the production, and the time to back up and save all the work as we went along. We also didn't have the experience to talk lucidly in front of the camera. We did our best work on the diary cameras but when we tried to do a staged shot we'd end up sounding like a pair of goats. Put simply, we were over scoped and under resourced, and like any business or project, when that's the reality, failure is certain. Had we picked a shorter project first and built up from there we would have had a better chance of success. If you go back to the example of the Long Way Round, that trip was 115 days long and was done with a film and support crew and a team of people working out of London on back up. Charlie and Ewan were also best buddies. We had signed ourselves up for almost a full year of traveling and working but barely knew each other. We lacked the ability to communicate with each other. We heard the words but didn't understand the meaning. Joe may feel that it failed because I left, in my opinion that's just the day it ended, it failed because the project wasn't properly scoped out. None of that will change the fact the Joe thinks I'm a complete wanker. The facts were, it had taken me till November 25th to get to Banos and I was well ahead of Joe at that stage. That left only one month to get the whole way to Ushuaia and film all of the stuff in between, there was no way we could have done it without redoing the route or canceling out of the Dublin to New York leg, which for me wasn't an option.

I then moved onto what I would do next in my head. The answer to that question came from the end of my last trip. I had just finished a Pan-American motorcycle trip which stretched all over the Americas and included what I thought then, was all of the Ruta 40, a notoriously difficult road in Argentina. I picked up a picture book in Buenos Aires called the "Ruta 40" and was dismayed to find out that I'd actually completed less than a third of the total distance which the road actually covers, 5200km stretching from Bolivia to Rio Gallegos in Southern Argentina. As I leafed through the book on the plane en route to London I made myself a promise, If I ever found myself in South America again, I'd try and do the entire Ruta 40 and not only that, I'd try and write a book about it. Admittedly it was a very strange road that brought me to this moment but I was done kicking the crap out of myself for failing, I was headed south to complete every single yard of the Ruta 40 in Argentina. I also told myself that maybe if I got through the Ruta 40 unscathed, maybe I could think about doing the Dublin to New York trip solo. They were very similar in terms of the level of isolation that you had to travel through, and if I was good enough to ride all the dirt and sand roads on it, maybe I'd also be good enough for Mongolia and Far Eastern Russia.

I scooted out of Banos that morning in a generally southern direction, I planned to spin round the Andes and make my way further south so I could make the border with Peru the following day. En Route, there were police everywhere, I think they were expecting some organized demonstrations, it was the most amount of police I'd seen in one day so no doubt something big was in the offing.

When I stopped for gas and went for a jimmy riddle I came out and found a young fella with his hand in my tank bag, I walked up behind him and gave him a clip in the ear. He denied any wrong doing but the way I look at it, if the hand is in the tank bag it's no different than if he had his hands in your wallet. To his protestations, I merely replied with the birdie, driving off before anymore hassle started.

The roads were mental in places. I was riding on seem-

ingly endless gravel roads as I passed once more over the Andes. There were lots of crosses on the roadside for those who weren't so lucky when they came this way. I was still struggling with the Minibars. From my Diary: The last couple of places I've stayed have all had mini bars. Now they haven't been the Ritz, averaging about

$20 a night, but they haven't been shit holes either. After four complete and utter mini bar wipe-outs, I have to admit I've the will power of a fox minding a bunch of chickens. I always walk in and say, "Please don't have a minibar, please don't have minibar " and sure enough there always is one with some crisps, peanuts, chocolate, salt crackers, Pepsi, beer, candy etc. My failure always starts with the salty stuff. "Sure you need to get some salt into you Ois after all that sweating on the bike", at least that's what I tell myself. As my mouth dries from eating the peanuts and crisps, "Jayzus I'm thirsty" and the drinks start to go. Of course the drink is too wet on its own, "I've the fucking munchies!!" Then it's all gone, all that remains is eight or nine wrappers and empty bottles taunting me. I made my way to the border with Peru moving from the Ecuadorian Andes into a flat plane where the landscape was dominated by Banana plantations. Did you know a banana tree only bears fruit once? When I heard that it caused me to emit a very high pitched girly sounding "Really?" I got the feeling that if I stood still long enough, one of the Banana companies would plant a banana tree in my ear. In the west there's a big drive to eat 5 portions of fruit a day, "You'll live longer and your arse won't fall off when your 85." It didn't jive in my head that if the western world was munching down on 5 portions of fruit a day, that the result was a sprawling monoculture of Banana trees for as far as the eye can see in Ecuador. I've never even heard it debated. The green crowd are all banana munchers but I wonder if they got their ass to Ecuador would they sing a different song?

As I continued south, in one day it went from 12degC in the mountains to 37degC on the planes I got to the border and even though I'd been through this one before, it was all terribly confusing. There was a sign which said "Frontera Ecuador - Peru" so I drove following the arrow, but it's only the Peru side which is working down that end. You have to stamp out of Ecuador in the town, then come back out and then go down a three lane highway to the Peru side, all a bit mental.

I think it showed that the Peruvians and Ecuadorians don't get along too well. There's been three military conflicts between the two countries in the 20th century alone and Ecuador has a major bee in its bonnet with Peru, who are allowing lots of counterfeit dollars to flood north into Ecuador.

I made it through fine and headed south till the light faded and I stopped for the night in the town of Mancora only to be confronted with yet another reed basket of

goodies and a fridge full of beer. "I can resist anything but temptation!" (Oscar Wilde)

Leaving Mancora I arrived smack bang in the middle of the Peruvian desert, and being from Ireland, I find this landscape a particular treat. I think it's a similar thing to the folks from the UK being obsessed with heading to Morocco to ride in the desert. In Ireland and Britain the whole place is green and all it does is rain, the opportunity to ride in what is essentially the exact opposite landscape to what we were raised in, is too much of a good thing. I've heard deserts all over the world are treated like large dumps, in Peru it's no different.

Outside every town for miles and miles, thrown onto

the side of the road is millions of tons of garbage and rubble, it's a shame but at least the junk isn't everywhere, it's mainly confined to the outskirts of towns. North Western Peru is a surfer's paradise, which is a pastime I don't really care for. The people in this part of Peru

aren't overly friendly and the cops are complete fuckers. I was in a hurry, I wanted to burn down to complete the

NOT DEAD YET

Ruta 40 and my mind had zeroed in on getting home for Christmas and I was riding big miles every day. My ass was wondering just what it did to deserve all the punishment.

There is no such thing as road etiquette in Peru and no one drives with any care and attention for other road users. I was nearly run off the road by oncoming trucks several times in the desert which I couldn't help think was deliberate. On top of that I found myself coming up behind grossly overloaded trucks shedding their loads as they drove along the highway.

The crazy desert winds rise up as the day wares on and

constantly threaten to push you right off the road, as each day came to an end there was a large part of me that felt lucky to have survived. However, the hazards you encounter are well worth enduring for the experience of driving through it. In some ways, I think there's a price to be paid to get to "great views" and as a result have great memories. For example to get a view from the top of a mountain, the price you pay is to have to hike up one, and to see the desert in all its glory you have to risk something in return, namely having to travel into one. All of which makes me wish I had a helicopter! All the great religions of the world started in the desert, and when you see what's out there, I think I can understand why. I stopped over and over again to try and soak it all up, to try and imprint what I was looking at somewhere in my brain. On several occasions I was looking out into the vast desert and in the distance the sand on the banks of the Andes was glistening from the light of the setting sun, I could feel myself welling up. I spent my second day in the desert as I continued to move further south. Much like the first day it began as the sun was rising. Even now I can see the image of the sun rising ahead of me as I made my way deeper and deeper into the desert. It gradually lit the desert into a soft peach color. The road bent south and with it the sun moved to my left side. The wind gradually picked up and started to send sand flying high up into the air dulling the color of the landscape turning the world a lifeless grey color. The wind is your constant companion as you ride south, it makes it hard going, but part of me wanted it to be hard. I had no interest in crossing a desert that was easy to cross. I wanted to look back and savor a beer that night knowing I'd fucking earned it, and had defeated the desert to get there.

Nazca

After three wonderful days in the desert I made my way to Nazca, a relatively short hop from Chincha Alta where I stayed the previous night. I was pounding out the miles as the whole emphasis of the trip had become to go and complete the Ruta 40 in Argentina. Peru was now just a country I had to ride through to get there. As I was driving along I passed through some of the most run down beat up towns imaginable. Only on the news when looking at footage of Afghanistan would you see stuff that would compare to it. The repeating pattern for all the towns is that either side of them there is rubbish and building rubble tipped for as far as the eye can see. Peru was starting to get very hard to travel in. Apart from the wind, there were lots of niggly things which back packers or conventional tourists may not see, but are things which motorcyclists have to deal with. I wrote

in my diary some recommendations for the Peruvian authorities (only some of them are tongue in cheek!)
Problem 1: The amount of noise from car horns is way too high mainly due to the fact that every fucker has a police siren built onto their car. Fix: Limit the use of every vehicles horn to just once a day, it will mean less noise, more sleep and more tourists, nuff said.
Problem 2: Gas stations giving out counterfeit Money: I was given a counterfeit 50 and a 20 sol note. They were so good that even when the next gas station held it up with a good one, I couldn't tell the difference. They give them out no problem, but when I tried to pay at the next station not knowing it was a forgery, the guy went fucking ballistic. Fix: Get some credit card readers at the gas stations, oh yeah and you'll cut out a counterfeit money laundering scheme at the same time.
Problem 3: Every bit of rubbish, garbage, shit and animal carcass is dumped at the start and end of every town. Fix: Put it in a landfill, you've enough deserts here. Put it in a couple of trucks and put it in a land fill. It fixes nothing in the short term but at least your towns don't look like they were just bombed.
Problem 4: Every fucking house in the country is unfinished, especially the upstairs portion. Fix: Instead of taxing people when the house is finished, tax them when it isn't, now your towns don't look like the fucking cookie monster was in nibbling all-round the house.
Problem 5: Every single cop on the road is a thieving bastard. Either they fine you a bullshit amount, or ask you for gas money for their truck. Fix: Just tell them to stop doing it
Problem 6: Gas attendants robbing you blind: It hap-

pened to me at least five times, either it was the wrong change, counterfeit money, not starting the counter at zero or starting to fill up the next guy before you paid, so he bills you for both. Fix: Kill them.

Problem 7: Oncoming trucks running you off the road: This happened to me at least a dozen times since getting to Peru. Fix: Fit all motorbikes with Exocet missiles to blow up trucks in the wrong lane, this will also be a help against thieving bastard cops

Problem 8: No Totty, there isn't a looker in the whole country! Fix: Ask Colombia for a few of their women, they've more than they know what to do with.

So like I was saying it's a really difficult country to travel in, in that you have to put up with a lot. That said the roads are great and the scenery is magnificent so it's worth putting up with. I managed to squeeze in about ten miles of off road in the desert the following day. Even though its sand there's a hard layer of stone compacted over it, so you can barrel through it pretty easy, I had a great time.

I headed south from Nazca early the next morning taking the coastal route south, most people at this point cut into the Andes and make their way to Cuzco, but having done that the previous year and also because I was making a B-Line for Argentina, I said I'd stay on the coast and in the desert.

Arequipa

I was prepared for lots of things leaving Nazca, but one of them wasn't 10degC. Keep in mind this is one of the driest and hottest deserts in the world. While I was out

there, I was starting to believe the world was in big trouble weather wise, I passed a guy who told me that it had rained for two days solid in this area of the desert, in his whole life he told me he never remembered more than the briefest of showers. The rain meant that the cliffs were raining rocks onto the road at a savage rate.
On top of that any of the more grassy hills and mountains were sliding all their top soil out onto the road. There's nothing like the thought of a mountain sliding down on top of you to keep you on your toes. Anytime I stopped I could hear the rocks rolling down. The sound was the sort of thing that they used to have in the western movies. Y'know when John Wayne is standing at the bottom of a hill, and a pebble rolls down and then he says, "Dem's apache's alright", except in this case it was going to mean a dose of rock coming down on top of you. On a serious note the road was littered with dam-

aged trucks and cars, caused by either hitting the rockslides or rolling over the razor sharp chards of rock. In some of the flatter sections the sand had almost completely enveloped the road.

I passed a digger working furiously to keep back the onslaught in one area. If the conditions weren't bad enough, the nightmare driving of Peruvian truckers nearly sealed my deal on several occasions. Twice a truck overtaking another truck ran me out to the hard

shoulder on a cliff. If you go off the cliff, you tumble to your death. You have about three feet to play with while doing 50mph, that's not a lot of wiggle room. I genuinely thought my number was up on multiple occasions, I'd even taken the time to say to myself, "Well there's worse ways to go..." as the incident was unfolding. I consoled myself with the fact that when they find my body, the sea water below would have washed away all the shite in my trousers!

Along the way I stopped in HANS's fish restaurant on

the coast, and when I went in I was stunned with how many bikers had left business cards. If you've driven this section of road you've probably stopped there, as the towns are so few and far between. If you're passing I highly recommend it, the chap who runs it is a gent and the grub is outstanding.

The other recurring theme along the way was people living in thatched houses on the side of the road, out in the middle of the desert. It's hard to believe that people can live in those conditions. No electricity, no floors, I'd go nuts! I had thought that Arequipa would be a quaint little Colonial town but as soon I hit the outskirts and

saw it sprawling away up the hillsides I knew I'd the wrong impression. It has a population of one million people, and the views everywhere in the town, much like Antigua are dominated by a massive Volcano, except Arequipa has three of them, with El Misti being the one that dominates the skyline. If man ever makes it to Mars, they'll be disappointed. Someone will say "Mmm" or make that "Nyeah" noise, "It looks just like South Peru!" This is about as alien a landscape as exists anywhere in the world.

Tacna

I left Arequipa and headed for Tacna, the most southerly city in Peru. Along the way I was scratching like a dog with fleas, I'd been eaten alive my Mosquitoes all night, I had heard that they only like humid conditions, and you don't get many in the desert, well if that's the case, no one told the mosquitoes. Along the way I got a puncture and was dismayed to see how much the desert riding had hammered the remaining rubber on the tire. I was hoping to find a tire in Arica in Northern Chile with a bit of luck. "Of all the places to get a puncture, right in the middle of the desert!", I had it sorted pretty quickly but I'd a mouth as dry as a Camel's heel by the time I was finished.

I was soon under way lapping up the views which were

all round me, Southern Peru is spectacular. Mountains, Canyons, Volcanoes, vast terracotta plains, dust storms, I was delighted that I'd come this way.

With my back tire in bad shape I could feel myself becoming fixated on it. Every tiny little wobble became "was that the tire!" I was also in the desert in a hugely

NOT DEAD YET

unpopulated part of Peru, if it went pear shaped, I would be in big trouble.

CHAPTER 21
CHILE

I spent quite a bit of time in Tacna trying to figure out a way to get tires to Iquique, which is in Northern Chile, about 200 miles south of Tacna. The rubber I had on the bike "should be able to get me that far", or at least that's what I told myself. The big question was how long the new tires would take to get to Iquique. I knew it was going to take at least three days so I took a day off in Tacna to see what it had to offer. The town itself is as modern and easy to hang around in as any I'd been in since crossing into Mexico. It's one of very few Oases in the Atacama Desert and it's like the whole town was just plonked out there in the middle of nowhere. The city was building up for Christmas and I found it hard to get my head round Santa in the sunshine. I guess kids in this part of the world have their mothers pestered with questions like "Mammy, if it's like 2 Zillion Degrees outside, how come Santy has a big red coat on him?"

I went to the war museum outside of town, the outer part of which are decorated with silver statues on top of white pillars. The whole thing is accentuated by the utterly blue desert sky and brown earth spreading out to the horizon in all directions, it was a great place to pass some time.

From there I went to the nearby war cemetery which is full of brilliant white crosses, again set off by the brown desert and blue skies all around. The Taxi driver and I were the only people there. I couldn't help but reflect on the amount of times I'd been at a major attraction in Latin America and had the whole place to myself. It was unnatural, whether it was because of the worldwide recession or that people just don't make it this far off the beaten track, or H1N1, your guess was as good as mine.

The following morning I rode south for the border with Chile. The route took me through one of the world's truly unique landscapes. It's all part of the Atacama Desert but in this particular section the road beat a path through red desert mountains and canyons which extended off as far as the eye could see. The sky was bright blue over a landscape which varied in every color shade from deepest darkest red to light yellow. I pulled off the road to follow a track down to one of the canyon edges. Beneath me was a vast sandy valley meandering its way through vast red cliffs. There was no breeze, just a brilliant blue sky which was uninterrupted in all directions until it touched the horizon. "People will never believe places like this exist", I told myself over and over again. I continued on the bike for as far as the track went, feeling like I was on Mars exploring a remote valley. I was on my way back to the road when all of a sudden the back tyre blew out. I totally miscalculated how much rubber I had on the rear tyre, and as I was going over some gravel the back tyre shredded, it was worn right through to the Canvas, and there was no way I could plug it. "Ah for fucks sake!"

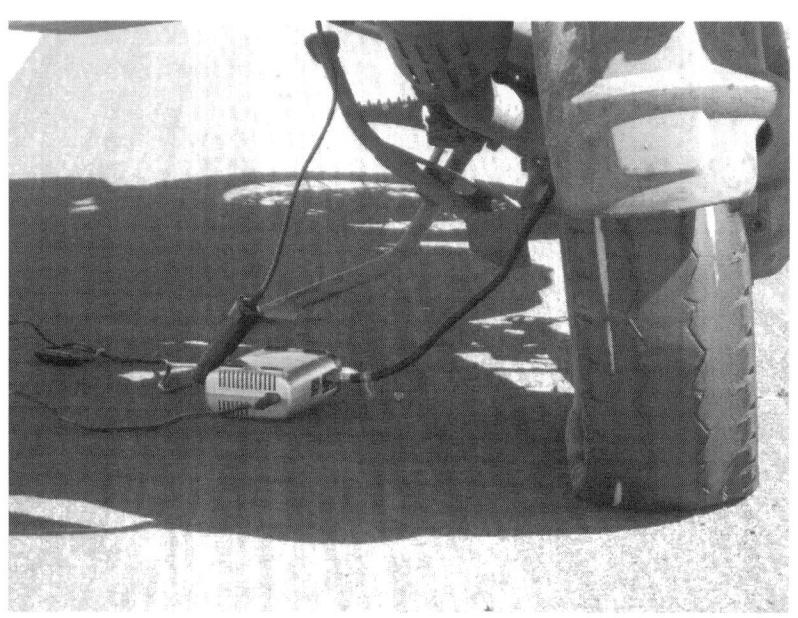

Iquique

I pushed the bike back to the Pan American highway, a distance of about a mile in the oppressive heat of the Atacama Desert and tried to flag down some help. The road was deserted and nothing passed me for the first 45 minutes. I had my mobile phone and got out the lonely planet to try and figure out how you make a call with an Irish mobile phone in Chile, I couldn't get it done, it kept returning an error message. Even if I did figure out "how" to make a call, who the fuck was I going to call, it's not like ringing anyone back in Ireland was going to help.

I knew the name of the guy I was going to get a new tire with in Iquique, and what I decided to do was try to flag down someone who was going to Iquique. The plan was that once I found someone I'd tell them to go to this guy and tell him to come and get me. It was a wild chance, but I guessed that seeing as he did tires he must have had to pick up some broken down gobshites every now and then as well. The day was getting away from me and I was burning sunlight at an alarming rate. I was stuck in the middle of the Atacama Desert with enough water to get me through to night fall, if I didn't find a way to get

to Iquique, it was game over.
Eventually a guy stopped, he had fuck all English, and I'd fuck all Spanish but I thought I got the message through. It was 90 minutes to Iquique, and 90 minutes back, so even if this guy scrambled I'd be out in the desert for at least another four hours with the bike before anyone came for me. I lay down in the shade of the bike and waited, and waited, and waited. As I was lying there I did the usual torture yourself to death routine, "It's your own bloody fault. Why didn't you get that tire sorted in blah blah blah. Why didn't you bring more water, you knew

you'd a fucked back tire. It's not the first time you've ran the tire down too low". I told myself to shut the fuck up and tried to go asleep. I knew one thing for sure, it would be dark by the time help arrived, I'd lost two hours at the border, and again I scolded the wisdom of how nations chose their time zones: "How the fuck can you go +2 hours in two steps." I have a vivid memory as the first hour passed of lying down by the side of the bike and falling asleep in the shade as the warm desert breeze blew all round my face, If I wasn't so worried about dying of thirst it would have been a great moment.

The sun was just about to set behind the hills and more

than three hours had passed since I'd talked to the guy on the road that had gone to get help. I was beginning to despair when the police showed up. In Chile, thankfully there's no corruption, so I didn't have to worry on that front. I told the guys what had happened, they had a look at the tyre, and I think started to say "what the fuck were doing running with a tyre that bald", so I did the whole "No pavimento routine", I doubt they bought it, but they had taken pity on me, so set about helping me. Every single truck that passed over the course of the next hour was stopped and asked if they could take me to Huaro, the nearest town about 30km from where I was stuck. Truck after truck passed but they were all too high off the ground and didn't have ramps to roll the bike up into. By this time it was the pitch black of night. Then a truck used for transporting large excavation equipment showed up, driven by a lovely helpful chap from Bolivia. The police chatted with him and I gave him my stupid Irish grin and within a few minutes we were wrestling the bike up a metal ramp. The ramp was designed for earth movers to go up it so it was more like a set of steps but we managed. I had some straps, nowhere near enough but at least the bike looked like it might stay in position till we got it to Huaro. We just had the bike in place when the guy who I'd sent for earlier showed up. What we decided to do was take the bike as it was to Huaro and then transfer it under the city lights to the smaller trailer. I continued to Hauro in the cabin with the truck driver who amazingly had a small bit of English and we chatted about all sorts of things. For a minute I was 18 years old again working on trucks. We got to Huaro and lined up the ramp with the small trailer. It was so dangerous, I was shitting bricks not only for the bike but for my safety as I rolled it from the truck down to the flimsy looking trailer.

We managed to take care of that part and then get the bike strapped into the trailer and set of for Iquique. At this stage I was just overwhelmed with how much these people had helped me. Two police officers, a Bolivian truck driver, two more truck drivers who the police had stopped and told to help me get the bike up the ramp, the lads who came to get me with the trailer from Iquique, the guy who sent them and the guy who went and told the guys in Iquique that I was broken down. All of these people had other things to do that day than help my fat hole, I thanked them all from the bottom of my heart.

The big problem happened when we got to the garage, we'd the bike in a trailer with no ramp and no way of getting the bike off the trailer. The bike fell over with one of our attempts to back it into the garage so what we decided to do, as it was past 11pm, was to just roll the trailer into the garage and ramp it off somehow in the morning. Dawn is ever the hope of man!

The guy brought me to a hotel close to the garage which was a steaming cesspit, but it was a door between me and

the night, about a 2% improvement on sleeping out on the Ruta 5 in the middle of the Atacama. I went to sleep telling myself, "tomorrow has to be better!"

I went down to the bike shop at opening time to see how long I'd be waiting on Sam. Today was Friday and I'd ordered the tires on Tuesday morning, would they have arrived? No was the answer. It meant a day of kicking my heels in Iquique. I asked the guys to do a service on the bike while we waited until the tires arrived. I knew I'd be around at least another night so first thing, I checked out of my shithole abode and set off to find myself a nicer place. A taxi came and we drove round and round and checked over ten hotels and hostels, but they were all either full, or over $150. That is one of the biggest eye openers that you'll get when you travel in South America, most of it is very cheap to travel in, but Chile is as expensive as hell.

I ended up back in the same place, the owner had a face on him which said "Ah here's the dumb fucking Gringo back. You decided we were good enough for ya, did ya?" I didn't have my light saber with me to take a limb off him, but it was a moment to utter the line from Lethal Weapon 4, "In Hong Kong you'd already be dead!"

I walked and walked all over town trying to figure out was there any virtue in the place at all. It's a town on the beach so there are plenty of surfers out trying to catch a break. I was out all day, so I went for breakfast in one spot, lunch in another and much like the rest of Latin America, the whole city was obsessed with soap operas, no matter where I went, everyone was glued to them. It doesn't matter what soap it is in the whole wide world, there's the same characters in all of them.

I was struggling to find anything l liked about the town, apart from some decent graffiti there seemed to be little to recommend. I'm sure that was mostly because with the bike in the shop, it felt like a prison more than it did a place to visit.

The tires never showed up the next day either so it was another day of walking around scratching my ring. I was bored out of my fucking mind. If the tires didn't show by Saturday I'd be stuck there till Monday.

The tires finally arrived the following day and Pepe had them put on in no time. Outside he had his Dakar Rally 4x4. He was the Dakar representative for that area of Chile and when the race came through, he was the guy who was front and centre. For those of you living under a rock, for the last couple of years the Dakar Rally has moved to South America due to Security concerns in

Africa.

Once the bike was ready I took the Ruta 5 south towards Calama. The road was almost completely straight, boring, and utterly unchanging with blue skies, flat brown desert, and a line of Asphalt which looked like someone had taken a black marker and drawn a line through the desert. The heat was savage.

I was bored so I said I'd take the bike off road towards what looked like a ghost town in the distance. I think it was an old Copper mine settlement and it was cool to hang out in. There wasn't a soul for miles. The ghost town even had its own graveyard and after a while the place was giving me the willies so I made my way back to the Ruta 5 and continued on south towards Calama.

San Pedro De Atacama

From Calama I made my way to San Pedro De Atacama, another much smaller oasis in the Atacama Desert. It sits in a valley and to get there you have to make your way down from a very high plane. As your altitude drops, the temperature rises to the point, that when you reach the bottom, it feels like you're in a frying pan.

This town attracts droves of tourists because of the surrounding rock formations. The Valley of the Moon is on the west side of the town, and like the name suggests, it feels like being on the moon. As you drop into the valley the view is dominated by a distant volcano and incredible rock formations either side of the road. The town itself has a lovely square and an old white colonial church. It's a great place to meet up with kindred spirits off traveling the world; no one comes to this part of the

world without visiting this town, so you never know who you'll bump into.

I left San Pedro the following morning before 8am and headed for the border with Argentina about a hundred miles away. If you come this way, remember to clear customs in San Pedro De Atacama for Chile, if you don't

they'll just sent you back at the border.

The first thing that you have to do is climb out of the valley in which San Pedro lies, up into the Altiplano of the Andes. I've never felt a sensation like it in my life. If you stopped the bike, you felt like you were being roasted alive, but if you drove you were freezing. I think what happens is that as the sun climbs higher in the sky, it heats up the air which was made frigid overnight. It was 6 degC with brilliant blue skies up until 11am.

I passed by a Volcano and took the bike off road for a spell to see if I could get closer to it, the desert here is very compact and any of the loose sand has blown away so it's not that difficult to ride on. I was also keen to take advantage of the fact that I had a new back tire, the restrictions on where I could and couldn't go had been lifted. I continued on the road without a sinner to be seen anywhere. All of a sudden a big black horse appeared on the road. He looked as out of place as I did I guess, but given I was miles and miles from anywhere and there wasn't a drink of water for over fifty miles where the hell

did he come from?
Right up to the border with Argentina I may as well have been riding on Mars, with just the occasional Al Paca and Llama showing their faces to remind you that you were still on Planet Earth. The moon was in the sky for the early part of the day and it reminded me of a quote I had heard when I was on the Utah Salt flats "Look you can see Earth from here!" I didn't see a single person for

the first 75 miles, and saw three trucks in the hundred miles to the border. At one stage I pulled well off the road to look at some interesting looking rocks. There was very few tracks around the area and I wondered how long it had been since anyone had come over to take a look at them. In a world so packed with people, it's hard to believe anywhere could be so empty. As the wind picked up, the view was dominated by the wind blowing the rising heat from the rocks and desert around me. I've never been anywhere like it.

CHAPTER 22
ARGENTINA AND THE RUTA 40

The Argentinian border was the easiest yet. The Argies are a great bunch, really friendly, and can't help you enough. I was through in twenty minutes and without further ado, I was off down the road heading for the start of the Ruta 40. I was trying to get confirmation from the cops and from the customs guys where exactly The Ruta 40 started in the town of La Quiaca.

The plan was to head east, then loop up towards the border with Bolivia, and then head due west and south on the Ruta 40. I met the turn off for the road coming down from Bolivia but the gobshite in me didn't want to drive over any bit of road twice unless I was absolutely forced to, that way every single mile of the journey would be

different.

I kept going looping north to meet the 40 at its starting

point in La Quiaca. On the way I passed through Paso Jama, a pass through the Andes and one of the most famous roads in the world. It bends and twists itself through so much natural beauty in such a short time, it leaves you feeling dazed. The passes are so high, if you get off the bike you find yourself breathless with any exertion at all. On the downside, with the amount of passes and valleys I found myself driving through over the previous days, I think it was turning my insides into a pump.

Purnamarca

On the way I passed flocks of llamas, a salt lake and some incredible looking cliffs and rock formations. By 4pm my internal scenery bucket was yet again completely full and I pulled off the road in a gorgeous little

town in the mountains called Purnamarca, which used to be part of the Inca trail.
I had been trying to psyche myself up all day for the "40", and was doing a bad job. "What the fuck are you doing this for? If you come off the bike in the middle of nowhere on your own, you are dead. No one is going to give a fuck one way or the other whether you do this or not. Almost no fucker has even heard of the Ruta 40, so why have you got such a hard on to do it. The bike has been acting the bollix a lot, if it breaks down, your fucked, there's no one to call out on the 40. The Mobile phone won't work out there. It's at least 2500km of gravel, 2500km of other shit, and 2800km back to Buenos Aires, will the tires hold up? Even if you do complete it you'll be fucked for a month after it and the only person who'll feel good about it is you, no one else." Those were the sorts of things that went through my mind as I made my way up La Quiaca. The other thing was that the 40 was an afterthought. I was really only doing it to salvage something out of the trip so it wasn't an utter failure. The following quote helped me get my head back in the right place:
You are capable of more than you know. Choose a goal that seems right for you and strive to be the best, however hard the path. Aim high. Behave honorably. Prepare to be alone at times, and to endure failure. Persist! - E.O. Wilson.

La Quiaca

I rode 244km to the official start point of the Ruta 40. There is no sign, and most people who live in the town

don't know and couldn't care less where the starting point is. I started asking for directions and got about three different answers eventually finding it in the form of a single lane dirt track beating a path out into the countryside. This road has iconic status in Europe. If you are into Adventure motorcycling this road constantly comes up, it holds almost legendary status in the psyche of any person who is planning to ride a bike in South America. For it to start without even a sign or a Mile 0

marker, felt very strange.

I've read a lot about bikers lamenting the fact that a lot of the Ruta 40 is being paved, well let me tell you, the gravel and sand is alive and well in Northern Argentina, the beast has plenty of kick left in it yet. Right from the very start it was corrugated roads made of gravel and sand, all of which meant I was getting the shit shaken clear out of me. It was a clenched teeth white knuckle ride all day and I was sweating bricks. I could smell the adrenaline and testosterone mixed with sweat wafting up into my helmet, it told me I was pushing myself right to my very limit.

I was so saturated with sweat by the time I got to a place to stay, I took off my enduro boots and showered with all my kit on, slowly stripping it off as the sweat was rinsed out of it.

I had seen only two cars all day, this part of North Western Argentina on account of it being primarily desert, is one of the most sparsely populated places in the world. The big challenge was the poor signposting and large sand build ups in the dips in the road. Any time I came to a Y on the road I had to go with my best guess because there was no one around for a hundred miles to ask. The GPS just gave the heading, as in North South

East or West.

I had been doing ok on the sand, but I'm never going to be good enough to actually enjoy riding on it, but I at least avoided having any near misses, so I was really happy with that. The rivets in the road at times were so bad that I thought I was on a wash board. I was worried with the weight of the bike that I'd lose the front or rear shock absorber but thankfully they held together, I wasn't sure the fillings in my teeth were going to make it though.

As the day wore on the wind picked up to the point where sand was blowing up into my helmet making it impossible to hold a line on the gravel tracks. I pulled off the 40 and stayed one more time in Purnamarca, I had 4,750km to go before I reached Rio Gallegos where the road ended.

Cafayate

The second day on the Ruta 40 kicked the balls clear off me. It started lovely with about 50km of asphalt curving over the Andes. Once you hit the top of the mountains you move onto Altiplano and from then on it was back onto a really crappy surface. The 40 navigates its way along the banks of a long since dried up salt lake, and I realized I was surrounded by mountains, all about twenty miles off in all directions. It was like I was in the

middle of a massive asteroid impact site.

The early going was easy, I was having thoughts like "Hmm is it that the road is easier today, or am I just getting better?" A piece of advice if you ever find yourself uttering the worlds, "Am I just getting better" the next thing you should do is head off and buy yourself a very good jock strap, because there's always a mighty kick in the balls coming. Things were going so well I even pulled over to have a look at two ghost towns and in keeping with the previous day I saw only two cars and one truck all day, somehow it seemed very appropriate to be in a ghost town given there was no one around for miles and miles. Once I left the second ghost town I thought I could hear faint chuckling, like the angels were saying

"let's see what the bollix makes of this next stretch of road." All the gravel went away and it was replaced with six inches of sand. At certain points it had the consistency of talcum powder and I was kicking up an enormous dust cloud which enveloped me any time I stopped, having a dust cloud catch up to you and completely surround you, is one of the biggest dude moments there is. To get through parts of it I had to stick my two legs out to act like stabilizers and just burn along in first gear, it was really hard going but it was early in the day and I told myself it couldn't stay this bad for long. Every now and then a line would appear which I'd jump onto and increase my speed hoping beyond hope that the really bad stuff was now over and what was ahead would be easier. Much like when you're queuing up in the supermarkets, the line that's next to you always appears to be just a bit better, but you can't cut across the sand track without either stopping or bumping through it. That leaves you ploughing along on the line you're on, forever tormented by the sexier looking line on your right or

left.

The early going in the bowl surrounded by mountains was awful. I was certain that if I could just get to the mountains the road would climb up and that would be the end of the heavy sand. It seemed that no matter how long I rode the mountains just wouldn't get any closer and by early afternoon, I'd a right royal pain in my hole

with the whole thing.
One of the worst parts of the run was the heat shimmer, it constantly gave me the impression that there was gorgeous sexy topless knickerless asphalt just ahead, but it never came, just more and more hardship.
Eventually as it always does the sand reduced as the road climbed out of the bowl, and as I climbed it was replaced with gravel, "Thank fuck for that!" As I crossed the peak of the mountains it started to rain which turned the whole path into a muddy fuck story. Whatever about keeping a line in the dry, when your visor is covered with rain drops you've no chance, so the going became very very slow. I couldn't believe how much the land-

scape changed once I went over the peak of the mountains, on one side desert and blue skies, and on the other clouds and rain. I made my way gingerly to a town called Cafayate where I stayed for the night. I was sore all over. My hips, knees, wrists, and back all felt like I'd been raped by a bull Elephant.

I worked out that I had driven greater than the length of Ireland on gravel and sand; I allowed myself a "du-uuudddddde!!" moment. Cafayate is a great town, I loved it. It looks and feels the way all towns should with a lovely square surrounded by restaurants. The people there were very friendly and the town had a really relaxed atmosphere. I met a couple from Ireland and we shared a beer and a bottle of wine over a chat, it was great to have a yap with someone from home after all

this time.

I left Cafayate late the following morning, I'd a bit of a hangover after knocking back the guts of a bottle of wine the previous night. The region around Cafayate is famous for its white wine, and believe it or not, the Ozone layer, or rather the lack of it in this region, is the reason for the special taste off the wine. So there you go, the hangover had nothing to do with the amount of alcohol consumed and everything to do with Ozone layer, which happens to be the best excuse I've ever had for a hangover. Can you imagine it back home in Ireland on a Sunday morning as people are popping some paracetamol, "Oh that ozone hole is a bastard!"

I got underway knowing that was I to survive the day I'd have about a 1000km gravel free stretch the following day, so I knuckled down and tore off. The first fifty miles were on asphalt and my first km marker pole that I met on the Ruta 40 said 4,322km. It was the first time I'd seen one on the Ruta 40 and it was also the first time I realized that Km 1 was in Rio Gallegos, and not in La Quiaca on the Bolivian border, not that it made much of a difference.

The dirt road was completely different than the other days, I thought it looked like I was in Africa, or at least when I've seen documentaries of some of the roads in Africa, I thought they looked similar. It was hard going at times, but in the 300 mile journey luckily only 100 miles or so was gravel and sand. About fifty miles into the shitty part of the road I was finding it tough going, it seemed like each km marker pole was taunting me with a song, "4331 km on the wall, if one km should accidentally fall, there'll be 4330km left for fatboy to ride…."

I pulled over to have a slug of water when a girl came over the hill driving a moped scuttling along without a problem in the world. If ever there's a red rag to a bull for a guy, it's to show him a girl doing what he was doing, except doing it with far less effort. Fuck that, I said to myself, jumping on the bike and gave the next fifty miles a serious pasting going at least 50% faster than I'd been going up to that point. I even managed to knock out a small river crossing.

The road then started to straighten and for over a hundred miles it was blue skies with white puffy clouds and mountains on either side of the road, quite simply a wonderful day to be riding a bike.
The sky and clouds reminded me of the Argentinean football jersey and I wondered if it's where they got the idea from. The whole country seems to be that bit bluer

than anywhere else I'd been. I've been in a lot of countries but in my mind's eye at least, Argentina always has a really bright blue hue.

The 40 is amazing mainly for the variety that you get in every day. It traverses mountains, deserts, small villages, rivers, pampas, and vineyards. When I look back through the pictures I took, I can't get over the number of things I saw every day. I made it to a town called Chiloceto, just shy of 300miles south of Cafayate. I had come to the section of the Ruta 40 which was asphalt. Where my head was at was, "Go like the clappers on the good sections of road, that'll give you time to go slower on the shittier bits." That being the case I planned to knock out some serious mileage over the coming days. I went out for a steak later that night and the good looking women switch had been turned on again for the first time since Colombia. There were also lots of fine looking women riding motorcycles, but I don't think it was because they preferred them, more that they were cheaper than a car.

So sitting there astride the beemer wasn't necessarily a draw, and to be honest it never has been.

The following day north of Mendoza I rode through a terrible storm. I could see it coming a long way off so I had all the rain gear on over my Enduro suit. As I rode into it, marble sized hailstones started lashing the shit out of me and the bike. With this sort of weather the only thing you can do is pull off the road and find shelter; however I was out in the middle of nowhere and had no choice but to do what you're not supposed to in a storm and shelter under a tree. It was a choice of being killed by lightning under a tree, or being pummeled to death by marbles of ice dropping from thousands of feet up in the sky. A car and a truck had pulled under the same tree and were pulling wood panels out of the truck to protect the car. The tree started to shed massive amounts of leaves and small branches as it was pulverized from above. The road turned completely white with the accumulation of hailstones. It was biblical stuff. Normally when something like this is happening I love it, "More thunder, more lightning, more hailstones", but for the first time in my life in a storm, I was truly worried. Eventually it passed and I rode on, taking my time to make sure I didn't catch up to it.

The Ruta 40 transformed itself into something like Sedona or Utah in the USA as it twisted its way through yet another Andean mountain pass on my way South. I was developing a love hate relationship with the road, actually more of a hate hate relationship as it constantly threw unexpected sections at me. Even though on the map the 40 was marked with a yellow line indicating asphalt, it would throw you a 50km stretch of gravel just to keep you awake. At that stage I didn't mind the loose surface, but when your mind has itself set on asphalt and a nice handy morning, to be bending around cliffs on gravel just added a couple of more grey hairs. The signposting was shocking in the remote areas the road passes through, some of the signs had been bleached beyond legible by the sun, and the only way to proceed was to wait for someone to come along and ask them which was

the correct way to go.
For the fifth day in a row the routine was as follows: Get up early, go, do 200km, stop for gas and water and hopefully something to eat. Do another 100km, get some more water and grub and then set about doing the last miles of the day. In the evening, as the gear I was wearing was saturated with sweat I would get into a shower with the whole enduro suit on, wash it while it was on

me, then hang the whole thing up. Then I would head out for some nose bag and then go to bed. On average I was on the road for ten to twelve hours a day and when I hit the bed at night, I was asleep before my head hit the pillow.

Out in the middle of nowhere, I met an English couple from London, Dean and Denise, they were pure cockney. They were on their honeymoon and were on a tour of the Argentinean wine region. Denise was fairly worldly and was anxious to see as much of the world as possible before having kids and Dean, a devoted hammers fan didn't know, "What the fuck I've been dragged down ere for!" This guy talked exactly like Turkish, from the film Snatch. We'd a good chat and I told them what I was up to, and that I was driving the entire 40. Dean's buddy had done the Pan American on a motorcycle the year previous and had heard all about the 40 from him. "You

NOT DEAD YET

doin fucking all of it?" said Dean, "I am", I replied. "Well your an ardcore cun in yaa!" was his response. It was easily the best compliment I've ever received. I've said it before, but there is no greater compliment for a guy, than for someone to use the word "hard-core" in a sentence with their name in it. South of Mendoza you cut off onto a 100km section of gravel as you make your way south to a town called Mallarque.

Mallarque

I was driving along on the shittiest of roads cutting through a wide open plane, under a completely black sky at 3pm in the afternoon. I was certain I was in for another beating from the storm clouds above. Knowing that it normally didn't get dark till almost 9pm was scant consolation for the fact that I could barely see. The rain

started to teem down and I really struggled to see my line through the gravel and sand. I was cursing the road, the wind, the rain on my visor, actually the whole world. A moment came when things went absolutely quiet, there was flare of pink lightning just ahead of me and for a few moments it seemed like time stood still. There was just the noise of the engine, the rain had stopped and the wind had eased. I was on a perfect line and there was almost no vibration coming up from the road to shake me and the bike. I passed a herd of wild horses on my left who were lit by a sliver of yellow sunshine peeking out from the storm clouds away on my right. When they saw and heard the bike they started to gallop alongside me. The feeling of riding alongside wild animals at full gallop under a completely black sky on a flat open plain with just the faintest yellow light illuminating our way made me feel like I was in a dream. The world seemed to

slow down as I realized I had drifted from my line into a track of heavy gravel and the front wheel was starting to wobble left and right. I tried to stay loose and correct it but every time I'd correct it, I'd be pulled back into the track until the bike fell over and we slid up the road together on the gravel. Even though the incident took only a couple of seconds, in my head it seemed to take an age. I'm not sure how long I lay on the road but next thing I knew a guy and a girl were pulling the bike up and putting me into the recovery position. I was lying on the ground in the pissing rain, not in pain or anything like that, but I knew I really didn't want to get up or start moving, it's hard to explain. In what seemed like an instant later, I was in an ambulance lying down on one of the beds about to head off to hospital in Mallarque. Then the thought came to me "Ok, time to get up" and I got up with the guys in the ambulance pushing me back down. All of a sudden I felt fine and the only thing on my mind was that I didn't want to leave the bike out on the 40 unattended. There was a big kafuffle but after about twenty minutes with the lads taking my blood pressure and doing the whole shine the light in your eyes routine, they were happy for me to go. I looked all-round the bike and bar some scratching on the pannier and my left fog light was broken, there was little enough damage. I said goodbye to the couple who stopped for me and thanked them for their help. When everyone had left I turned around and there was a horse standing with a Volcano behind him in the distance, it was like he was winking at me saying, "You're a lucky bollix!"

I continued into Mallarque where I booked myself into a hotel, had a shower and went to bed. The following morning I woke up sore from head to toe. I passed the halfway point on the 40 the following day, taking the time to put a bit of Graffiti on the back of the 2500km marker post, don't worry, it was washable ink, first sup of rain and it'll be a distant memory. I was really in the boonies at that moment. In over ten hours on the road I barely saw a soul. The reality is that most people avoid the gravel roads to preserve both their tires and shock absorbers. Why would you go the hard way when you can take the easy one? The solitude was unnatural. It seemed so strange to be in such a beautiful place, but for no one to be there, it's a bit like climbing a mountain that way I suppose.

Perito Morena

The following day I planned to make it as far as Perito Moreno. This is the part of Argentina where the winds really pick up. Sailors out to sea in this region refer to the wind as the Roaring 40's because the wind never drops below 40mph. Is it too much of a coincidence that the road is also called the Ruth 40 and also has brutal wind?

All day the wind howled, the rain pissed, and I was covered from head to toe in muck. It was absolutely brutal hard going. For a good hour I was doing a chant of, "Fuck off wind, fuck off wind, Fuck off wind" as it did it best to let me know how it felt to be pulled around under Hulk Hogan's armpit.

There wasn't much in the way of scenery in the early

going, it was just flat pampas where you can see for miles all round you. There's nothing to block the wind and rain so you get pummeled all day. The only thing of note that I saw all day was a bunch of Emu's running across the road, other than that I spent my time being brutally assaulted by the elements.

The road was empty, if anything was to happen in all likelihood I'd lay where I fell and die from exposure. Like I said earlier, there's a different way to get to all of the major towns and tourist sites so it's only the "benny biker brigade" who bother with this stretch of Satan's alimentary canal. You might be asking yourself, why bother at all? Well it's all for style points. If while in Ireland and the UK you were to meet another biker and you told them you rode all of the 40, assuming they believed you, they are honor bound to let you have prima nocte with

NOT DEAD YET

either their missus or best looking daughter of legal age. They'll say "This is my wife, please pleasure yourself with

her!" That will be swiftly followed by the sound of her brushing her teeth and spraying perfume.

I was scared through almost every minute of the days riding, but never enough to turn back, or give up. I think its ok to say you were scared or afraid, if you weren't feeling that way it wouldn't take an enormous amount of courage to keep going. Isn't that what courage is? To keep going even though you're scared, thanks for that one RFK.

El Calafate

I left Perito Moreno the following morning with over 400 miles ahead of me, two thirds of it would be on gravel and dirt and I was preparing myself for incessant gales. All day I was doing the best technical riding of my life, I was in right gear, had the right road position and was bombing along at a ferocious speed, the further I went the better I was getting.

I was pushing myself hard because I wanted to get home for Christmas, and the British Airways cabin crew union had announced that they were going on strike from 12:01 on the 22nd of December for 12 days. That meant I needed to leave Buenos Aires on December 19th, which also meant I would have to get the bike to Lufthansa by the 18th.

It would also mean riding 3200km in four days. I left El Calafate with 515km to go on the Ruta 40. Once done I'd have about 2700km to ride north to get to Buenos Aires to ship the bike. I'd been to Ushuaia the previous year so didn't mind skipping it. The 40 out of Calafate takes you south to a town called 28 Novembre, and then veers east to Rio Gallegos. You can take a different road to Rio

Gallegos, its all asphalt and it's about 50km shorter but honor dictated that I take the 40. I was in a garage in 28 Novembre and they couldn't believe I was going that way. They told me "no one will be on that road", if you get into trouble you're fucked. I replied, "The story of my life mate!" Of the 515km, about 380km or so was gravel, sand, shite and muck. I've never felt so isolated and alone. At times I would come over the crest of a hill and be looking out onto a plane so vast it would send a shiver of loneliness right through me. Once I started to go east I saw no other forms of life apart from sheep. As the minutes and hours go by, and you continue to not see

anyone, you can't help but feel tiny. It brought the quote "Oh God thy sea is so great and my boat is so small" into my head without me having to think about it. I even-

tually made it to Rio Gallegos, and had a potter around looking for any sign which might say mile 0 of the Ruta

40 but there wasn't any much like La Quiaca.
In a way I thought it was a fitting end as I looked out at the ocean and a beached ship near by. It took me 5,200km to finish it, some of that includes time spent doubling back or driving around a town to find a place to stay etc. From there it was a 2700km hike north to Buenos Aires. I completed the 40, I didn't particularly feel good about it, I wasn't punching the air or anything like that. In some ways I knew I'd get it done, so I didn't feel like Conan, I just had a mild feeling of studliness. I finished the day after 850km in a coastal town called Puerto San Julian. They've a replica of the boat Magellan discovered the Magellan Straits in, moored by the seaside. Let me tell you, they were brave men to take on the south Atlantic in a boat so small. I walked around the town that evening hearing nothing but echoes. I was there the previous year and met a biker called Graham, we a good chat over dinner about us both having finished the Pan Am. A mate of mine John Mundy was there only a few weeks previously and now I was there pottering around on my own, feeling like a bag of shit. Every day I'd torment myself about the failure of the project, and when I'd stop in the evening and walk around the various towns by myself, the feeling of regret was the worst.

The next morning I got up in an awful way with tiredness and went for breakfast, which leads me to my only moan about Argentina. The breakfast in the country is brutal, normally made up of stale bread and jam, with coffee so strong you could walk across it. The whole time I spent in Argentina, it was the same everywhere I went. If there are any Argies out there, just in case you've been misled all this time, the white bit in the middle of the roll is supposed to be soft!

I was trying to feel good about finishing the whole Ruta 40. I had never spent so much time on my own in my life. For anyone who feels that the world is packed and who wants to get away from it all, this is the route. I travelled for thousands of miles on that road and barely met a soul.

As I tried to leave Puerto San Julian I discovered they had no gas. In all of Puerto San Julian that there was no gasoline, none! Not a lick! Every station had run out. I had about 50km worth of juice in the tank and the nearest gas in the next town was 115km away. "Fuck!!!!, Why the fuck did there always have to be a fucking drama, why is it the day I'm in a rush up to Buenos Aires that a whole town runs out of fucking juice!, Fuck!!!"

Gas showed up eventually, and by midday I was back riding on one of the world's straightest, flattest and most windswept roads, the Ruta 3. It really is a bastard of a road, not just because it's so straight, but because it also has km marker poles to count you down one by one the whole way to Buenos Aires. The chief reason it's a bastard though is the wind. It's not enough to blow you off the bike but it wears you down over the course of the day and by the time you stop in the evening your ears are ringing and you've a roaring headache. You just wish you were anywhere but on that road. The tedium continued the day after. The road almost never bends, and the land is as flat as a pancake. There isn't a hill nor a lake, absolutely nothing to take your mind off what looks like an unravelled ball of twine running through a sea of blue green pampas.

When I was close to the coast, I was getting knocked right to left by the wind, and when I moved away the wind knocked me from left to right. The amount of truck traffic increased as I rode north and when I wasn't getting clobbered enough by the wind, these boys clobbered me with their slipstream. What you really need to help you out is a sidecar with a pig in it. A real pig. A pig is the only animal that can see the wind so what you want is a side car with a little pig, a helmet, and a microphone and earpiece to tell you when the gusts are coming. If he gave you any cheek you could just threaten him with a frying pan "You'll be in there ya bollix if there's any more out of you."

I kept breaking the journey up into 80km/50miles stages, either stop for gas, some water, take a picture, anything to get you off the bike and take your mind off the monotony of this the land. The wind is too loud for an iPod so it's just you and the helmet, thinking to yourself, "C'mon Ois, you've done over 22,000 miles on this trip, what the fuck do you normally think about to make the miles go by?" I couldn't think of anything just the relentless count down of the kilometer marker posts 451......450.....

Later on I hit a goat head on. He was standing in the middle of the road, I was beeping the horn like a whores bastard and he looked like he was getting out of the way so at about 30mph just as I was about to pass him, he doubled back and I hit him. He bounced off the wheel and out of the way of the bike. I jarred both ankles, knees, and my hips trying to keep the bike from hitting the deck. The other casualty was my right bollock which had slid up the seat along with the rest of my under carriage and collided with the petrol tank. It hurt like someone had clubbed it with a nine iron. I pulled over to see if I'd done any damage to the bike. I couldn't see anything but I was sore as fuck. I can see me in 40 years when I'm walking with a limp and some young lad says to me "Is it the arthritis?" I'll say no, "it's the goat!"

Trelew

I stopped in Trelew the following night in a motel, identical to the ones you see in North America, it was a great little spot. I woke up the morning after my incident with

the goat feeling like I'd been hit by a train. Incidentally the goat was fine, or at least he was limping around the place after it but didn't look like he was in too bad shape. I think goats have been known to survive large falls in mountains, they're quite hardy. Certainly I think he was doing better than me.

The list of things that were sore that morning included both ankles, both knees, both hips, my right nut, my left nut, the bit at the back of your balls which I don't know the name of, my ass, my lower back, both shoulders, and both wrists. I told myself, "C'mon ya fat fuck, you are nearly there."

The Gaucho Gill shrines knocking around this part of the world were the only thing to help break up the boredom on the road but they were only a temporary respite. The next morning I bit the bullet and went to see about my sore ball. I looked up Google and it mentioned torsion, never look up ball bag issues on the web, you'll be scared to death. Anyway the pain while not getting worse, wasn't getting better and I was worried I'd a twist (which is what Torsion is) so I found out where the Doctors was. I had shower and put on a fresh set of underpants and together with my fresh sore ball, I went off wondering how the fuck I was going to pull this one off. Think about it for a second, you've pigeon Spanish, and an issue down town with a delicate area and you've got to try and explain it, I wasn't looking forward to it, but one of the descriptions of torsion involved putrification of the nut, "Fuck that!", I'd grin and bear whatever lay ahead of me.

I walked in the door of the surgery and they had a nurse standing there at a desk who was taking details after which, they take you in to the to see the doctor. She gave me a form to fill in with all my personal details and asked what's wrong. I pointed down town and inhaled sharply through my teeth while frowning. She blushed and told me to take a seat.

In situations like these I wonder if it's better to have a guy or a girl doctor. Like most guys the mere thought of a guy touching the crown jewels is enough to ruin my next 5000 hard on's, so I was hoping it would be a woman. Her name was Sabrina Sorhobigarat, no doubt she was desperate to get married to lose that second name, jeez what a moniker. Thankfully she spoke English, so I explained to her what happened.

Our first awkward moment was when she was bending over to examine my ball bag and said, "Emm you're left or my left?" I roared laughing and couldn't stop for a full minute. She told me to hold the big fella out of the way while she did a quick exam.

Of course she was a doctor and knew what she was doing but holy fuck you'd think they were conkers I had. She checked the good one first and then gingerly checked the bad one at which point she said If I'd torsion, I'd be a lot sorer - this she said as she passed my sore ball between the palm of one hand and pressed it with the thumb of the other hand.

In the end she gave me ibuprofen for the swelling (on the nut) and told me to wear supportive underwear, and to avoid any sexual activity. "No fucking problem there, darling!" I said to myself. The last time I'd a shag, there wasn't even a recession!

I had driven the same distance on the Ruta 3 as it is from Dublin in Ireland to Moscow in Russia and still had a more than 800km to go. I won't bore you with the details on the rest of the journey up to Buenos Aires, I'm sure you trust me, it was like trying to count the hairs on a German Shepard dog.

The final sprint into Buenos Aires was done in the pissing rain which kind of gave the trip a bit of symmetry for me, when I started 135 days earlier in Calgary it was pissing rain for the first few days as well.

Buenos Aires

I drove to Ezieze airport in Buenos Aires to ship the bike. It takes a good bit longer than say for example to ship it from the UK to Canada, or from Panama to Colombia but all the steps are straight forward, they just

take a bit of time to complete.
Once you've the paper work done you roll the bike up onto a pallet and the guys tie it down with metal straps and then shrink wrap it, I would have it back in Ireland

NOT DEAD YET

on the 27th of December. I headed off into Buenos Aires to have a steak freshly torn off a bulls arse. The final 55 miles were to just ride the bike home from the airport when I collected the bike in Dublin.

The trip was a failure in the sense that the project failed, the only thing I salvaged out of it was the satisfaction of completing the Ruta 40 and the confidence that it gave me to go forward and do Dublin to New York solo.

CHAPTER 23
ITS ALL YOUR FAULT

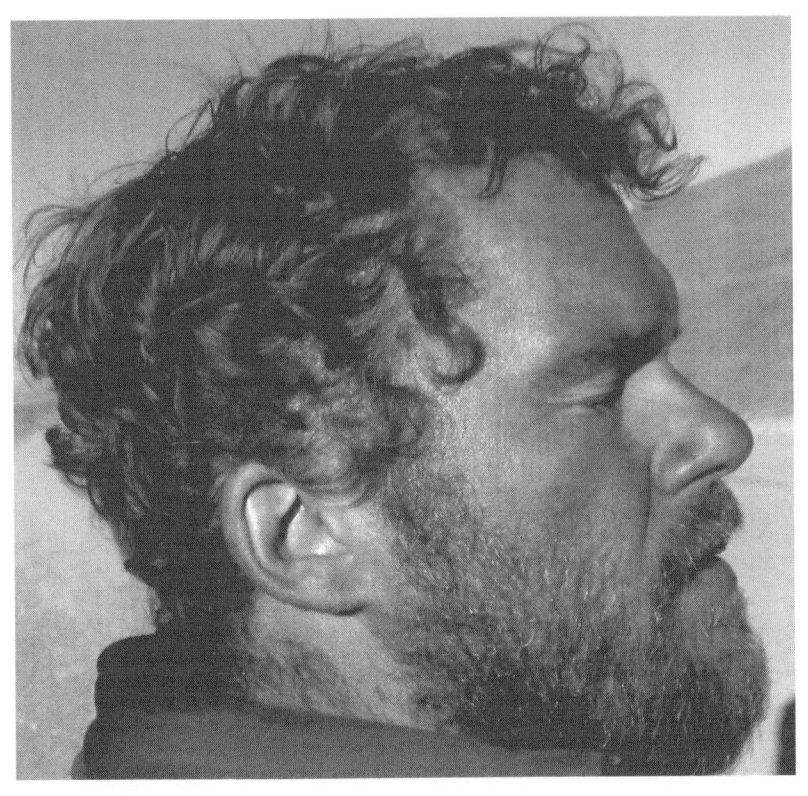

Riding a bike round the world teaches you severe lessons in character.

Many times during the trip, I was in a terrible situation but constantly told myself "Well, it was your choice to come on this trip and that's why you're in this situation, so get on with it, you're to blame."

When I had a puncture and it was because I'd let the tire thread run down too low, I'd tell myself, "That's what you get fatboy for letting the thread get too low, it's your fault, get on with it."

It was torture knowing that no matter what problem I had to face, it was my fault for choosing to go on the trip in the first place, and I'd no one to blame but myself. I often thought back to normal daily life. Smokers constantly blame other people for the fact that they smoke, "Your stressing me out", "My parents are visiting, I'll give them up when they go", "You made me smoke because you sparked up", you name it, a smoker will find someone or something else to blame for the fact they are smoking. So when the ultimate consequences of smoking arrive in later life, it's hard to look in the mirror and say "It's my fault, I'm to blame."

Fat bastards like me are no different. "I had to eat the pie, sure I was visiting their house and it would be rude to say no. It was a date and sure we had to go out for a meal or she'd think I was cheap. It was a family get together so I had to eat. It's my birthday. It is Christmas", on and on it goes. So, heaven forbid I was to have a heart attack tomorrow, I'd only have myself to blame. Let's face it, no one is putting a gun to my head as I scoff back the apple tart and cream.

I started to ask myself "Is everything bad that ever happened to me, my fault?"

For the purposes of the conversation let's just apply the following filter, You are living in the Western world, over the age of 18, and not a gimp with an 8-ball in your mouth trapped under someone's stairs. I went through the list of stuff I wasn't happy about in chronological order, starting with the most recent first.

The project failed, yep mostly my fault, I got too caught up in the emotion of it and didn't plan it out properly. I was overweight, absolutely my fault. I went on and on, even back to my marriage failing and no matter what question I asked myself, I kept coming back with the fact that it was my fault.

Now you might think that I'm being too hard on myself, but I look at it slightly differently. If you take personal responsibility for everything that ever happens to you (within reason) then you get to be in control of your life. You can choose not to do certain things which create consequences you don't like.

You make a decision and then have to live with the consequences, but get on with it. I find it stops you getting into a spiral of looking for someone to share the blame with. It's also about taking aggressive control of your life and making informed decisions and if you get it wrong, so be it, I made the decision, I got it wrong but I made it. There was no point wingeing about it, everyone's got their own shit to deal with.

A topical example in Ireland is unemployment. If you lost your job you can choose to blame your employer, the bankers, the government, your boss, even the worldwide recession. You can then go on to blame foreign nationals living in the country, let them go back to their own country and get a job there. You can then blame people from the countryside coming up to Dublin and "robbing our jobs." Maybe you'll even have a go at women, sure if they would only go back into the home and look after the kids, there would be loads of jobs for us men. When you're done with all that, you'll move onto the size of the social welfare payment that you're getting and "why isn't it bigger". You'll start saying things like, "I'm not incentivized to work". Eventually, a long way down the road you'll realize that you need to go and get retrained and find yourself a job. Blaming yourself up front, short circuits all the bullshit and forces you to pick up the pieces and get on with it, it won't feel good but you'll be moving again and like I said earlier, emotion is driven by motion. The powerful mindset says, I am in control of my destiny, I am not a victim. I choose to ride solo around the world and will live with the consequences no matter what.

BOOK 2
DUBLIN TO NEW YORK

NOT DEAD YET

CHAPTER 24
IRELAND, WALES, ENGLAND, FRANCE, BELGIUM, GERMANY AND THE CZECH REPUBLIC

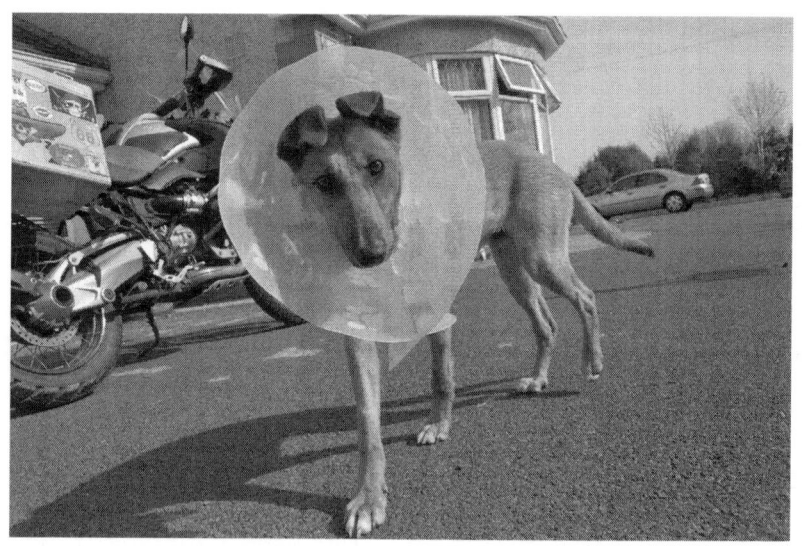

I won't bore you with many details on the trip prep for the second leg. I was going alone but some of my friends would show up at different stages between Dublin and Moscow, I was very happy about that.

I'd over three months to get ready, and given this was to be my third big trip, I was pretty certain about what I did and didn't want to bring with me. The hard part was getting a multi entry visa for Russia. For this I used an agency in Moscow who issues an invite to the Russian embassy in Dublin, Ireland. Once they receive it, they invite you to apply for the visa. The multi entry visa is more expensive but it gives you the maximum flexibility. On this leg there was going to be far more opportunity for things to go wrong, so flexibility was paramount.

It also wasn't clear that I would be able to get out of Magadan in Far Eastern Russia, the air shipments from the city airport had ceased two years previously, the rough plan was to get to Vladivostok by ship and then somehow from there get to North America, but it all seemed so far off I didn't give it too much attention.

I also picked up a Mongolian visa which was very straight forward.

I never bothered learning a word of Russian or Mongolian, nor any language from any of the countries I'd be traveling through. If I'm honest about it, I was being a bit cocky. Having completed two back to back Pan Americans, I really thought I could cope with anything the trip would throw at me.

All my gear was tailored for surviving in Mongolia and Far Eastern Russia, so there were lots of thin fleeces and things to keep me warm as well as lots of camping gear. I only made one physical modification to the bike as part of getting it ready and that was to add a gel battery. My thinking was that if it got very cold in Siberia and Far Eastern Russia this would give me the best chance of being able to get the bike started every morning. I was going to try and make a documentary about it so I had a host of cameras and film equipment to video and photograph as much of it as possible as I went. I packed detailed maps of the countries I was riding through, with the exception of Mongolia where I had to make do with a standard wall map of the country. Reading the sentence back now I can't believe how dumb a move that was, I was utterly unprepared for one of the World's hardest country's to travel in.

After finishing the Ruta 40, I was as proud as a dog with two mickeys and was skipping over a lot of the planning. Lots of folks back home had serious concerns about me heading off alone into the wilds of Russia and Mongolia. Many asked me if I was afraid. I was, but not enough to not do it, if that makes sense. I'd survived before in incredibly remote locations so I was reasonably confident that things would be ok.

I left the house at 6:30am on April 12th. The plan was to hook up with my buddy Dave at the Nass roundabout (a place between Portarlington and Dublin) for 7:05, he was coming along for the first two days. We had been great friends since I was 18 yrs old and he was the one who brought me along to my first bike show. When I got to the roundabout Dave was already gone, I looked at the watch and I was over 30 minutes late. It took me far longer than I'd planned to get ready that morning.
I burned up the road for Dublin Port only to find that the Ulysses ferry gate was closed, I was too late. I heard

my phone ringing, which when I answered turned out to be Dave, he was waving at me from the ferry. I think he said something along the lines of "Y'know what Hughes, your some fucking gobshite!" I couldn't believe I had missed the ferry, with months of planning behind me I had managed to screw up on Day 1! Luckily, I was able to get on the Swift ferry which was sailing 45mins later and we hooked up in Holyhead in Wales none the worse for wear.

Snowdonia

We drove south and went through Snowdonia National Park, the largest National Park in Wales. The Park is full of mountains, valleys, rivers and hiking trails and its also home to the largest lake in Wales. Mount Snowdon is a very popular mountain for hikers to climb and

the view from the top is spectacular. I'd no clue how to pronounce any of the Welsh towns we passed through, or spell them from how they were pronounced, even though its a Gaelic language, its alien to Irish Gaelic. Most sound like they're pronounced with a handful of marbles in your mouth. The Welsh greeting is about as good as a greeting can get, "Good health to you now and forever."

All day we had gorgeous hazy sunshine, the locals were telling us that it had been raining solid there for ages, so we should make the most of it. We spent the rest of the day jumping on and off the bikes taking pictures of the Welsh countryside before making our way to Aberystwyth in time to catch a lovely sunset.

Aberystwyth

We stayed in a B&B and had to hike all our gear up three flights of stairs. The thought that I'd packed way too much stuff was quickly starting to grow in my head. It had been a great day and we headed out for a walk which we followed with a few pints. The locals refer to the town as Aber, and its chiefly a holiday town with a string of hotels and B&B's along a well kept beach promenade. The great weather continued the next day as we ambled through the Welsh countryside in the general direction of Bristol. The towns in Wales are lovely, most have very narrow streets and the houses are made almost entirely of stone. With the good weather, the amount of bikers on the roads was way up and we met every type from Japanese Road rockets to Honda 50's, all enjoying a day's riding without the rain gear.

The Welsh are a friendly enough bunch and easy to get on with. We were both surprised at how much the locals swung between Gaelic and English and wondered if it was for our benefit. We talked with several folks on the road about which towns were worth having a look at but what they pronounced and what we could later find on the map, gelled like oil and water.

Bristol

When we got to Bristol we hooked up with an old college buddy of mine, Joanne O' Rourke and went out for some grub. As we walked down to meet her we passed a statue of an elderly Queen Victoria, we both commented "I wouldn't". After a great chat and catch up over dinner and a few beers, we called it an early night. As we walked back to the Travelodge we commented to each other that we were like a pair of old men, if this was ten years ago we'd have been out in a nightclub till all hours.
I said goodbye to Dave the following morning at 8am, he was burning back for Holyhead and home. It was great having a riding buddy for first two days and I was very sad and more than a bit lonely to see him ride off.

Felixstowe

I put the head down and crossed England riding mostly on the M4 in the direction of the town of Felixstowe, north east of London. I was going there to meet up with John Mundy for a few hours. John is a guy who was supposed to come along on the first Pan-American motorcycle trip I did, but he couldn't make it, instead doing it the following year. It was about 9degC the whole day and

I was freezing on the bike. I kept saying to myself, "Jesus if you're cold now, you are going to be fucked in Siberia!" I got to Felixstowe in the early afternoon, and while I was getting gas I had a laugh at a tabloid headline revealing that one of Jordan's (English glamour model) boobs exploded while she was on holiday.

Felixstowe is best known for its docks where some of the biggest container ships in the world are loaded and unloaded. I called into Johns place and we went out for a cup of tea and a round of sausage egg and chips. We shared lots of stories from our recent Pan American trips and had a good laugh catching up. We said good luck and I went into the seaside town which is near the docks to find a place to stay. The town had seen better days, and the place I ended up staying in, was as rough as a badgers arse, but I was conscious of the need to keep the costs down, so beggars can't be choosers. After a couple of walks up and down the promenade I headed back to the hotel to get a kip. Trying to have a wash that night was a disaster. If you can imagine a scene where I was kneeling in a bath trying to wash my hair under a tap with a tiny trickle of cold water running from it, definitely not my best look.

Weston

The next morning I left Felixstowe and headed over for the town of Weston in Hertfordshire, about an hour north of London. I'd arranged to hook up with a chap by the name of Simon Race who was planning on doing a similar trip to me, in a years time. We were going to trade notes on our routes. Simon's house was a dude layer, the garage had a serious sports car, a KTM scrambler and of course a big BMW 1200 GSA, the same bike

as my own. We went out for a dose of German beer and yakked on about Mongolia and Siberia. After some grub, we went out for some more beer and then met up with Simon's missus Suzie in the local pub. We then had a huge round of shepherd's pie followed by apple tart and even more beer. After all that, I had as sound a night's kip as I'd had in years, the Races were great hosts. Simon sorted me out with much more detailed maps of Mongolia than I had, and also gave me a water proof hold all to replace the one which I'd wrecked the zip on the day previous. He also went on to be one of the biggest helps to me on the trip as I travelled. I've told him many times, "I can't wait to do the same for you amigo, I'll be your fixer in HQ Irlandski!" I left at 8:30 the next morning giving myself plenty of time to catch in Channel Tunnel train booking.

Around about this time a huge Icelandic Volcano had

gone off and airlines were starting to ground their fleets. I was headed for the Channel tunnel and wondered if I'd get caught up in all the traffic chaos. As it turned out it was no problem.

It was my first time in the Channel tunnel. It's an awesome display of engineering and a great way to get onto the European continent. You just drive the bike up onto a train, and away it goes and you arrive in France about 25 minutes later, it couldn't be easier.

Once in France and taking Simon's advice I headed for Vimy, one of the few places left where they have preserved the trenches from the Western front from World War one.

Vimy

The scene is very well preserved. The ground surrounding the area is all lumpy and hilly, left intact from when the shells and bombs went off all those years ago. The only difference between then and 95 years earlier was that it's covered in grass and they have some trees growing in the area. Back then it would have been a sea of mud. The population of Canada in 1915 was a little over 7 million people and 60,000 of those died in World War I. I left Vimy and rode cross country avoiding dual carriageways as much as possible in the direction of Normandy, about eight hours away (taking it very handy). Along the way I stopped at one of the many WWI mass graves for which that area is famous. I walked in and had a look around. The sun was shining, there was barely a breath of air, the only noise to be heard was the singing

of birds. The most stunning thing, apart from the vast number of graves was the ages of those buried there. Most were 18 or 19 years old. I thought back to when

NOT DEAD YET

I was that age and tried to imagine, what I would do if someone gave me a gun and said go and fight. I was looking out for Irish names, and there were lots, over 50,000 Irish men died in World War I, (Southern Ireland was part of Britain back then) with over 30,000 soldiers from Southern Ireland never making it back home. There were over 37 million casualties in WWI, it was the first time that war and killing were done on an industrial scale.

Normandy

From there I moved across the countryside towards Normandy where the World War II D-day invasions took place, on the way crossing the spectacular Normandy Bridge. It was like riding along the back of a massive green dragon, I've no other words for it. I drove first

to Gold beach where the British landed. When I went there it was hard to know what to expect, I guess part of me wished there would be some preserved battlements, or ships lying on the beach or something, but all have long since been cleared. It's easy to see why they picked that beach, the land is flat so they wouldn't get mowed down from a height by the Germans as they stormed the beaches. All that's there now is a beach, with nothing to tell you that this was the site of the largest invasion in human history. The weather was amazing and the countryside was full of color, it seemed like half the fields were full of yellow rape seed. The next day started as the previous one ended. I spent an hour in the early morning trying to find a statue I drove by the previous day, it was of a young American Marine taking a rest with his buddies on a bench after storming the beach. I couldn't find it and was really beginning to think I'd imagined it.

NOT DEAD YET

My next port of call was to go down to Omaha beach where the American's came ashore on D-day, and then go on up to the American war memorial. The beach, much like Gold beach is just a beach, the only thing that marks the occasion is a silver memorial sitting above the tide line. The American cemetery reminded me very much of Arlington cemetery in Washington DC.

While I was there I was asked questions by a local historian and got some surprising answers to questions that I didn't know.

The first question was, "Did you come here because of the film saving Private Ryan? My answer was about 90% yes but it was also a place I wanted to come to since seeing the movie, "The Longest Day." The second question was, "Do you think the graves are just memorials or are there American soldiers buried there? I answered that I wasn't sure, maybe the soldiers were repatriated to Arlington cemetery in Washington DC? It turned out that they are actual graves, over 40% of those killed in France are buried at Omaha. The third question was, "Do you think that the characters in Saving Private Ryan are fictional?" I answered that I thought it might be loosely based on actual events, but no I didn't think the characters were real. The answer was that the plot was inspired in part, by the true story of Fritz Niland, one of four brothers from New York State who saw action during the war. Two of the Niland brothers were killed on D- Day, while another was missing in Burma and was presumed dead, although was found to have survived later on. Fritz was located in Normandy by an Army chaplain, the Reverend Francis Sampson, and taken out of the combat zone.

On a side note, there are also thirty three other sets of brothers buried there. Then another historian came along and chatted with me for a while. He told me that Saving Private Ryan is one of the most important war movies ever made because it depicts how things really were, after all that I felt like going out and buying the movie. If you're from America, and get a chance to go to this part of the world, you won't regret it. On so many occasions you can feel the air getting sucked out of your lungs when you see the scale of the crosses lined up in perfect rows. It's critical that present and future generations understand what those who came before them had to sacrifice, so their way of life could be maintained.

I'm not a big lover of the French as a nation, but I have to commend the integrity, pride and care that they put into

NOT DEAD YET

the grave sites in France. It's a credit to them and anyone who has visited these areas can't help but be touched by the diligence they put into it. I took a last look at the ocean, it was the last time I'd see it before pulling into Magadan port in Far Eastern Russia, only God knew when that would be.

Bruges

I made my way north east for five hours to Bruges in Belgium. The reason I was going there was the movie "In Bruges" with Colin Farrell and Brendan Gleeson, if you haven't seen it, its well worth a look. I got there around 6pm, quickly showered and headed out to take a few snaps of what is one of the most picturesque towns in all of Europe. My buddies Barry Dunne and Philly Fitz finally showed up at 10pm in the main square after riding

the whole way from Dublin in one day. (15 hours in the saddle) After the lads had a shower and downed some Hot dogs and chips, we went out for a couple of pints. No matter where we went we bumped into people being impacted by the Ash Cloud over Europe. We met two girls from Scotland who were supposed to be in Lanzarote, but the flight was cancelled so they took the ferry to Bruges instead. Similarly one of the girl's boyfriends was stuck in Singapore and couldn't make it home either. If all that wasn't enough, one of the lads (Joel) who was supposed to come along for the week as far as Prague couldn't get out of the south of France. He had planned to fly home and ride down to Dublin to meet up with the lads.

We'd a great night in Bruges and all of us ended up as drunk as skunks! The following morning, beset with hangovers, Barry, Phil and I went out and about in the

NOT DEAD YET

town. For the great unwashed out there, it's a world UNESCO heritage sight where some of the buildings date back as far as Medieval times. On every corner there's something cool to look at. It's the ultimate town to wander in and then go sit down and grab a coffee in one of hundreds of outdoor restaurants and cafes. Half the town pottered around on bicycles and if you wanted, you could take a horse drawn carriage tour or a boat tour through the cities incredible network of canals.

The town has a very orderly, well run feel to it, very Belgian you might say. That night the three of us met up with a friend of mine who I met in Cuzco 18 months earlier, Vanessa. We've stayed in touch over the years and she's a great pal. We'd a couple of civilized pints as we all inhaled Vanessa's rollies. (Belgium is one of the few countries left where you can still smoke in bars)

Nurburg

We left the following morning in the direction of Germany. The countries were clocking by as they do when you travel in Europe, so far since leaving Ireland I'd been through Wales, England, France, Belgium, clipped the bottom right corner off The Netherlands, and then all of a sudden we were in Germany, it was mental to think that in less than a week I'd be in Russia. One of the places we were most looking forward to was the Nurburg Ring, a place of pilgrimage for people who want to go fast. Anyone can show up at the track and pay to do a lap. As we were waiting around we saw everything from Porches to Nissan Micras, a Volkswagen van, and even a family going round in what I would describe as a granny car. When you consider that you have to share your lap with people who are going round at speeds of up to 180mph,

NOT DEAD YET

it's an absolute free for all. As people race around the track, its insane to think you have Porches and Micras competing for the same racing line. While we were there we met two folks from Cork, James Coleman and his sister. James offered to take me round the track in his Ford Mondeo so I could film Barry and Phil as they went around. I couldn't chance going myself on the bike, it had to get me to New York (Yeah I know, I'm a wimp!) We had a fabulous time doing it. When we were done with that, we found some vantage points to watch the cars racing around having a great time in the process. If you're in this part of the world, I really encourage you to go, even if you don't go out on the track, it's a great spectacle. Just go to a viewing point and watch all the various cars getting pushed to their limit on the track. From there we went into the town and had a few pints as we retold the story of going round over and over again,

"Did you see that bollix in the black corvette!? I thought that Porsche was going to kill you!" So it went until long after the sun went down.

Nuremberg

We left Nurburg and rode in the direction of a city called Nuremberg, where the post WWII Nazi trails were held. About five minutes into the journey our visors were covered with sleet as the temperature dropped to one degree. I think we all thought the weather had been great so far, so we were due a bit of bad. It stayed freezing cold all day and we stopped often to drink tea, coffee and anything hot we could get our hands on. We kept saying to each other, "Can you believe it's nearly May and it's fucking snowing!" We kept the heads down and the arses up, finally getting to Nuremberg where we went out looking for something to do, harder than you might think in that town. We gave up after a couple of hours and had an early night.

The next morning Phil had a serious dose of the Ringaskiddies (KFC at 10pm, nuff said) so we strolled around the streets trying to get him something to settle his stomach. We took some pictures of the town, which had a serious collection of ugly statues dedicated to women with really hairy bushes.

We left the town early and were only twenty minutes on the road when we pulled over for some tea to warm ourselves up. As we were coming out to pack up and leave, I noticed a leak on my final drive. The 1200 GSA has two major weak points, one is the electronics on the ignition system (Ref: Colombia) and the other is the final drive

NOT DEAD YET

(Ref: Phoenix), for the second time in a year, my final drive had shit the bed.

So much for making it to Prague that day, but all was not lost. I pumped "BMW dealer" into the GPS and there were heaps of them within thirty miles, this was Germany after all. The first one we tried didn't have the parts but the second one did, not only that, as soon as I arrived they put the bike straight up on the lift and started working on it.

Phil and Barry continued on to Prague and I told them I'd catch up with them there tomorrow, it was only 200km away. From the moment the bike docked in BMW they had between one and three guys working on it flat out and got me back on the road by 6pm that evening. The silver lining on this problem was that the final drive was one of the key mechanical things I was worried about for Mongolia and the Road of Bones in

Far Eastern Russia. The fact that it had been completely stripped out, had the seals and the bearing changed, meant I was probably golden until I got to New York. Even though time was pushing on, I said I'd burn on for Prague, getting there just as the sun was dropping below the horizon in my rear view mirror.

I knew where the lads were staying so they were there waiting for me and helped me unpack the bike. One hour after I docked at the hotel, the three of us were settling down to a seriously good steak and some great beer served by the seriously hot Monika. Man, how a bad day can turn good!

After a skinful of beer, we got up the follow morning to go out and see what Prague had to offer. All three of us were nursing wicked hangovers, at about a buck fifty a beer, we'd been doing the whole, "The more you drink the more you save!" routine, and we saved a lot! We were

blessed with glorious sunshine and we spent the day walking from one touristy spot to another.

Much like Bruges, Prague is a place where around every corner there's something to take a picture of, not surprising then that it's wall to wall tourists.

At one point, Barry really felt the hangover biting and had to lie down on the ground, as he said himself,

"couldn't walk another step!" To give him a break we pulled in and got a caricature drawing of the three of us. It couldn't have been in a better spot, sitting on a bench on the river bank with the Royal palace in the distance with lots of boats cruising up and down the river beside us. We went to all the big stuff. The two main squares, the astronomical clock, the palace on the hill, the bridge with all the statues (these all have names I know, but I'd a serious hangover and wasn't paying any attention) and then we finished off with the Jewish graveyard where a tiny plot of land has the graves of 100,000 folks who all wanted to be buried there.

The Czech women are gorgeous, we were rubber necking all day, "Bar Dunne 12 o clock, Phil, rear view mirror", they didn't seem as taken with us, three hungover paddies with the lads dressed in track suits. After the site seeing was done, it was time for one more night on the lash. After we got washed and changed we went off on a pub crawl passing several stag nights who were painting the town red. I was packed for Mongolia and Siberia and the only pair of shoes I brought was hiking boots. We hit a lot of disco bars and you wouldn't believe how hard it is to get down to "Daddy cool" by Boney M, in a pair of Hob nail boots.

The next morning I said good luck to Bar Dunne and Phil as they turned for home, I was feeling pretty blue when they left. A fairly big chunk of me wanted to just go home as well. I think it was the thought of what was coming. I was closing to the end of the easy stuff, once I

NOT DEAD YET

got to the Ukraine it would all be, "The unknown." The other thing was that Barry and Phil were a great laugh and we spent all day laughing and joking. To go from that to being on your own staring down the barrel of a trip to Magadan was a brutal transition.

I left Prague heading east for the town of Kutna Hora, its famous for having a church full of human bones used for

398

decoration within the church building. When I got there however, there wasn't anywhere to park the bike and it was too dodgy to leave the bike alone with all my gear on the back. I had to pass on going in, it was a major pain in the ass. It was just one of the downsides of traveling alone.

From there I made my way across country roads the whole way to the border with Slovakia. Only a couple of years ago this border would have been quite difficult to cross into, now since Slovakia had joined the EU, you can roll right through. If ever there was an advert for the EU this was it, driving from country to country unhindered. If only it was so easy everywhere else.

NOT DEAD YET

CHAPTER 25
SLOVAKIA AND UKRAINE

Once in Slovakia the countryside turned more mountainous and with Spring in full bloom, it was very picturesque. Everywhere took the Euro which was dead handy and it was about 30% cheaper than the Czech Republic. I didn't know what to expect of the country really, but much like the rest of Europe, you don't get any hassle and everyone is friendly enough and do their best to help you.

I ended up in the town of Bojnice famous because it has a wonderful fairy tale castle. At this stage I was following the Long Way Round route, piggy backing onto their trip preparations. It saved me the hassle of trying to find out what was worth seeing on the way to Moscow. I'm a lazy bastard. When I was five minutes from the hostel I came upon an accident where a car had hit a motorbike, I couldn't help but think that if I hadn't got lost on the way there, that could have been me. The routine every night now involved a map and a highlighter pen as my GPS had run out of maps since I'd left the Czech Republic.

Kocise

I continued east in the direction of the town of Kocise, the second biggest city in Slovakia, not far from the border with the Ukraine. Along the way I stayed mostly on the E50, a road which runs east to west almost the width of Slovakia, but did take the opportunity with my acre sized map, to go cross country and cut off some loops in the road.

The sun shone all day, the roads were good, and it was about as uneventful a day as it's possible to have. The further you go east the towns get poorer and most had a big

NOT DEAD YET

dirty chimney stack in the middle. I passed what I think

was a natural gas outlet which they run along the road above ground. The pipe is then looped up over entrances to factories and roads. It's mad looking, but would be a feature of towns from this point forward as its how they plumb cities which suffer the intense cold of Central Europe in the winter. The architecture was non-existent in most of the towns, mostly just rows of square communist high-rise buildings, an ever-present reminder of when the country was part of the Soviet Block. In 1993 it split with the Czechoslovakia to create the Slovak republic.

I couldn't believe how different the people were in Slovakia versus only a couple of hundred kilometers further west. The mix included Russians, Ukrainians, Slovaks and Hungarians. It was like a different world to where I was only 8hrs earlier. In the Czech Republic most of the folks had a good smattering of English and German, in Slovakia no one had a clue what I was on about.

I stopped near the town of Turna nod Bodvou, an absolute non-event of a place, but it had somewhere to sleep and that was all I was looking for so I could prepare for crossing into the Ukraine. I left the next morning in the pissing rain, it was almost as if it turned on to coincide with the beginning of the hard-ish stuff.

After about ninety minutes I arrived at two tanks which were parked close to the border and hung out for a while, you don't see too many tanks knocking around after all.

I puckered up and continued to Ukraine, never having left Europe over land before, I hadn't a clue what to expect. I met some border guards who were very friendly and helpful on the Slovak side, it went really quickly, they told me it might not go so well on the Ukraine side.

NOT DEAD YET

I drove up to the Ukraine checkpoint and was stopped by two soldiers who started making a big deal that I didn't stop when they asked me to, I'd been through this

a few times before, the shakedown was on again. After keeping me for about ten minutes and bullshitting on about the fact that I didn't stop and was also missing a sticker, I handed over the ten euro bribe and was on my way to another pack of freshly castrated crocodiles in customs.

They told me I didn't have a green card and that I needed to go back. I had done the research and had no idea what they were on about, but one of the other lads there had one, so it looked like I was fucked. Just when I was about to head off for Poland which would mean entering Russia via Lithuania as you can't get through Belarus (about a 1000 mile detour) one of the girls who worked there called me back and processed me.

I asked them was I ok to go, and they gruffly waved me on. After a reasonably distasteful time at the border, I was officially in Ukraine. Obviously by this stage I was well used to bribes, but it confirms that if you get in trouble in some countries it's the guy with biggest wallet

who gets off every time, simple as that.

Before I get into describing Ukraine, it might help to describe what I was expecting. Here's what I knew going in. It was the wealthiest region of the ex Soviet Union and very richest in oil etc. Modern historians reckon that had Hitler's army headed further south in Ukraine and taken its oil fields, instead of heading north to Stalingrad, Germany may have gone on to win the war in Russia. It separated from the Soviet Union a number of years

NOT DEAD YET

previously so I was expecting it to look about 33% poorer than Slovakia, if that makes any sense. In summary, I wasn't expecting an improvement on Slovakia. As it turned out when I looked up the numbers, the average weekly wage in Ukraine was less than $100.

Once I crossed the border, the question that jumped into my head was, "Who flicked the poor switch!" The fields in the farms were worked with horses pulling ploughs and people tilled the soil with hoes and shovels. Anyone who has ever used a hoe before will tell you it's a bit of work, now imagine hoeing for an acre!

The road which I took was in terrible condition and the towns I passed through were very poor. The area I was traveling in actually used to be part of Poland before World War II, looking at how it looked then, I doubted they'd be looking for it back anytime soon. The country has a population of about 44 million people and is a little

smaller that the state of Texas in the USA, or a little bit smaller than France. The country uses the Cyrillic alphabet, so pronunciation of the road signs as they looked on the signposts was a thing of the past. I really regretted not studying up on a few phrases before I got there, and doubly not regretted at least learning the alphabet so I could decipher what the Cyrillic letters meant.

Lviv

I made my way to the town of Lviv, a beautiful city in the North West part of the country. The roads along the way were somewhere between terrible and ok. At one point I turned around and drove back twenty miles because the roads were so bad, I thought I must have taken a wrong turn, "No way this is the road to such a major city."
As the day wore on a couple of trends were starting to

emerge. The first was that the Western part of the country was as poor as they come. Secondly, the churches and graveyards, all Eastern Orthodox, were incredibly ornate and well maintained. No matter how small the town, they all had fabulous churches with shiny gold and silver roofs, the contrast between them and the surrounding poverty couldn't have been starker. Thirdly, the people seemed very gruff. In the first day I interacted with say ten people, and of those, only three of them were in any way polite. The others were like trying to take a bone off a pit bull. Now it's not like I was debating politics with these folks. The extent of what I was looking for was gas, grub and a room for the night.

I made it to Lviv and booked into a hotel. The folks that I met in that town were ok, a welcome change from the folks I'd met thus far. I tried to figure out why people behaved differently towards strangers than in Western Europe and I came across an interesting story that brought it home for me. The article I read detailed the fact no one trusted anyone during the days of the Iron curtain. The only people who you talked to were your family, everyone else was liable to report or inform on you to local officials. Ukraine only got its independence from Russia reasonably recently, and up until that point, people were thought to mistrust westerners. They also learned the hard way to only answer the question they were asked. Knowing the history didn't make traveling there any more pleasant, but it's not like I was moving there, I was only driving through it. I went out and about in Lviv to see what I could see but the weather was crap so I gave up pretty quickly. The first day was tough, a total culture shock, but I'd lived to fight another day.

Kiev

I had passed into a new time zone when I got to Ukraine, I was officially two hours ahead of home and it really gave me a tremendous feeling of movement and progress. The fact that it got dark now two hours earlier than it did at home made me feel quite far from home. Incidentally, you don't say "The Ukraine", they don't like it and consider it an insult, you say Ukraine much the same way you'd say Ireland or England.
That day I was headed to Kiev, and spotted Chernobyl to the north of it on the map. In case you born after 1990, Chernobyl is the site of world's largest ever Nuclear disaster. As the story goes, had the winds been blowing differently on the day of the nuclear incident in 1980, it

would have taken out Kiev.

Such was the extent of the brain washing that we in Ireland received growing up from the mass media, that in my mind, Ukraine was a place where the sun seldom shone, the people were oppressed and afraid, and the buildings and structures were dull and lifeless. As I left Lviv it was a dull and cloudy day and as I hit the outskirts of the town I couldn't help but think how much of the stereotype seemed to be true.

I made my way out onto the loop road for the city which joined up with the main road to Kiev and was stopped by the police. They brought me over to camera which showed me doing 74kmph in a 60kmph zone. I was barely moving as far as I was concerned, and certainly didn't see any sign, and was by no means the fastest thing on the road. They brought me over behind the car and showed me a book which I didn't understand. The book detailed the fines and they indicated to me that I would have to go to the police station to pay it. I asked them could I pay the fine there and then. I knew the drill and before I left the hotel that morning I had left about $15 in various notes and currency's in my wallet so that when I was stopped, I would be able to empty it out and hopefully fool them into thinking I'd no more money. They looked very disappointed that this was all I had in the wallet but were happy enough to take it and let me go.

It was my second day in Ukraine and already it was the second bribe I'd given. The other way of looking at it is of course, that I was speeding and I had an on the spot fine imposed on me, of course this argument is only sound if the money they took off me goes to the state and not into the coppers arse pocket, which I seriously doubted. The journey to Kiev was a little over 550km, and it took all day to do it. A lot of the road was marked as dual carriageway on the map but it seldom had both sides open and in many places the road was completely closed for road works, making the going very slow.

Along the road there are hundreds of petrol stations, and petrol prices are roughly half what they were in Ireland. They also had lots of very good garages, one in a particular is a chain called "A La Minute" which sold quality hot food and drink. Up until that day, I thought the Americans had the Apple pie gold medal sown up, well move over lads, Ukrainian apple pie is a hum dinger. The pastry was really thin, and was stuffed with huge big pyramid shaped pieces of apple all served with a scoop of ice cream and some Raspberry sauce! It went a long way to curing me of my "Ukraine is crap" buzz.

The countryside between Lviv and Kiev is flat fertile farmland, in other words boring and in over 350 miles I

NOT DEAD YET

barely saw a thing worth taking a picture of, all there was to see was beat up towns with poor farmers working the land outside the towns and villages. I got to Kiev in the early evening and made my way to the old town, which is the touristy area (except they don't really get many tourists). I found it really hard to find a place to stay. The

old town was cobbled just like Lviv and the dated tram lines represented a major hazard for motorcyclists. After about 90mins I flagged a taxi and asked him to take me to a hotel. When I got there the receptionist was about as helpful as Gonorrhea. I kept telling myself, "Dude, you're in a different country, you need to be more tolerant and adapt to how these folks live and act in their country!" The following day I got up early and started working my way through the tourist sites in the city. The average Kiev dweller appears devout, most blessed themselves as they passed a church, and where one church faces another they blessed themselves twice, doing a quick shuffle as they turn around to face the other way.

I learned some new stuff walking around as well. If you want to look like a Ukrainian dude, you needed to get yourself a leather jacket which goes down to your pants pockets and make sure its flat fitting. Then get yourself a fairly snug set of black jeans, black shoes, and 20 cigarettes, being sure to always have one smoke in your hand. Finally, brush your hair straight down so it looks like a bowl cut and you're all set, you too can look like you are from Kiev. I'm certain I was the only male in the entire city of Kiev with curly hair.

The politics of the country is dominated by "Those who hate Russia" and "Those who really really hate Russia!" While I was there, a riot broke out in the parliament over the government allowing the Russian navy access to one of its ports. I learned that over 8 million Ukrainians died in a famine in the 1920's which they believe was engineered by the brutal Russian communist regime and also that another 8 million Ukrainians were killed by German and Russian troops during World War II, it

NOT DEAD YET

went a long way to help explain why people acted the way they did. People were very suspicious, if I tried to get directions from anyone, they'd walk right by me and shake their head. Nobody made eye contact, it was all very "head down and arse up."

I made my way to freedom square which is where the Orange revolution happened. The whole thing was watched worldwide, it was when the KGB tried to poison the President of the country, the Presidents face aged 20 years over night.

I had my first scam played on me while I was there. I was getting a lot of looks from people, I stood out, they seemed to be making it clear I didn't belong there. Well, these two men were looking at me while pretending not to. I said to myself, "Ok this is a bit dodgy" so I went to cross the road to one of the statues where there were a lot of police. To cross the road in Freedom square you have to go underground. As I went down the stairs, I rubber necked back, only to see that they were following me. Fuccckk!!!!!!" I pulled over to the left of the tunnel which led to the stairs and pretended to look in a shop window as they overtook me. They passed and I started walking again. As I walked up the stairs behind them, one of them paused for a second, and then "accidentally on purpose" dropped a plastic money holder full of US Dollars, I walked sharply to the left of him and his friend and as I passed the guy on the left, I shouted at them, "You dropped your money" and kept walking. One of them continued with the charade by thanking me for telling him. He was holding his hand out for me to shake which I pushed away and told him to, "Get the fuck away from me" and did a Benny Hill impression walking as

fast as I could over to the Police. When I got to them, I turned around and the guys were gone. "Fuck, what did they want!"
I'm certain I wasn't in physical danger, they were using some scam or another, maybe if I picked it up they'd say I robbed some of it or something like that. I looked around for them and then for the next twenty minutes I walked like I was Jason Bourne in the Bourne Ultimatum, down roads checking windows to see if they were following me. As I was burning down the road, two separate SUV's mounted the footpath right towards me, I said "Oh fuck, this is them" but it wasn't, it was either the secret police or some other rich boys flouting the law. A woman who they nearly hit further up the road glanced back towards me and shrugged her shoulders. It was almost like she was apologizing.
After about 30 minutes with no sign of them I relaxed and went into the "Belfast Irish Pub", and had something to drink. I'd no idea what had happened but it was enough for me to say that I wouldn't be back to Kiev in a hurry.

Kharkiv

I left Kiev very early the next day, certain I was going to spend hours lost in the traffic. As it happened I found my way out really easily, on the way passing a massive statue cleverly named the "Mother Motherland monument". It's immense, and when it was built 40 years ago, it was the worlds largest statue. It reminded me of something from the Lord of the Rings.
The road north to Kharkiv takes you towards the airport

and the early going is all an eight lane highway. However, once you get by the airport, the road turns right back to shitty one laners peppered with masses of potholes. By 8am I'd a hundred miles done and was pulled over having breakfast.

The countryside continued to be all flat agricultural land with barely a landmark or even a hill to be seen in any direction. The closer I got to the Russian border the more I noticed that the towns retained the statues of Lenin. My guess was that the folks on the border aren't convinced the Russians are gone for good just yet, and are keeping the statues out just in case the Russians ask them where the statue went when they come back.

I made my way through the countryside to Kharkiv, a city just south of the Russian border, a base for me to get set up to cross the border with Russia. I met two chaps from Kiev and Germany in the car park who were really great fun. The guy from Kiev, when I made mention of all the fine looking women in the Ukraine, said that it was "compensation" for all the other crap.

The next morning I headed off in the direction of the border with Russia as nervous as a cat in a dog pound. The place was mayhem and I'd to drop another bribe with Ukrainian exit guards to get through. This was after queuing for two hours and as I was just about to get out of the country, it gave me a royal pain in the hole. I joked with the guard, "So is this a big problem ($20) or a small problem ($10). As I passed the money over and the guards walked away saying bye, I said in my best Arnold accent "I won't be back!" Summing up on the Ukraine. The highlights were the incredible churches especially St. Andrews in Kiev and beautiful looking women. It was also very inexpensive to travel in. The downside was that its very corrupt, I was there four days and was the victim of a scam and three bribes, and the people aren't in the least bit friendly. In summary, give it a miss.

CHAPTER 26
ERNAN AND THE GUY FROM THE CHURCH

In 1994 my mother suffered a large stroke and was permanently paralyzed down her left side. At the time I was 24 and was just out of college. I had just started working and was finally bringing in some money. I had big plans to try and help her out, to buy her some stuff that she had gone without for years and years, as a way of thanking her for putting me through college. I can remember thinking, "God's a bollix."

We moved Mam into the dining room, which we turned into her bedroom, it was also close to the fridge and kitchen which meant fixing her something to eat was easier. We all did our best to help out and got some home help support to help take care of her.

Around about that time, my older brother had recently stopped going to an evangelical Christian church and was back out on the town living life to the full. Well, one night he brought home a girl and went upstairs with her where no doubt he was shagging her silly. Thirsty, after his night of endeavor he proceeded to head back down stairs for a couple of cans of beer from the fridge. He, being drunk out of his mind thought it would be a good idea to go downstairs naked.

The beer was in the fridge and the fridge was in my mother's bedroom, the converted dining room. Without further ado, my brother walked into where my mother was sleeping and opened the fridge door pulling out a six pack of beer. He then turned to walk back out. My mother was fully awake the whole time and looking out through disbelieving eyes shouted at Ernan, "What are you doing?" Ernan standing there in his pelt replied, "Just getting some beers" in a tone which said "What's the problem?", notwithstanding the fact that he was naked in my mothers bedroom and it was 4am. My mother gave him an incredulous look and then asked in a slightly higher and significantly more agitated tone, "Who is upstairs?" For some reason best known to himself, Ernan replied, "A guy from the church." He then walked out of the room and made his way back upstairs, six-pack in hand.

My mother with the little power that still remained in her body after the stroke, proceeded to make her way out of the bed and staggered to the bottom of the stairs. From there, somehow she managed to get herself up the 14 steps to the upstairs of the house. She hobbled over to the door of my brother's room and with the one arm that still worked, pushed the door in. She was greeted with the sight of my brother doggy-styling some unknown girl while he simultaneously took a slug out of a bottle of Budweiser.

I think the only thing that didn't bring about the onset of a second and almost certainly fatal stroke was the fact that, as it turned out, Ernan wasn't shagging a guy from the church.

NOT DEAD YET

CHAPTER 27
WESTERN RUSSIA

As I moved over to the Russian side of the border, I was very nervous. As usual I needn't have worried, bar the fact that the computer system had crashed it was reasonably straightforward, taking about four hours all all in all. I'm not sure getting there earlier would have made any difference. If you were a normal punter, who had come from Ireland without any experience of second and third world borders, this would have been a very stressful day. However, once you've been through Central America, nothing will ever faze you again, at least when it comes to borders. One of the things that was very noticeable was that when the Russian guards were checking my passport photo, they really took a lot of time to compare you to the photo, almost as if they were counting the freckles on your face!

I was dying of the thirst when I eventually got away from the border and pulled into a garage and slaughtered two bottles of Diet Coke. From there I made my way north to the town of Orel, about two hundred miles north west of where I was. As I was riding along, I kept saying to myself, "I'm in Russia, I can't believe I rode my bike the whole way to Russia!" The landscape was almost identical to the Ukraine, mostly flat agricultural land with the exception that there were murals with the old Soviet Hammer and Sickle on the occasional wall. It's still slightly different than you'd think though. For example, say you had to drive across Saskatchewan in Canada. The roads are utterly straight and the countryside absolutely flat with nothing but fields of barley and wheat extending off to the horizon in all directions. There you'd be bored. However, because your in Russia, your never bored. Your constantly thinking about what's coming up,

NOT DEAD YET

you've no clue what is going to happen next and a piece of your brain is constantly telling yourself to be a bit on edge because of where you are in the world.

Bill, a buddy of mine in Moscow had arranged for me to meet a friend of his in Lenin Square in Orel, she'd get me a place to stay before I headed to Moscow the following day. On the way, I got stopped by the Police and they gave me the rubber glove treatment but eventually let me go. There was nothing bad natured about it, they just had a lot of questions that I couldn't answer, actually I didn't have a clue what they were even asking me. I just kept pointing at Vladivostok on a map to let them know where I was off to. If you can picture the scene with me and two Russian police officers holding Kalashnikov's leafing through the lonely planet Russian phrase book in

search of words, it was comical.

In Russia, when you arrive in a new town you have to register your arrival. This is normally done by hotel staff at the local bureau, in fact if you're from another country, you really don't have any choice other than to stay in a hotel when traveling in Russia. Now that doesn't mean that you have to stay in a hotel every night, but you when you try to leave the country, they will look for your travel documentation and you have to show that you registered in every town you stayed in. That's another key difference between traveling there and everywhere else in the world, they don't want you there and aren't in the least bit interested in you or your holiday. A foreigner showing up at a hotel in the middle of Russia is just work for them, they don't see it as revenue. They don't get too picky when you're out in the boonies because they know that there isn't always a place to register, but certainly

NOT DEAD YET

whenever you get to a big town, you have to register.
I arrived in Orel having missed my connection with Bill's friend, Irina. It turned out that when you cross north into Russia you go forward an hour so instead of being just a little late, I was very late. I stopped beside these bikers and asked was there any hotels nearby. One of the bikers, Max, a sound man, brought me to a hotel and even helped me unpack the bike and bring my stuff up to the room.

Later on we met for what I thought was going to be a couple of pints in a pub or a bar, but it turned out to be

a good round of street drinking. I was introduced to a great bunch of lads from the town and we'd a great night. It was also the first eye opener I had regarding Russian Women. It became very clear to me that the real reason Hitler invaded Russia was for the women, if the men in

Ireland knew how good it was, they would all take up arms and invade, it was too good to be true. The only problem was that I couldn't speak a word of Russian, and they couldn't speak a word of English.

The next morning, dying with a hangover the lads came back and helped me get packed me up and escorted me out of town, past the police checkpoints. From there I made my way North to Moscow, one of the world's largest cities, home to almost twenty million people.

I found Bill Finn's house very easily following the instructions that he had emailed me. As I was riding the route, I could hear his voice in my head describing in

detail every turn off I was to take and what were the land marks to look for. I got to the house and they were having a barbecue in my honor.

I showered quickly and it wasn't long before I was ferrying Bill's kids up and down the street on the motorbike. Liam, Aine, Sean and Evan, four of the cutest kids I've ever met and they all got a tremendous kick out of being on the bike. There was a Scottish Irish couple there also with their kids and we shared beers and sausages till late into the evening. Later on we went out for a couple of pints and met some of the other expats living in Bills "reservation", a mini expat community on the outskirts of Moscow.

The next day we went into Moscow City Centre, I was full of excitement. For Bill, this must have been the tenth time he'd been in showing people around, but he did his best to feign interest. We went down through the main shopping area and then over to the Kremlin. I couldn't believe I was standing in Red Square, it was such a thrill and I was overcome with a tremendous sense of achievement. I couldn't get over the fact that I'd ridden my bike the whole way to Moscow from Ireland. From there we travelled to some other places around Moscow all done via the very impressive underground Metro system, which is as modern, clean and efficient as anything in Europe or the US. Some of the Metro stations are works of art and you feel like your on the way to an Opera rath-

er than entering a train station. It runs every 5 minutes during the week and services seven million daily users. We rode the Metro to go as far as the World War II equipment exhibition. When we were going up the escalator I saw an altercation at the top. By the time we reached there, the police were handling a dead body. He had been killed only a minute or two earlier by a blow to the head. There was blood flooding all over the floor. The way the police were treating the body wasn't fit for a dead rat, but the most disturbing thing, was how run of the mill the whole thing seemed to passers-by. We were both stunned to silence for a while. The whole incident reminded me to buck up and be a bit more careful, I wasn't on a city break for the weekend, Moscow's got warts like most major cities and I needed to watch out a bit more.

Bill told me in his time there, he'd seen several murders, a tale repeated by several of Bill's expat friends. As if to turn the moment completely on its head, when we turned the corner there were two guys playing Bach on a violin and a cello as if nothing had happened. We didn't say much for a long time after. Having seen enough of Moscow, we went back to Bills place and went for grub with his wife Oksana and the kids and had a nice evening sipping beer and talking crap. I spent the next day organizing my gear for setting off. I worked on the route and also arranged with Oksana, Bill's wife, about where we were going to ship spare tires to, Barnaul and Ulan Ude were the two most logical points. That way I'd have fresh tires for both Mongolia, and Far Eastern Russia. It was time to get rid of all the emotional crutches that I'd built into the trip. From the start, Dave was coming with me as far as Wales, I'd meet Barry and Phil in Bruges and when I got to Moscow I knew I'd stay with Bill and Oksana.

This was the day when no matter how far I looked ahead, I couldn't tell the next time I'd meet someone I'd met before, maybe it wouldn't be till I got back to Ireland in August. With that in mind I said good luck to Bill,

Oksana and the kids and thanked them for all their help. Only a couple of minutes later I was rocketing towards the "three o clock" position on the MCAD Moscow loop road. In case you haven't heard about it, it's a ten lane superhighway which completely encircles Moscow.

People refer to their location in Moscow based on what time they are at on the circle, e.g.: Bill lives at 11 o clock, I was heading east so therefore was burning for the three o'clock position. I made my way to the M7 which I'd be staying on till I got to the town of UFA over a 1000km further east.

Kazaan

Russia covers one ninth of all the land in the world and its population is about 142 million people. The vast majority of those people live in a very narrow sliver in the southern part of the country, much like Canada; any further north is virtually uninhabitable for more than six months of the year. It has the world's largest amount of forests and 25% of all the fresh water in the world. There are 83 nationalities in Russia, so there is no such thing as a typical "Russian".

I had intended to stay in the town of Lizney Novgorad about 250 miles east of Moscow but I got there too early to pull in and I'd been off the road for three nights, so I just kept going in the direction of the city of Kazaan. This part of the world has almost no mountains, it's mainly flat boring farm land. Now before anyone starts jumping up and down, I'm not saying that farmland isn't nice, it's just that in over 400 miles, an oul hill here and

there would be nice. The only thing of interest I passed was a long line of whores standing at the side of a road near a truck lay-by. Based on the look of them, they were bargain basement, high mileage models.

Gradually as you go east the amount of cars on the road dries up to almost zero, and everything you meet is a truck. In a way I was glad, I wanted to get some "East" miles under my belt. It was time to get the head down for a couple of days. Along the way I stopped in several garages meeting lots of nice folks eventually pulling into a truck stop for the night about a hundred miles short of Kazaan, 430 miles from Moscow.

Once I'd checked into the truck stop, a guy who hadn't a word of English had me phone this guy, "Barry in England" who the trucker had met in Omsk (about 1200km further east of where I was). I phoned him, Barry answered and I said, "Emm, A guy just gave me the phone and told me to talk to you?" "It's Oleg from Omsk?" It wasn't long before Barry hung up.

I went out to stretch my legs and got talking to truckers from Poland, Estonia, Russia and even one from Kazakhstan, he didn't really get my Borat impersonation, "Very nice!" I went through my route with the guys and they gave some great tips on which sections to avoid based on traffic and which were more difficult towns to get through. They told me I was staring down the barrel of a seven day hard ride to the Mongolian border after I'd included some time out to change my tires in Barnaul.

I said good night to the lads as they were ordering in whores for the night.

UFA

A little more information on Russia in general is probably appropriate at this point. Petrol prices run at about $2 a gallon, about one third the price of juice in the UK, and about 40% of what they are in Ireland, when you consider the size of Russia it's just as well. The Russian average monthly wage is $303, a really really good job pays about a $1000 a month. The average price to rent an apartment (1 bedroom) is about $1000 in Moscow, but even in the crappy towns, it's as high as $500. As a result of the high cost of renting whole families share one room in a lot of instances. The average life expectancy of Russian men is only 64, whereas for women its 76, the result is that there's a lot more women than men knocking around. If you are a single man and you want to get a girlfriend, take some Russian lessons and go to Russia. You'll be batting way above your station in no time, I promise. I've said already that a lot of the hotels don't

actually want tourists to stay with them, especially if they have the hassle of registering you when you arrive. They have to go to the immigration office and get some paperwork stamped and if you change your mind and stay and extra day they have to repeat the process. On no level are the hotels competing for your business, it's very much a "take it or leave it" setup. Customer service does not exist.

Back to the story. I was on the road at 6:50am the following morning after dropping into yet another time zone, by the end of that day I'd be in another, a full five hours ahead of the folks back home in Ireland. It was a scorcher of a day, the sun never stopped shining. As I slowly roasted with every mile that passed, I was calling myself a dill weed for getting the clothing so wrong, although I knew it would be freezing at times in Siberia, I never thought it would be 30degC in Central Russia in

NOT DEAD YET

early May. I knocked out seven hundred or so kilometers through an unendingly flat agricultural plane and ended up on the eastern side of the town of UFA. This place took the word "shithole" to a place it's never been before. The motels whack up the prices for foreigners and for my little corner in the pig sty, I was being gouged to the tune of about a hundred bucks.

The Cops were everywhere on the road and thankfully most of the folks who are coming towards you will flash you to let you know they are ahead. In most countries the Police normally need a probable cause to stop you.

That is not the case in Russia, they can and do, stop you without any reason. The average Police patrol isn't sitting there waiting to catch you when you do something wrong, they just stop you anyway, so to stay grief free, you need a bit of luck. To stop you, they stick out a baton and point it right at you till you slow down and pull into the side of the road. Although I was stopped a lot, there was never any hassle. I always showed them a sketch of the route I was taking and they'd smile, look at me and then wave me on.

The countryside continued to be all flat farmland and hadn't changed for nearly three days. I couldn't wait to arrive at the Ural Mountains which I hoped would be a welcome break from the monotony.

Along the way I passed many truck stops which cater to "trucker" needs. You can get everything from tires to whores in these places and on several occasions I saw lines of six or seven prostitutes all waving in trucks. There's something so weird about seeing hookers all geared up and ready to go at 10am in the morning, obviously seeing a line of them anywhere is pretty weird too.

NOT DEAD YET

I moved into an oil rich region of Russia, passing several mid sized oil fields and a massive refinery. As was the case in Slovakia, they pump the oil up and over the roads forming metal pipe bridges in the process. I think it must have something to do with how cold the ground gets in winter. I would not want to be in the car that goes out of control and hits one of those pipes. These days were the equivalent of the doldrums on the trip. In order to get to the really scenic places you have to drive through the not so scenic and I had driven almost 1500km without seeing a hill. The Ural's could not come quick enough and I knew they would be soon followed

by the Altay Region, the "boring part" was almost over. The more remote in Russia I went, the more poverty I saw. On the outskirts of each town, large settlements of wooden houses appeared, I felt bad moaning about not having internet when these folks didn't have running water or electricity. One thing I always wondered about was Russian brides. I'd often ask myself why they do it, marry a man they never met. Well the answer was starting to grow on me. The man to woman ratio in Russia is a mile out and the women there are tripping over themselves trying to find a good man. There is massive poverty and very crammed living conditions in the cities. If you were "that" girl and you had the opportunity to marry a nice guy with a few quid from the west who'd take you away from it all, of course you'd go. Your problems would go from "No toilet" to "I wish the spare bedroom had an en suite." I don't think that it's beyond reason that a woman would fall in love with a man who could transform her life in that way.

I drove a total of 700km the following day and in the process passed through the Ural Mountains. They are

important in history because prior to World War II starting, Stalin moved all of Russia's important industry to the East of them, so that if Germany ever invaded Russia, the country could continue to function. It's the main reason there are so many cities that Far East with such huge populations, and even though the risk of invasion has long since passed, the cities have continued to thrive and prosper.

To call the Urals Mountains is a bit of a reach, I doubt any of them are above 700m but it was a great change from the flat landscape I'd been riding in for what seemed like an eternity. The disappointing thing was that there was no place to pull over and take a picture, if you did pull over you would end up being dug out of a truck. This part of Russia doesn't get many tourists so it's not altogether surprising that they haven't spent any cash on lay-by's. I spent the rest of the day hugging the northern border with Kazakhstan, something which made me feel like I was a million miles from home.

For days now I'd been living the life of a trucker, eating where they ate, sleeping where they slept and sharing the same bumpy line of tarmac for well over 2000km. The trucker pit stops are awesome places. No matter what goes wrong with a truck, these boys seem to be able to get you back on the road. They are a constant hive of activity and the drivers all seem to be experts at fixing their trucks, really just using the truck stops to get parts, or use their welding stations. The grub they serve is all baked fresh, that's not to say its great grub, it's always hot and tastes mostly like stew.

The people's skin tone darkened a notch as the road wore on, the majority of folks now looked like what I'd expect to find in Kazakhstan or Mongolia, not a major surprise when you consider Russia is made up of so many different ethnic groups and I was over 2200km from Moscow. The scenery seldom changed but was a bit more like the golden flat planes of Montana than what had passed before.

I had just passed into Siberia and a lot of the land was under water, no doubt on account of the massive thaw. It occurred to me the local farmers have to sow and harvest a crop between late April and early September otherwise they'd lose it all when the winter came. In 640km that day the views to my left and right barely changed, it was all flat farm land for as far as the eye could see, the resemblance to the prairies of Saskatchewan in Canada was uncanny.

The roads got significantly crappier the further I went into Siberia. Most had significant snow damage created by the trucks ploughing long ditches in the road as they navigated their way through the snow in winter. It wasn't long before I was contending with long stretches of gravel.

The scale of the loop roads around the major cities was hard to comprehend. For example, around the town of Chelyabinsk, to avoid going into the city you end up detouring almost 100km, which is about the width of two counties in Ireland. It packs miles onto your trip journey, but I suppose it beats having to spend your time in city traffic.

Getting to Omsk had given me a tremendous feeling of accomplishment and it now felt like Mongolia was within touching distance. I could remember when I first saw the town of Omsk on a map and remembered thinking that it may as well have been on the moon.

Nova Sibirsk

The following morning I packed in 1degC with a north wind blowing like it was pressing ice directly onto my face. I put on the vast majority of my cold weather gear and set off. It didn't get above 5degC all day. For the record: I set off with Winter motorcycle socks which go above your calf, motorbike boots, motorbike pants with fleece liners, a pair of shorts, 2 body armor layers, a motorbike jacket, a rain jacket, a buff, fleece glove liners, leather gloves, a neck and face wrap, a helmet and a pair of sunglasses and to top it all off, some ear plugs and I was still absolutely freezing.

Every forty minutes or so I was off the bike stopping for a coffee or heating my hands on the piston heads. After about three hours I could start to feel every injury I'd ever had, it's like the cold seeks out your weak points and makes them ache. After about five hours even my balls started to hurt with the cold. It was a new one for me, normally they'd just hug to my plumbing in the cold and stay warm that way. When I went for a number one, a couple of times I cupped them to make sure they hadn't vanished altogether. At one stage, with my hand still in my fleece gloves, I put them on the piston head for about 20 seconds and then put my hands down my pants and gave my town halls (balls) a little cuddle, it felt so good. I started to wonder if my ball issues were related to hitting that goat in Argentina, I started to imagine the goat laughing at me.

Along the way I passed a huge helicopter parked up outside a gas station, it was just sitting there. It was a long time since it had flown, but that's the sort of thing you just don't see back home! Later on that night, I spent about twenty minutes defrosting my balls in the shower. I'm not sure if defrosting balls fits into the masturbation pigeon hole, but it sure felt as good as any wank I've ever had. It was May 9th, the day Russia celebrates victory over Germany in World War II. Every TV was playing old war movies portraying the bravery of the victorious motherland. When I was in a roadside café thawing out, they had live footage of the march in Red Square demonstrating Russia's military arsenal, I smiled when I thought to myself, "Dude you were there last week!"

I continued to go through time zones like pairs of socks, and I could really feel like I was going "round the world".

NOT DEAD YET

For example I left at dawn from just outside UFA and drove for ten minutes before I saw the sun rise, two days later, at the exact same time it was well above the horizon; I'd pushed further east by 1200km at that stage.

I was getting no hassle from the police at all. Anytime I was stopped I start with a handshake and then did the whole "Ireland, Magadan, Vladivostok" (You need to say Vladivostok like you're a Klingon) explanation and they just waved me through. The hand shake is a massive deal in Russia. If say, you're with a party of five guys and another arrives, he'll shake the hand of everyone there, and if anyone else arrives they'll all do the same. I reckon it's the number one way to stay out of trouble, start with the shake of a hand. I think it fires something in us that goes

way back, along the lines of "I mean you no harm" or

"I'm your friend", things just seem to go well after that. On top of that, the mention of the word Vladivostok is a big thing to Russians. It's "the" epic journey in Russia, to travel from Moscow to Vladivostok. I think most folks in Russia dream of doing this journey, so by saying that's what you're doing, the locals identify with you straight away. The men in Russia are all "Men's men" They love football, girls, motorbikes and fast cars, so when the cops hear you're off on a crazy adventure they tend to give you "dude" points and let you off on your merry way.
I stopped about twenty miles short of the town of Novosibirsk and put the head down for the night in a truck stop motel. I got something approaching a panic attack about Mongolia being so close that evening. I was lying there thinking about crossing it and having to camp in many unknown and strange places by myself. I had to get up and leave the room. I went across the road to a café and played a game of, "let's pretend not to look at the strange men in the camouflage uniforms looking at my bike!"
The motels allow you to check in for 12 hours and then move on, so it meant getting on the road very early even though I'd only 250km to go to Barnaul. The first obstacle was to get through the city of Novosibirsk, Russia's third biggest city and winner of the world's most beat up town award. The roads through it were in appalling condition, not helped no doubt by the terrible winter they get in this part of the world.
I was riding my way through the city with the temperature stuck at -1degC, which might not sound that cold but when its accompanied by a Siberian wind chill, it had my teeth chattering like a set of maracas. On the

NOT DEAD YET

way out of the city a bridge traversed a frozen lake and I pulled over to have a look at it. It felt like I was in one of those Discovery channel programs as I stood by the bank of the lake listening to the sound of the ice cracking as it thawed. It was May 10th and the lake was just starting to thaw now. In my head I'd always assumed that the thaw would be well underway in Siberia, note Magadan is much further north, so if it wasn't thawing here yet, then there was little chance it would be thawing up there. What I'd been hoping and praying for as I rode along was that the snow would melt, and then obviously flood the rivers, but that by the time I got to Far Eastern Russia most of the water would be long gone. Something told me things were not going to work out the way I planned them, as if they ever do, where Mother Nature is involved.

Barnaul

I spent the rest of the morning meandering towards Barnaul where I planned to get the bike serviced and the tires changed. After that it would be a straight shot south in the direction of Mongolia passing thought the Altay

Region of Russia. It was probably from this moment on that every single thing got harder and harder to do, and no matter which way I turned, all I ran into was problems.

It was my second day in Barnaul when I got a call from Oksana in Moscow to say that the crowd who were shipping the tires had shipped them four days late. It meant I was stuck in Barnaul, but I told myself I could use the time to get the bike and my brain tip top, before going into Mongolia.

Barnaul is a strange place. You can't help wonder what the hell it's doing there, out in the middle of Siberia. The place was freezing, it was May 12th and it was snowing, sleeting, and pissing rain all in the same breath. It was as bad as any winters day in Ireland with a Siberian wind that cut you right through to the spine. Much like Orel in South Western Russia the place was overrun with fine looking women. The style of them was like something you'd expect to see on a catwalk in Paris or Milan. The priority in these parts appeared to be very much on appearance, based on several conversations I had, the typical Russian girl would prefer to have nice clothes or a nice car than live in a nice apartment. I've said this before, but when I think back to all the times the lads and I went out on the "pull" in Dublin when I was younger, we'd often find ourselves saying "Jayzus where are all the women?" or "Jayzus, it must be gay night in this place, there's no birds!" All the while in Barnaul, in the middle of Siberia you can't throw a stone without hitting a fine thing.

The town is also the capital of the Russian Bride scene, in all likelihood, were you to go and find yourself a Rus-

sian Bride online, the town you would most likely end up in, is Barnaul. How do I know all this? I met several lads from Middle America in the hotel lobby, who over a couple of beers told me that was why they were there. These guys were very genuine. I asked them was there no women in America? One of them went on to explain that he was a farmer living in a small town in Pennsylvania. He had no opportunity in his daily goings on to meet women. Like most people he wanted to get married and have kids but living where he was, he felt like he was never going to get the opportunity. The women he was meeting there were also from rural backgrounds and he felt it was a perfect match. The guys also went onto explain that Russian women have a very traditional outlook on life. Everything they said gelled with what I had encountered crossing Russia.

I wouldn't describe Barnaul as friendly, but I think that's more down to the culture than anything else. For example if you go into a hotel and ask, "Do you have a room for the night?" the most likely answer you'll get is "Nyet" (No). In the west, there is a bit more lubricant in the language, "I'm very sorry Sir, but were fully booked out, maybe you could try…." At first blush it comes across as rude and can rub you up the wrong way, but it's a cultural thing. I think it comes from years and years of, "Never answer more than you are asked". At various times the people have had to deal with Polit Bureau, Cheka, KGB, FSB, OKHRAN and most of them are still around, so people being a bit guarded is not altogether surprising.

It was my third day in Barnaul and it looked like it would be another three days before the tires showed up. I spent most of my days wandering around the city and

some of the stuff I came across included tanks (every towns got one), a metal bear, a Russian advertisement for Robin Hood, a woman selling ice cream out doors in -1degC and lots of statues of Lenin. The whole town was decked out with 9th of May regalia (65th anniversary of the war ending with Germany) and a couple of times, I had been asked if I was from Germany. I got that quite a lot in Russia actually. Apparently in Russia, they think a German looks like me, I wonder what they thought I looked like when I was in Germany. The old ladies who sold stuff in the stalls all spoke to me in German, but no English, so several times I had to ask for stuff in German. Actually its fair to say I travelled in Russia more on the strength of my German than English or Russian. I asked Irina back in Orel why so many people in Russia could speak German. She told me that when they were going to school they were thought that the Fourth Reich was going to come marching over the Steppe and try to conquer Russia, it was therefore a useful language to have.

The town has quite a few drunks knocking around, enough to make you feel uncomfortable, but not enough to make you stay indoors. There happened to be a military convention going on in the hotel where I was staying, it meant when I tried to book a longer stay due to the tire delay I was told I had to leave. In almost every country in the world changing hotels is not a big deal, pick up your bags and go check in some other place, it couldn't be easier. That is not the case in Russia. You register in the hotel for a certain period, which is also the length of time you are registering to stay in the city. Any lengthening of your stay means more paperwork and furrowed brows by all the folks behind the counter in the hotel. I hailed a taxi to take me to the Hotel Barnaul, recommended by the Lonely Planet. I went through the whole registration buzz one more time. This time I registered for a further 5 days hoping to be gone in two. This would hopefully cover my remaining time in Russia before I crossed back in after Mongolia. I wasn't sure how

picky they would get when I left the country to cross into Mongolia so I wanted to make sure I had the bases covered. I then went back into the taxi to get my stuff and I followed him up to the hotel on the bike. As we came to a cross walk this chap had dropped his car keys and my taxi guy accidentally ran over them, smashing up the bit that you click to turn on the alarm / central locking. He then ran after the taxi booting the fuck out of the door. I was following thinking, "ok… this can't be good." Anyway after a stand up row and lots of what I'm certain were Russian swear words in the freezing drizzle between the driver and the other guy, we were back on our way to the hotel.

The day cleared up in the early afternoon and I went out to see if there was anything I had missed on my previous laps of Barnaul. Over the course of the day the place slowly grew on me and the more I walked the more I found little bronze statues, another tank, ferris wheels, mosaic's, murals, and then the highlight of the lot, the War museum. It commemorated all the wars which Russia was involved in.

I also bought an English translation of a book on Russian history; it was full of incredible information. E.g. The Death toll for Russia in World War II was 20 million people, vs. 7 million for Germany, 2.5 million for Japan, 600,000 for the UK, and 400,000 for the USA. It was for this reason, that Stalin was able to negotiate the slice up of Eastern Europe. Almost 30% of all the men in Russia of all ages in 1939 were dead by 1945. I asked Bill when I was in Moscow whether or not the May 9th celebrations were dying off, Anyone who fought in WWII must now be at least 85? He commented that if anything they were getting bigger and bigger. Most modern Russians consider it "the" defining moment in their history.

I got the call from Oksana that the tires would be in the post office by early afternoon so I headed off to collect them and bring them down to Bikeland, a local motorcycle shop to get fitted. Alexi, Roman, and Maxim were there and had me on my way in no time. With the knobblies fitted, brake pads and all the fluids changed I headed back to the hotel to get packed up and get ready to leave.

I said to myself, "Ok, I haven't been locked in Russia for a while", so I headed out on the town to put that straight. I went to a restaurant/bar called Carte Blanche and got the ball rolling over a steak and three Carlsbergs. Any of the literature about going out in Barnaul talked about the Pilot club so I headed off down Lenin Street to find it. On the way I bumped into two students, Anastasia and Kate who told me that it had been closed and re-

opened under another name. They said that it was crap and that the place I should go, is a place they were headed, so we jumped in a taxi and headed off. Much to my

surprise the happening place, Club 13 was actually only a one minute walk from my hotel, which would come in handy when I was staggering home a few hours later. The bar had a live band knocking out loads of western rock, and these guys could play; although at this stage I'd about eight pints so they could have been castrating cats and I've have thought it was pretty good.
Knowing I was headed off to the Altay Region in the morning, I said goodnight to the girls and headed back to the hotel. In the lobby, the security lads were watching porn on the TV. I saluted them good night and said something to the tune of "Giddy up outta that!"

Altay Region

The next morning I woke up with a brutal hangover and packed up the bike to head south to the Altay region, it would be my first night camping on the trip, and also my last night in Western Russia. I knew when I left Barnaul there were probably no more "comforts" between me and Ulaanbaatar in Mongolia.
Packing up a bike with a bad hangover is about as much fun as getting your balls waxed and I kept saying to myself, "What the fuck did you get locked for ya gobshite!". I also had to lug all my gear from the fourth floor down and out into the car park so I was sweating bullets by the time I was ready to go.
The hangover had at least taken away my nerves about camping out in the boonies in Russia. I drove south passing through the town of Biysk and continued south for another 200km. The Altay region was starting to turn on the style as hills turned into mountains and before I

knew it I was skirting along a beautiful valley surrounded by incredible snow-capped mountains.
These were the first mountains I'd seen since the Carpathians in Ukraine. The further you drive south and the closer you get to the border with Mongolia, the roads

completely and utterly empty out. It was like I had the Altay to myself. Simply put, almost no one uses this road, the Russians are not inclined to visit Mongolia for whatever reason. The area is close to the Kazakhstan and Chinese border so is heavily patrolled by the Russian secret service, just another reason which keeps the visitors away.

With sunset about an hour away I started looking for a place to camp. If I'm honest about it, camping in Russia scared the crap out of me. It's one thing camping in a campsite, or even in touristy areas like Alaska or Canada but Russia? There was one too many AK-47's knocking around for my liking.

I found a spot by a stream which had a mound blocking the view of the tent from the road and had a look around to make sure I wasn't pitching the tent in someone's farm. I had my first outdoor crap of the trip, a seminal moment in any journey. I've been there before, but this was my first in years where I didn't have to do it out of pure necessity. It's a highly over rated experience, I was certain someone would come round the corner while I was mid-log. Give me porcelain, some kittensoft roll and a good magazine any day. With everything locked down I climbed into the tent just as the sun dipped below the horizon and wondered how long it would be before dawn. I was lying in the tent saying that sentence which all reluctant campers use, when they find themselves in a tent in the early evening "So now what the fuck are you supposed to do now?" I played the zip game, which is where you start to count the zips in the tent, my jeans, the door of the tent, my tank bag, my bike trousers, each motorcycle boot, my jackets, my hold all bags etc. etc. Oh the things you do to pass the time.

The following day I rode the remainder of the two hundred miles to the Mongolian border through epic countryside. This area should be an outdoor sports Mecca with whitewater, mountains and wonderful roads, however in the whole time I was there, I didn't see a single place where you could get a room for the night. It is one of the world's last great unspoiled areas, hurry, it won't stay like that for long. Before I got to the border I used up the last of my Russian money filling the bike up to the petrol cap with gas, I'd no idea when I'd next pass a gas station. The border was ahead of me, it seemed like it was completely deserted. I was more apprehensive than the night I had my first shag.

CHAPTER 28
SCORPIONS

NOT DEAD YET

When we were growing up there was a lot of crime. Houses and cars all around us would get robbed regularly. Even people who had almost nothing were robbed. I used to ask my Dad, "How come they are robbing from poor people, why not rob from just the rich people?" My Dad told me that those who rob from the poor didn't care who they robbed from. The moral part of their mind was broken. They could no longer tell right from wrong. They had nothing to lose, there were no more levels beneath them. To these people, prison was no worse than what they were living through on a daily basis. He also gave me a severe warning to never confront a person who had nothing to lose, it was a fight you couldn't win.

It seemed pretty brutal to me. I was sure that people could change, sure weren't they always doing it in the movies. He went on to make the point that they had nothing to change to. It didn't occur to them to change, because the bit inside them that would have driven them to want to change, namely their moral compass, was missing.

Many years later, I was working in a shipping company and there was a strike. I was 19 years old. One of the guys was caught swimming out in Bray, a seaside resort on the east coast of Ireland, when he was supposed to be delivering stock to a local shopping center. One of the managers happened to be driving by, spotted the truck and spotted him in swimming, even taking the time to wave at him. The guy was subsequently sacked for not only going off swimming while he was working, and for putting in for overtime that day as well, saying he was caught in traffic. Perversely, the guy denied it. He then called in the Union who took us all outside the gate on strike. I couldn't believe it. Everyone knew he was lying but no one would take a stand. It was pitched as "The MAN" beating up on the humble worker.

When the Union rep came out from Liberty hall, I asked him if he was going to do an investigation. He replied that, "It's my job to believe the worker, if he says he wasn't in swimming then he wasn't in swimming." I talked to the guy who was with the truck driver on the day he was caught, he said he was in swimming and we were all outside the gate based on lies. Even when the word had spread that this guy had lied, we stayed outside the gate. He continued to lie and deny everything. The average age of the work force was high, there was no way they would get another job if they lost this one. The union money they were receiving was a pittance and the company was about to close.

It was only at the point where some of the older guys realized that the dole queue was waiting for them, for possibly the rest of their lives that they acted. The liar was sacked and we all went back to work on worse conditions than when the strike started.

I talked to one of the older guys to try and understand why the driver did it. He told me that the guy didn't know the difference between a lie and the truth. He came from a background that was "Us against Them!" Every job he ever had was always done under adversarial conditions with the employer. He could in no way see that he was at fault, it was the "Man" coming down on the little guy one more time. Logic no longer played any role in the man's reasoning, it was all dominated by bitter and twisted emotion.

This story dovetails well into the parable of the Scorpion. A scorpion and a frog stood at the bank of a river. The scorpion said to the frog "Will you carry me over the river on your back?" The frog said no, telling the scorpion "You will sting me and I will drown." The scorpion replied that, "If I sting you, we will both drown. Please won't you carry me over the water?" The frog calmed by the scorpion's logic said ok. When they were halfway across the river, the scorpion stung the frog. The frog cried, "Why did you do that, now we will both drown!" The scorpion replied "I couldn't help it, I'm a scorpion!" The moral of the story is that some people cannot change, a scorpion will always be a scorpion, it's just who they are.

CHAPTER 29
MONGOLIA - PART 1

NOT DEAD YET

There is some stuff about Mongolia that's worth knowing before I begin this part of the story.

1) It's the 19th largest and most sparsely populated country in the world with just 2.9 million people inhabiting its 1.6 Million Square kilometers. So, what does that mean exactly? Well to personalize it a bit for you, if the UK and Ireland had had the same population density, between both islands, there would only be 400,000 people, the same amount of people that currently live in the city of Leeds.
2) More than 20% of its population live on less than one Euro per day
3) 30% of its population are nomadic, living in yurts and 38% of its population live in just one city, it's capital, Ulaanbaatar
4) When Genghis Khan was around, back in the 12th century, the Mongols ruled the largest contiguous land empire in history, stretching from modern day Poland to South Korea.

First Camp

I made my way through the first Russian border checkpoint and then proceeded down some asphalt to a set of large green gates. A large Russian Soldier walked out and checked my paperwork after which he walked over and opened the gate. I was looking through the gate in a state of utter disbelief. The road had turned into a track over the mountain and was completely covered in snow and slushy muck. The track extended off to the horizon, where it turned up and made its way up and over a nearby peak. "What the fuck is that?!", I said to the border guard. "That is Mongolia!", he replied as he smiled and waved me through. "Fuuccckkkkk!!!!!"

I passed through the gate and made my way slowly through the snow, slush, muck and gunge. I got 800 meters past the gate when I became completely bogged down in snow, right up to the level of the bike panniers. This happened again and again and each time I'd to strip the bike completely to get it out of the snow, then I'd have to pull the bike to harder ground and then I would have to reload it and start the whole process again. One time in particular I was stuck so bad, a passing truck driver had to give me a hand to push the bike out. I was starting to panic. Was all of Mongolia going to be like this? Why the fuck hasn't this snow melted? I was reciting that most famous of sayings to myself "Dude, you are sooooo fucked!" How could it be that everything up to this point was asphalt, and merely the act of passing through a gate had turned the whole world to shit? After two hours and barely 2km done, I looked back up

the road and had thoughts about heading back up to Russia. The sort of things that were going through my head were along the lines of: "Who cares if you don't go through Mongolia? It's not like anyone back home knows this place from a cabbage anyway. You're the only person making yourself do this, so why do it, just go back up to Russia where there are roads, dodgy soup and fine looking women, from there you can ride around to Ulan Ude." I tend to go negative first and then once I've called myself every name under the sun, I come back and push myself that bit harder. It's not like there's any cheerleaders in these parts to chant "Oisin's the king, Oisin's the king" so either you find the power within, or you quit and turn back. I decided at a minimum I was going to try and fight through to the Mongolian border post. There I'd get some local information on the road conditions and try and figure out what to do. After six grueling kilometers taking a total of three hours I arrived at the Mongolian border and was greeted with the following words from a female border guard, "Welcome to Mongolia, Where are you from? Are you married? I am not married!"

It's a great thing to hear the words "Welcome." I've crossed a lot of borders in my time and the only other country I can remember hearing it in was Argentina. At every stage in the processing at the border, the person welcomed me to Mongolia and was very generous and helpful. It was like they knew you just rode through a quagmire to get there, and were trying to make up for it. I picked up some insurance on the Mongolian side and had a conversation with a guy who spoke English about the way to Ogliv, the town I was aiming to get to the following day. He said 28km west, 100km south. That was a defining moment for what was ahead, from then on it was all heading and distance, signposts were a thing I'd have to do without.

It was getting very late in the evening so I was anxious to get going, I planned to camp in the first available spot and get underway at first light the next day. I said goodbye to the Insurance vendor and his son and drove off into what was, for me at least, the complete and utter unknown. The most important thing to understand about this part of the world is that there are no roads, there are just trails through the rocky earth sprawling off in all directions.

Before I got to Mongolia, one of the things I was interested to find out was, how did a country which was so dominant back in the 13th century, become so poor and inaccessible. I wanted to meet the typical Mongolian and see whether or not the sinews of those great Mongol

warriors still lived on in today's Mongolians. In Ireland we use the phrase, "Outer Mongolia" to refer to being in the middle of nowhere, for example if a lad was to arrive home late for his dinner, his wife might say to him "Where the fuck were you, Outer Mongolia?" I was only a couple of miles into Mongolia when I realized I was somewhere very special. Everyone I passed on the bike was waving and when I rode off a trail to get some gas, loads of people came over to shake my hand. If I stopped on the road to take a picture and a car passed they would all get out to make sure I was ok, shake my hand and then all pile back into the car and head on their way again. Everyone was smiling, I've yet to encounter a welcome like it.

Nothing could prepare you for the traveling conditions there. The ground in the North West region is hard, a mixture of gravel and sand. My guess is they just marked on the map, the ways which people happened to have travelled over the years. This was traveling as they used to do it in the old west, across country, navigating the shortest distance between two points around mountains and lakes. It was at all times, incredibly challenging. I was living in the map, constantly looking for way points and land marks to make sure I wasn't driving off course. The land didn't look like it had changed since the time of the Khan's and traveling there is the closest thing you can do today, to experience what traveling the world was like in the 12th Century.

As you drive along you can see three or four trails all bending off in different directions. It freaks you out at first but you can be confident that some miles down the road the tracks will converge on each other again. All it takes is one articulated lorry to say, "Hmm I fancy taking a slightly different route" and there you have it, a new trail. There are absolutely no signposts in the North West, at least I didn't see a single one on the first day. Directions are calculated using the compass. I kept hearing the echo of the insurance guy's directions in my head "Drive 28km west, 100km south". I spent my time constantly cross referencing the distance I had travelled with the direction I was driving with any and all landmarks on the map. "Ok so I'm driving south east, good. I've done 24km so I should be coming to a lake on my right and a big mountain on my left, good." And so it went for every single mile that I rode. I couldn't believe how tiring it was. Between concentrating on the trails, doing my best to not come off the bike, x-raying the map, looking at my distance travelled, looking at the heading on the GPS and trying to enjoy where I was, I was flat out.

The other thing I was dealing with was exploding emotions. This was the most intense experience of my life and with every mile I traveled, I felt like I was on the brink of an emotional overload as I traveled further and further into the unknown.

The early going was cold and all the mountains were covered in snow and the lakes frozen over with ice. All I wanted to do was make sure I was on the right trail to the town of Ogliv, once I was sure, I would pull over and camp for the night. I found my way with a lot of difficulty on account of all the different tracks and trails which split off the main trail like tributaries off a river. I looked for a reasonably sheltered spot and pulled a mile or so off the trail and set up a camp. I boiled water and made myself some pasta and a cup of tea, despite the relentless howling wind. I felt silly for feeling so nervous the day before. Just being there was exhilarating. I told myself "Dude, You are Luke Skywalker and you don't even have an R2 unit to chat to!" I looked around as I was chowing down and for nearly an hour not a single car nor truck passed. Even though I was a mile off the road I could see traffic coming from miles off due to the dust clouds they'd throw up into the air. With the camp set for the night I dressed up in some warm clothes and walked up to the top of a nearby hill and looked out on the plane, like it was my newly conquered kingdom. The wind rose to meet me as I held my arms aloft, roaring and screaming with raw naked emotion. The air was strangely chilled and filled my lungs in a way that I'd never felt before, it was like I was suddenly aware of how big my lungs were. I could feel the energy from the landscape vibrating through me. Once the sun dropped behind the mountains the cold became unbearable. I got into the

NOT DEAD YET

tent and slept the night away oblivious to the howling wind and bitter cold. The wind at least kept the frost away and just before dawn I got up. I stepped out of the tent and for not the first time on the trip, it was like stepping out onto another planet. The sky was dark purple all around me with the first hints of orange coming up from the east as thick dark clouds made their way across the mountains on my left. I've never felt so alone and isolated in my entire life. It felt like there wasn't another person on the planet.

I got ready to leave for my first full day in Mongolia with not even an inkling of what lay ahead of me. I packed up the camp full of enthusiasm, I'd survived a night camping in the bitter cold of Russia and now I'd a night under my belt in Mongolia, the bike was running great and I'd the town of Ogliv ahead where I'd get some grub and some local money. Everything was going according to plan. I was feeling quietly confident. At these moments

Irish people have learned to keep the head down and say nothing. The moment you say, "Things are going well" is the moment fate will deal you a kick in balls with hob nail boots that you're likely never to forget. So, the way you're supposed to deal with it is say nothing, don't even allow yourself to think it. Well, I allowed myself to say it out loud and those words carried on the wind to Loki, the god of mischief and chief tormenter of bikers. The next 100 hours were the toughest I'd ever known. Riding through Mongolia is like being in a movie, I constantly had an epic soundtrack in my head. As I passed over a hill, I was Aragorn galloping a horse across the plane, I've never felt so free, so alive and so full of energy. My heart and lungs felt like my chest was too small for them, I was bursting at the seams. I was the conquering hero in every movie I had ever seen. I was Luke Skywalker blowing up the death star, I was Frodo

making his way to Mordor and I was John Wayne kissing Maureen o' Hara in the Quiet man. I was invincible. I didn't think it was possible to feel so good. It could only go downhill from there. My first blip happened as I was coming up a snow covered muddy mountainside trail. I crossed some snow lying on the ground which

was mostly ice and the bike skidded, I instantly fell over breaking the right hand guard, battering the right mirror, denting the right pannier and windscreen and driving the left mirror so far into my left tit, that it would be black for days, and lastly my knee hurt like a mother. The bike had fallen over on the side of a mountain, I tried to lift it but it was facing the wrong way round so I couldn't budge it. I was in the process of stripping it down when a 4x4 came along and two Mongolian chaps gave me a hand getting it up off the ground. They were also kind enough to show me which trail to follow going over the mountain, I thanked them and waved them off as they drove down the mountain. After a quick run round the bike to make sure nothing else was broken I was back on the trail.

Ogliv

The track straightened out and along the way I stopped off to take some pictures. Just then a guy came along on a horse. There didn't seem to be any yurts about so I wondered where he lived. His face was red and weather beaten with deep wrinkles carved by the harsh conditions all round his eyes and mouth. He seemed to be happy where he was, in that he seemed to fit that loca-

tion, if that makes sense. He was coming over to say hello, he didn't speak English and obviously I didn't have a

NOT DEAD YET

word of Mongolian so I pulled out the map and showed him where I was headed. He made lots of appreciative noises, but from the way he looked at the map I could tell that he'd never seen one before, or at least never seen one of the country of Mongolia. He looked at the map like you or I might look at a school class photo, going through naming all the people you can remember. I pointed to the Russian border where I came from on the map, and then with my finger traced the direction I was headed and he nodded, and then pointed to the nearest town, Ogliv. He looked at the map for ages, it seemed to be giving him tremendous comfort. I wished I had a

spare map so I could have given him one, it was like he found a long forgotten photo album. I shook his hand and was sad to say goodbye.

It seemed like every time I stopped before the town of Ogliv, someone would come along on a bike or in a jeep and stop and get out to make sure I was ok and to have a chat. I didn't pass that many cars but if I was stopped, they always stopped, and always got out for a chat which was more hand signals and smiling than anything else. The people were friendly beyond anything I'd encoun-

tered before. Later that day I saw my first Mongolian signpost, it stood like a sentry with three arrows to three towns detailed in Cyrillic text, my map was in English. The one road sign a day would continue to be a trend for the remainder of my time in the cuds. All of a sudden about 35km from Ogliv I hit a stretch of tarmac, gorgeous! I thought to myself maybe the Mongolians have come across a few bob and the roads will be better than I expected.

Ogliv is a place to get some food, petrol, money and not

NOT DEAD YET

much more. All of the Mongolian towns are like that, I can safely say there isn't a town worth visiting in all of

Mongolia, by western standards they are too poor for us to assimilate, they'll only depress you. The only reason to go is if you need supplies or for somewhere to stay. (With the possible exception of the ancient capital Kharkhoran) As I was sitting in a restaurant in Ogliv, one of the guys I met at the border the day previous walked in, noticed me and walked over and gave me a big kiss on the cheek, shaking my hand vigorously.
The next town I was headed for was Hovd. I scouted around the town for the way south and saw a dirty oul track leading out of town. I pointed to the road and said "Hovd?" to a local, to which he nodded in the affirmative. I secretly hoped I might get a bit more asphalt, I wouldn't see any more for nearly 1600km
Not long after I left the town of Ogliv in the direction of Hovd, it started to rain and sleet, and just a bit further on I had my first minor bit of water to cross. The

lakes were still full of ice and were still in the process of melting. They were sending water in various amounts down paths of least resistance, which in many cases happened to be right in the path of the track that I was following. I should have known something was up when I hadn't seen so much as a car or a truck since I'd left Ogliv, the way I was taking was not being used by the locals due to all the water draining out of the lakes. It was the third water crossing of the day, where I eventually came unstuck. I was faced with a huge river of water and wondered whether or not I'd be able to get through it. I scanned all around and no matter where I looked, it didn't look like there was a way through. The raised banks which surrounded the water were soft and mushy and dropped off into the water after a couple of feet. I allowed the bike down a bank with the intention of parking on its shore and to my horror found that the ground was too soft and the bike was starting to sink. I said to myself, "Ok fuck it, barrel through it." Halfway across, the water rose above the piston heads, the bike cut out and I jumped off the bike to hold it upright in the freshly unfrozen ice water. I tried to push the bike out of the water over and over again, but the front tyre was stuck in mud. With the water over the piston heads, I was shitting myself that I would draw water into the engine. I stood there freezing cold, shouting for help, but none was going to come, the locals were all going a different way, they knew the lake melt was too high in that area. The bike was too heavy and was sinking further and further into the gunge at the bottom so while I was standing in the water I starting unpacking the bike and throwing the stuff from the bike onto the bank of a nearby island.

If the bike fell over in the water it would be fucked, I'd have to wait till someone came along to tow it out and then wait for a truck to bring it somewhere to dry out and get it fixed up. When I threw my helmet it bounced off the bank and started floating down and around the melt water, somehow it didn't sink. It was a momentary comical moment, in what was otherwise a very serious situation. Twenty of the darkest minutes I'm likely to ever go through passed. I stood freezing roaring for help getting more and more disconsolate and descending into a darker and darker mood. I tortured myself till I went absolutely mental. The sorts of things that went through my head: "Fuck it, push the bike over and thumb it to Hovd, fly to Ulaanbaatar and go home. At least roll the bike out so you can have the pleasure of burning it out while you dry yourself. You are an arrogant fucker to think that you could do this on your own. Oh yeah, and

NOT DEAD YET

by the way fat boy, no one gives a fuck, now put that in your pipe and smoke it while you stand here and freeze to death! You won't be able to get through, you're a useless worthless fat fuck and when you go home with your tail between your legs, all those cunts will plague you with "I told you so!" Granted it's not healthy but you just have to do it, or at least I have to. I drove myself into frenzy of negativity and channelled the rage into pushing the bike out. I moved the bike about eight feet which was enough to move the water to the midpoint of the piston heads. I turned the key of the ignition with the words "Oh please God, let it start, please God let it start!" The bike started and I walked it out of the river while thrusting it forward with little bursts of the throttle in first gear. The effort to do it left me feeling like I was going to have a heart attack and my legs were so cold they were shaking uncontrollably. Once I got the bike across, I'd

to walk back across to the island to collect the stuff I'd thrown off and then change out of my soaking socks and jocks. The wind was howling and it was raining. I didn't know how many more of these I'd have to cross so I said I'd try and find a place to stay in Hovd for the night to get all my stuff dry, assuming I could get there. I'd no idea how much damage I'd done to the bike, there was a slick of oil in the water, where had it come from? Was there water in the engine oil? I'd no clue.

Hovd

I was lucky as it turned out, in that this was the last river between me and Hovd. As I pressed on the weather picked up and the sun did its best to try and break through the clouds. I wasn't sure I was on course but started to get confident when I saw several trucks com-

ing from the direction I was going; "Well they must be coming from Hovd, there's nothing else on the fucking map!" Given the tracks were a little bit busier I stopped if I wasn't sure, got out the map and asked passing trucks if I was on course, "to be sure to be sure!"

The tracks turned into gravel roads even had a few markers at the side so I was feeling confident. Then, in the distance the town appeared. It's an amazing thing to find a town after riding across country through every manner of obstacle to find it. The sense of achievement left me feeling like Lawrence of Arabia. Like I said earlier, none of the Mongolian towns are worth visiting. They're all (at least the ones I've seen) incredibly poor and wretched. If you're planning a trip to Mongolia, don't expect anything from the towns other than gas, some grub and if your desperate, a bed for the night. I happened to be soaked and freezing so I'd have slept on a briar as long as it was warm that night.

When I got to the outskirts a guy pulled up beside me and asked "Are you looking for a hotel?" I said I was, he said to follow him and he even helped me bring my bags upstairs in what was a nondescript decrepit building. It looked like a blast site and didn't actually say it was a hotel, the sign said "sauna, pool, smoking", but the room was what I needed. I took off all the wet stuff and washed it and then hung it up. They didn't have any hot water so a cold wash would have to suffice. Washing cold balls with even colder water is one of life's best left undiscovered secrets. I went out in the town to find myself some warm grub. The restaurant I went to happened to be in the town's actual hotel, and the grub was grand. They even took time to put two nipples onto the mounds of

rice on the plate to make them look like boobs, or maybe I'd been "Sans woman" for too long and just misinterpreted it.
That night I lay in the bed thinking about everything that had happened, I thought about having a wank but for the first time on the trip, my wank bank was emp-

ty, I couldn't think of a single thing. The next morning I packed up and stocked up on water and food, it was 450km to Altay and my plan was to camp about 250km down the road. The sun was shining, and the road started with about 2km of hard top, "Lovely start to the day" I told myself.

I was making good progress and by about 11am I had 150km done and was in great spirits. My stomach started to feel a bit rumbly, the Ringaskiddies were on the way. I had a bit of a giggle to myself thinking about a Billy Connolly sketch where he talks about women feeling listless and constipated. I was thinking that the cure should have been described as, "What you need is some Mongolian broth, it'll turn your alimentary canal into the London Underground!" With no traffic or people around you can just drop the tweeds anywhere and let her rip. This one was going to be pure slurry and there was a terrible wind so I decided I better strip off from the waist down, slurrying in a gale might have some unfortunate consequences. I pointed my ring in the same direction the gale was blowing and fertilized a good acre of the Mongolian desert, although unlike Yak crap, I'm pretty sure you couldn't use this stuff to light a fire. I looked up mid chamber evacuation and noticed that the unrelenting gale had caught hold of my tank bag. The wind had lifted out the maps from the top sleeve and all the laminates which I'd taken from Simon in England had started blowing down the valley. In only a couple of seconds they were fifty yards away and by the time I'd finished my impression of a slurry spreader the maps had made their way to Norway. Fuck! Fuck! Fuck! Fuck! Fuck! Fuck! If you'll excuse the pun, it was a crap mo-

ment. So, if you happen to be out and about and you find a laminate of a detailed Mongolian map, treat it well, for its travelled a long way. I didn't get too disconsolate, I reckoned I was on the main track to Altay and if I just followed this and used the GPS to tell me I was heading east or southeast, I should be ok. WRONG!! WRONG!! WRONG!! WRONG!!

The trails were heavily riveted and the vibration the bike was putting up with was almost comical. All of a sudden the ride got a lot shakier, I knew what had happened, the rear shock had blown. Fuck! Fuck! Fuck! Fuck! Fuck! Fuck! I had no idea what that meant for the bike. I knew there would be a lot less suspension and it would be a much more bumpy ride, and I would probably be shaken to shit along the way, but I didn't know if I could continue on riding the bike or not. If I just rode slowly would I make it to Altay for instance? How long would it take to get worse? My lack of knowledge on the general functioning of bikes had finally bitten the arse clear off me. I asked myself, "I wonder could I make it to Altay? Maybe I could get the bike up on a truck there and send it to Ulaanbaatar, and I would fly?" Over and over again I asked myself the same questions. I'd left Hovd which didn't appear to have any facilities and I was

about half way between the two towns so I decided to press on. Looking back, I find it amazing that somehow I had come to the conclusion that Altay would be a better option than Hovd. I knew where Hovd was, I knew it had a place to stay, some people who spoke English. It was obviously a much better option than pushing on for Altay. It was a complete unknown and I didn't even have any maps to get there.

I got going again, moving very slow and cursing the incessant rivets which were shaking the marrow from my bones. Hour after hour passed and on and on I went. At this stage the traffic had completely dried up, it was hours since I'd seen anyone and I wondered if I had gone off course again. The rivets got worse and worse, the bike shook more and more and slowly started to fall apart. The thing causing all the problems was the rivets, if it was smooth sand or just normal gravel I think I'd have been fine but with no rear shock and all the paths heavily riveted, the bike was shaking to pieces. When the spring which sits around the shock started rubbing off the back tyre I said ok that's it, you can't go any further. You have to pull in and wait for a truck.

In the distance I saw a small cluster of yurts and made my way towards them. I parked the bike close to one yurt and changed out of the motorcycle gear into my civilians. The longer it went without any trucks and cars passing the more the realization grew on me that I was completely lost. Given that was the case I thought my

NOT DEAD YET

best bet would be to hitch a ride to the nearest town, see if I could get a truck and then come back for the bike and all my stuff. I was despondent from fighting with the bike and elements all day and I was in a terrible place emotionally. I was 40% sure I was going to burn out the bike. At that stage I was in a complete and utter state of depression. I couldn't see a way out of the problems I was having and thought that maybe the only option would be to give up and fly home. This kid showed up called

Fatso and we gobbled on in each other's dialect. I gave him the packed food I had in the bike, no way I would be camping tonight I told myself, it's a town or nothing. Now giving food away when you're in the middle of nowhere might sound like a dumb idea, but this kid needed some grub way more than I did. I'm a big hefty

bollix who could do with a few days of abstinence so as long as I had water, I wasn't panicking. He went into the yurt and I presume gave the grub to his mother. About an hour later, two dudes showed up on a small Russian motorcycle.

Starsky and Hutch

These guys were about 28 years old or so I thought, and proud looking men. They sat huddled looking at the problem with the bike and next thing I knew from deep within their coats they pulled out a multitude of mobile phones and SIM cards and started making phone calls while continuing to study the bike. I explained as best I could what had happened and they kept silent in that squatting position that Asians seem to be able to keep up for hours on end. Meanwhile, two more men showed up and a woman came from a nearby Yurt and thanked me for the pasta and oatmeal. Next thing I knew I was handed a phone and there was a girl who could speak broken English on the other end of it. I explained everything that had happened so far and where I was headed. She told me that I wasn't where I thought I was, I wasn't even close to the road to Altay and I'd veered over a 100km too far south. As the words came into my ears, "100km off course" I had the most vivid flashback of when I was taking a dump on the Mongolian plane watching my maps flying off into the distance. "Oh fuck", I said. She

said a sentence which sent a shockwave right through me: "No help will come to you where you are, do you understand? No help will come that way?" Time Froze instantly as the words sent a shockwave through me, "No Help will come that way!" I asked her what I should do.

She told me I had to make my way 28km to the North to a small town, and that the two guys (Starsky and Hutch is what I was calling them) would show me the way, but I had to get myself and the bike there. From there, maybe I could find a truck. The lads took one of my luggage straps and tied up the back shock so it wasn't rubbing off the back tyre and they set off, with me following them to a town I'd never heard of. As I followed them, I got a great lesson about riding in Mongolia, stay to the edges of the tracks, there is less rivets and if the ground is flat, just get off the road altogether and go cross country. With the shock tied up I felt that I could nurse the bike a long way and started to grow ideas of maybe getting it to Altay and shipping it to Ulaanbaatar from there. We got to the town but there were no trucks, we were too far off the beaten path. Feeling good about the band aid we had in place on the bike, I got Starsky and Hutch to show me to the road to Altay. It was now 5pm, so I said I'd nurse it along till 9pm, then camp and go again all day the next day. From what I had gathered I was 50 km from another small town and could get more water and something to eat if needed there. I was overcome with gratitude that these lads had come so far out of their way to help me out. They were powerful looking men with great temperaments. I thought to myself, "With an army of these guys, Genghis Khan could have conquered the world." I rode out from the town and continued along the track which was the way to Altay, and continued to be pulverized by the rivets. No matter what part of the road I drove on, I was getting the shit shaken out of me. The bike was shaking uncontrollably and every 10 km or so I had to get off and reseat the panniers and give the bike a quick look over. Then disaster struck. The clutch lever cable went loose and I couldn't change gear. I looked under the bike and what had happened was, the rear shock, as a result of being tied up, had pushed forward and damaged the clutch cable, all my clutch fluid had drained away into the desert. Well, that was it, I told myself, you are well and truly done. All the while this was going on the wind was blowing ferociously and a sand storm was gathering. I was out in the middle of the desert getting pulverized by the elements. I was 25 km from the town I had just left, and 25 km to the town which Starsky and Hutch had mentioned. The path through the desert was all sand, even walking in it was difficult. Without any passing traffic I had no idea what I was going to do. An hour passed and no one had come. Another hour passed and I had lost all hope, I was crushed.

I pitched the tent close to the road nearly having a nervous breakdown as the wind did it best to blow it and the cover sheet off into the desert. I climbed in out of the wind and looked forlornly at the single liter of water I had left. I grabbed my rosary beads and started to pray that someone would show up.

CHAPTER 30
KNIGHT RIDER

NOT DEAD YET

For the purposes of this book I've tried to think back to before I was a teenager so I could match it up with the images I had floating around in my head during the trip, and as I've mentioned previously I find it very difficult. Any memories I do have, I'm the same age in most of them. So for example, if I have a memory from when I was eight years old, and say compare it to one where I know I was twelve years old, in my mind's eye, I haven't changed. Why that should be the case I don't know. Is it even normal to have a memory where you can see yourself in it? Shouldn't the memories be you looking out of your eyes or is normal for you to be actually in a memory? And then if you are actually in the memory as opposed to looking at it, then it can't be a memory right? It has to be imagined? I haven't a clue!

When I was 12, we didn't have a pot to piss in at the time. (Poor) Lots of the houses in my area had started to get the Irish version of cable, which meant that instead of having just the two domestic TV channels, you now had six: RTE1 and 2, BBC1 & 2, UTV and finally Channel 4. We were down in a friend of my older brothers house and Knight Rider was about to start. I can't begin to tell you how big a deal this TV program was to a kid growing up back then. My brothers friends mother came in and because it was close to dinner time, ran us out of the house telling us that the TV program was also on RTE1. The three of us raced up the road and burst through the door turning on RTE1 to find no sign of the program. My mother, seeing how disappointed we were, sat at the TV in a futile attempt to try and tune in the station. It was never going to work, we didn't have cable connected but she still sat there twiddling the station knobs clockwise and anti- clockwise to try and tune in a station that wasn't connected, she continued long after the program would have been finished. We all sat there miserable. It was a dark shitty old dirty rainy Wednesday night in Dublin. For some reason, that particular memory, always comes back to me. My two brothers and I are standing around the TV wearing matching blue rain coats with the hoods still up, willing my mother to find the signal, even though there was no hope. The image will stay with me forever, and it's a constant reminder to me that despite everything, she did her best for us.

It's hard to explain how this links to the next bit but I'll do my best. I often get a vision or a dream of myself sitting on the Mongolian plain. I'm on my knee's desperately trying to fix something or other with the bike but obviously struggling. Strangely, when I see the scene in my head I'm about two hundred yards away from it. Even more strangely there is a guy standing over me

obviously giving out to me while pointing his finger at me. Though I'm a long ways off, I can tell he's telling me I'm useless at fixing stuff. I draw closer to the scene to the point where I can hear their conversation. As I circle around to the right, I come face to face with the guy who is shouting at me. I'm not surprised to find that the person I'm confronted with is me. I roar, "Fuck off and leave him alone!" Then there is only one person there. It's just me on my knees in Mongolia trying to fix a broken

shock absorber with no clue what I'm doing. My hands are trembling as I fumble with the bits trying to cobble some form of a solution together in the deafening wind. The very next thought that always enters my head is my mother trying to tune in the station with no hope of success.

CHAPTER 31
MONGOLIA PART 2

I waited and waited, desperately hoping someone would come. Close to dusk, on what seemed like the wings of an angel, a small truck showed up. I stopped it by standing out in the middle of the track, even if they hadn't planned on stopping, there was no way they were going to get up that road unless it was over my dead body. I needn't have worried as they all jumped out and shook my hand. I told them where I was trying to get to and showed them the problem with the clutch. All three guys went hell for leather trying to fix the clutch problem. I was quickly learning that everyone in Mongolia was able to throw their hand at fixing anything mechanical. They have to be able to. They don't have the money to replace parts, so everything on cars and trucks was run to absolute and total failure. The landscape is so harsh that they constantly have to fix broken suspensions, wheel arches, shredded tires and every other manner of problem.

I asked them could they take me and the bike to the town of Altay, or even better Ulaanbaatar. They told me to come with them, they seemed to be saying that we should sleep first and make decisions tomorrow. The four of us loaded up the bike into the back of the small truck without a ramp. The BMW 1200 with gas in it is about 300 KG weight, a heavy bastard! After a torrid time, we got it in doing some cosmetic damage to the bike in the process, I didn't give a fuck. As far as I was concerned the trip was over and now it was only a matter of getting to Ulaanbaatar, from where I would fly home.

The four of us bundled into the trucks cabin and I had one of the men sitting on my lap as we drove to a town over the heavily riveted trail. The town wasn't the one I was in previously, it was even more southerly, if I read the direction right. We got there around 11pm (wher-

NOT DEAD YET

ever there was) and went into a yurt which adjoined a tiny mud walled cottage. The house was full of kids, I wondered would they let me pitch the tent in the yard, I didn't want to be putting anyone out. As it turned out we had only stopped there to get some grub and do some welding on the underside of the truck.

The people in the house treated me like I was a king, and I was touched by how much kindness they were showing a complete stranger. In the midst of the scene were two picture posters on the wall. The first had a topless woman getting kissed by a Romeo type figure, with the banner "Love is love" written overhead. It was bizarre in the extreme to be in a room with ten kids and five adults in Mongolia, not understanding a word, in a darkly lit room with a pair of jugs hanging out on the wall. Once the welding was done, we went on a night ride to another strange town in the absolute and utter boonies

where a yurt was situated beside a small house. Everyone got out and went in and had tea. A cot in the yurt was allocated to me, to which I said, "Could I just camp instead" (I've a thing about sleeping in a big room full of people who I don't know, or can't communicate with.) I started to try and pitch the tent, by this stage it was well after 2am and I was making a balls of putting it together in the pitch dark. As I fuddled on, I knew one thing, I didn't deserve the kindness these people had shown me. Imagine it, picking someone off the road, loading up his stuff and bringing him back to your house where you put someone out of their bed to give to him. You give him

food that you can ill afford and welcome him like he's a long lost uncle. I felt ashamed of myself when I thought about what I would do if I saw a Mongolian broke down by the side of the road in Ireland. (Nothing)

NOT DEAD YET

I have subsequently heard people say that the Mongolians help each other because they live in such a harsh environment and that they know at some stage down the line it could be them. There is an inference in that statement, which suggests that no matter where you went in the world, as long as the living was tough, and it was isolated, someone would help you if they passed. It also gives comfort to westerners that, were they in the same situation; they would do as the Mongolians did. Personally I don't believe it for a second. The Mongolians are a different breed of people. The people I met do not care who you are, where you are from, what you do for a living, what car you drive, who your parents were, how old you are, how rich or poor you are, they simply know that you need help and they give it to you without any thought of reward or reciprocation. When someone, who has nothing, gives you half their meal to share as they beam a smile at you that would melt the coldest heart, it feels like you have reconnected with what it means to be human. I felt like I finally understood that the secret of life was to be a good person and to do your best to help others. I have never had the mirror held up to me in such a fashion.

One of the guys gave me a hand pitching my tent and before I got in to go asleep. I shook his hand clasping both my left and right hand around his hand and while making eye contact, I thanked him from the bottom of my heart, for all that he and his friends had done for me. I fell into an exhausted fitful sleep and woke the next morning to the sound of what seemed like the whole village clearing their throat. With all the sand and dust that's in the air, in this part of the world there's a whole pile of that, "hold your finger to one nostril, and blow the snot out the other" (I think they call it a snot rocket in the states) thing going on, Mongolia is not for the faint hearted.

There is no running water in most of the towns and there seemed to be an etiquette, that if one is doing a number one, that should just go straight on the ground to keep the dust down, and if it's a number two, well that should go into the crapper, a wooden frame built around a hole in the ground. The girl in the yurt boiled me some water for my noodles as the rest of the family ate their breakfast. The sound of slurping had been on the rise since I'd got to boonie Russia, and in Mongolia it was like a concerto. I was pissing myself laughing at the noise of the slurps, even if I tried, I wouldn't have been able to get up to the pitch that these guys were at.

I walked around the village to find a shop. It's hard to spend money in Mongolia. It's not that things are particularly cheap it's just that there's nothing particularly appetizing for sale in any of the shops. Most don't have refrigeration so it's chiefly dry goods for sale. You can buy water, two liter bottles of Coke, lollipops, sweets, packets of biscuits freshly chiseled out of bomb shelters, cooking oil, salt, sugar, beef fat and other stuff which is edible but that you wouldn't really eat. It's all bought based on having a long shelf life. I still hadn't managed to walk out of a shop yet with anything to eat that wasn't sweets or water. I'd gotten into the habit of buying lots of lollipops every time I went to a shot and then distributing them to the curious kids who constantly came up to me, to say hello. The way the children take stuff off you is very gracious. They cup one hand under the other and wait for you to place it there, as opposed to take it from you. It's a small thing, but feels infinitely polite. The kids are so poor, with dirty faces and hands, you can't help but feel that kids shouldn't have to live like this.

As I was picking up a couple of packets of biscuits to give to the family who let me stay by their yurt, I heard a voice behind me saying, "Where are you from?" It was Tushig. He worked as a construction lead building one of the roads taking coal from Mongolia to China. He used to live in Manchester and we got chatting about how the hell we both ended up there. I explained to him where I thought I was, he started laughing, by the depth of the laugh I knew I wasn't even close. He invited me to stay in his place, he had a cook, and there was room,

I could speak English to him and he would sort out the bike stuff for me. I nearly fainted with a mixture of relief and gratitude. The plan was that the guys who lived in

the town would move the bike to another truck and then that truck would come and collect me the following day at his yurt and take me to Ulaanbaatar. I was as most westerners are, initially suspicious, why are you helping me?

Tushig

I followed my heart, Tushig seemed like a good guy, and to be honest next to camping in the village, it sounded like a great deal. His driver drove the two of us over to where he stayed. We followed a small path out into the middle of nowhere and we stopped along the way to talk to some folks who were working for Tushig on the road, a really friendly bunch of fellows. Then we continued on to his place.
It turned out to be three yurts in the middle of nowhere, nestled under the shelter of some large mountains. Once again I was stunned with his generosity but initially I was disappointed, at least in the village I could buy some water, I couldn't do anything there. At that moment it was just Tushig, the camp cook whose name was Namchie and I. I asked him how many people normally sleep in each yurt, he replied seven. "Ah for fucks sake" I thought to myself.
We also talked about the truck going to Ulaanbaatar, how long would it take, when it would collect me and so on. The bike had picked up some more collateral damage driving it around in the small truck and with a 1000km run to Ulaanbaatar coming up on these roads, the bike would be a bag of bolts by the time we got there. He told

me not to worry, they would pack it softly. I wasn't overly concerned, I reckoned the bike was damaged beyond my ability to get it repaired in Mongolia and with that, the trip was probably over so a couple more dents and breakages wouldn't make any difference.

In all likelihood I'd be at the camp for two days, I looked around and asked myself, "What the hell am I going to do out here for two days? A dark mood had descended on me again. These people were doing their best to help me but I felt like I was a million miles from where I wanted to be. I just wanted to get to Ulaanbaatar as fast as possible so I could go home.

Some people might say that I should have tried to make the best of the situation, maybe even use the time to connect with myself, and use the isolation to meditate, it was a unique place to be in the world, I should be happy. I had that debate in my head at the time and came back with "Fuck those fuckers, and fuck the horse they came in on! That sort of dribble is easy to dole out from a comfortable arm chair in the West before they pop down to the gym to do a yoga class." Think of how things are in the West. Take a coffee. How many ways do people drink their coffee: latte, espresso, americano, black, soy, iced, cappuccino, sugar, milk, foam, with our without a biscuit, the list is endless. In Mongolia's outback you'll be thankful just to get water to boil, so you can toss a ruffled up tea bag into it. That is it. It's either drink it, or go hang your bollix off a rock. Obviously in some of the cities in Mongolia you can get whatever you want, but once you get out into the cuds, forget it. At that moment my bike was wrecked, I had no clue where I was, I was dehydrated and absolutely starving. I missed home and was at my wits end. Tushig told me that I needed to sleep, that I needed to rest, that I was stressed out. Once I'd slept, things would be much better. They made room for me on one of the cots in the main yurt and I fell sound asleep to the sound of wood burning in the stove.

The turning point

I woke up a different man. I was seeing the world from a whole new point of view. It was like I had gone through the wall and come out the other side. I wasn't "trapped, stuck, broken down, stressed and tired" all of a sudden I was delighted to be getting the opportunity to stay in a yurt for a while. I also started to think that if I hadn't broken down, I wouldn't have the opportunity to experience how Mongolians live. Hell, the whole world was one big opportunity.

For the first couple of hours it was just Tushig, Namchie and I in the main yurt, while everyone went back out to the roads to work. Tushig was the boss, it was his job to make sure stuff got done and he occupied the Top dog spot in the yurt, which is always directly facing the door. He was married with one child, both of whom were in Taiwan, where his wife was studying a Masters. The whole crew are out there six months at a time, working seven days a week without any holidays. In winter the weather is too harsh to do any work, even in late spring early summer, the gales that pick up are ferocious. At that point, they would all return home to Ulaanbaatar. Namchie was the work camp cook, it was her responsibility to feed everyone, a group of about 15 people, three times a day. She cooked, cleaned and worked her ass off, putting in 16 hour days with just an hour for a nap in the afternoon. She was the only girl in the setup. I asked Tushig was it not hard for her being the only girl, he replied Mongolian women have to work very hard. As the hours passed I was amazed at just how hard she grafted. All the guys treated her with great respect, there was no horseplay or acting the maggot, she was like a sister to them all. She had a very young daughter in Ulaanbaatar, who was being looked after by her brother and his wife for the six months she was away working. For working seven days a week, sixteen hours a day she drew down about $400 a month. This was considered a very good job in Mongolia. I think the only thing that made her job doable was the fact that because it was a company yurt, there was wood supplied. Most yurts use Yak crap as a fuel as there are almost no trees in Mongolia, and almost no arable land for that matter. Having wood to burn, meant avoiding having to trek many miles with bags collecting Yak crap.

Another point of interest is that the majority of the water

in that part of Mongolia comes from snow which has blown down from Siberia in the winter, which goes on to melt and fill its lakes.

All the meals are prepared from scratch ingredients; flour, water, potatoes, rice, lard, etc. The meat on account of there being no refrigeration is all dried. They smoke it by burning Yak crap and it's hung up in one of the yurts. All the bread is made with flour and water and is either fried in lard, or steamed. After that its potatoes, rice, and whatever greens they can get from the local town (very little). Everyone drunk water which came from a small metal tank outside, this was all the water available to the whole camp for washing, cooking, cleaning and drinking, so everyone used it very sparingly.

I talked to Tushig about living in a yurt and seeing he had lived in Manchester, Ulaanbaatar and even a little in Taiwan, I was surprised to hear that he preferred a Ger. I asked him why. He told me that life is simpler. It's safer, calmer, you can hear yourself think. There's nothing to worry about, you only have to do your job, then come home eat and sleep, and then do it all again. The workers all came home around 8pm and ate dinner. I was always served second just behind Tushig and was getting embarrassed with all the special attention I was getting. The grub was simple and all cooked in the same pot over the stove in the middle of the yurt. It contained potato, meat, some bread, garlic, and onion, it was really good. It was very high in fat but that's what the lads need when they are working out on the roads for so long each day, there wasn't a pick on any of them. When the heads go down to eat the grub out of the bowls, they don't come up till it's all gone. There are never any leftovers. Directly after

dinner a bunch of us would head out and kick football, every time I hit a good ball, I was doing the eagle dance which the Mongolian wrestlers do. The lads all got a great kick out of it and joined in.

From my Diary:

They fire up the generator around 9pm and turn on the TV, there is one channel and it normally has a film showing and everyone huddles around to watch. At about 10pm, everyone puts on their coat, walk outside and jump up onto the back of a truck. They are all heading to a place where they can get a mobile phone reception, several miles away. It had been six days since the mobile phone transmitter had failed on the mountain, and no one had been in contact with home. Namchie was especially stressed out, her little girl had fallen and hit her head in Ulaanbaatar and she didn't have any news as to how she was. They all came back two hours later and everyone got ready for bed. One of the guys gave up his bed for me and slept on the floor in the next yurt. I tell them I'll camp in the tent, but they won't hear of it. As I'm lying in my sleeping bag, the same guy comes back with his jacket rolled up and gives it to me as a pillow. For the second day in a row, people I never met before, brought me to where they lived, gave me a bed to sleep in and shared their food with me.

Tushig had organized for me to be collected by the truck and was continuously on the phone to make sure all was on track. He even contacted his brother in Ulaanbaatar to meet me when I got there to make sure everything worked out ok. I offered them money but they shooed my hand away. The Mongolians continue to teach this westerner what it meant to be a good person.

Day 2 in the Yurt

The next morning most of the guys headed back out onto the road and I started my vigil of peering down the valley waiting for the truck to come. In terms of duration to Ulaanbaatar, a 4x4 normally took 24 hours solid driving to get there. In my head I said, "Ok, maybe 36 hours for a truck." The initial messages I'd gotten were that it would pick me up before 2pm. When the lads came back for lunch we ate and then went out kicking football for a bit. We took a heap of pictures together, after which we all said goodbye and wished each other luck. I went in for a nap as the wind was picking up and in the early evening went out to stretch my legs. When I looked to my right the yurt which the road workers slept in, had been completely totaled by the wind. Namchie and I went through the debris for the lads stuff and moved it into the second Ger. I couldn't help thinking what an

awful thing to come back to, tired after a day's graft in the biting wind, only to find your accommodation is flattened.
When they got back, to my complete surprise they spent about 20 seconds at the, "Ah for fucks sake" and then just got on with segregating it and finding out which parts they'd need to get from the local village to fix it the next day.
At this stage I was supposed to be long gone, but there was still no sign of the transport. It was well after nine before the lights of a truck appeared in the distance. It turned out to be the original truck which had picked me up in the desert two days earlier. I said to them, "I thought we were going in a bigger yoke?" They said that they were going to take me to the truck which was parked up in the desert, about five miles off.

Within a couple of minutes, Tushig was driving me behind the truck to the rendezvous point, where I'd finally restart my journey to Ulaanbaatar. We saw the lights of the truck in the distance and converged on it moving slowly across the desert in the pitch black of night. When we got there I saw it was a rigid lorry, for the purposes of the story I'll call it, Hilda. It was driven by a tough looking customer who I'll call Jengis and the spare driver, who I'll call Bantu.

I couldn't believe what was happening, there we were, two trucks and a 4X4 all with the lights on, out in the middle of nowhere in a howling wind under a sky full of stars, all chatting away like we'd just come out of church on a Sunday. It felt like I was in a drug smuggling movie. I said a final farewell to Tushig and thanked him profusely for all the help he gave me. The truck was of Chinese origin and was made in 1971. There were two seats in it, neither of which leaned back and Bantu and I had to share the leg space available in front of the right seat of the truck. The truck smelt pretty bad, or maybe it was the two lads, or maybe it was me. Looking at them while giving myself a quick sniff under the armpits, all three of us seemed to be far distant strangers to a bar of soap.

It was only when we got moving I realized that we'd no chance of making Ulaanbaatar in 36hours, this thing was as slow as a one legged donkey. I asked Jengis, "So how long will it take for us to get to Ulaanbaatar"; He just shrugged his shoulders. I pushed him a bit more, "36 hours, 40 hours" to which he just laughed. He then said in broken English "If we're very lucky, three days." I replied with a, "You must be fucking joking me!"

Within one hour of leaving the camp, Hilda had already

broken down three times. I was trying to stay positive saying things like, "Ah that's all the problems happening at once, we'll get a good run soon." The truck was a bag of bolts. The window on my side didn't work, there was no heating or air conditioning, no radio, and to top it all off, the door would only open with sorcery. You had to open and close the lock, pull the door to you, then open the latch, and at that exact instant, throw your shoulder at it like it was a stranger humping your missus, and then it might open!

I could hear angels talking, "Hughes is going to fucking blow any second! He's cracking, any second now that fucker will blow!"
Bantu didn't really like me, my size 15 feet were now in the small area where he kept his legs. There was a small

area behind the seats where you could fit a small leprechaun or a large mosquito and he spent most of his time sprawled between there and my seat.

How Jengis was able to navigate was beyond me. Every now and then he would stop, turn off the lights in the truck, look at the stars and the mountains and then continue on. There was no GPS, no maps, and no signposts, it was a marvel. He drove all night with the exception of when he took a one hour nap. To navigate in this country using memory during the day is one thing but to do it at night, this fella was my hero.

The seat I was on was made for a little Chinese fella with a boney arse. Stuffing a 6ft4in 250Lb Irish man into that space made me feel like I was a plucked and tied up turkey going into an oven.

Jengis at one stage pulled over for a snooze, and within two breaths of closing his eyes he was snoring like a

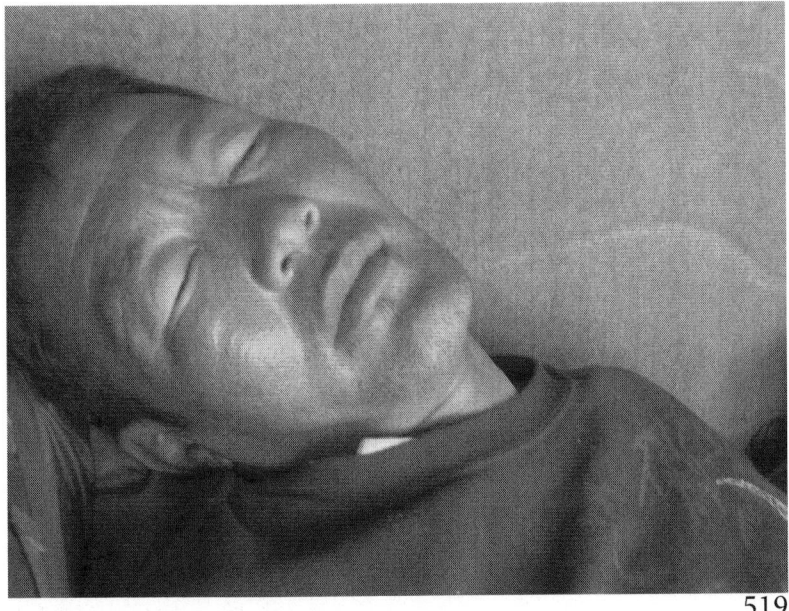

hippo. Close to dawn, he again stopped for 40 winks, just before we came onto a flat plane where there was lots of surface water. There were many streams flowing any which way took their fancy, I had to keep reminding myself, "This is the main road to Ulaanbaatar!" Once we got through that the lads pulled over and made themselves some tea and soup using water that you wouldn't let cattle drink. I declined, I didn't fancy a bout of colon-blow while in the truck, these lads obviously had iron tanks for stomachs.

Later, we stopped at the Mongolian equivalent of a road side café which is where you go into someone's yurt, they cook you grub along with their family and you give them a few quid for their troubles. It's all very wholesome and they all have a great chat, it seems like the truck drivers are the chief carriers of news and scandal and their company is much appreciated. The kids all come in from where ever it is kids go in these places and stand by the wall listening attentively to what the truckers are saying to the main man in the yurt.

We left and continued on our way. My guess was that in 8 hours we'd done less than a hundred miles. The truck was forever breaking down. The list of problems included overheating, break failures, complete gauge malfunctions and regular stops to keep Hilda topped up with oil. Every hour of the three days was punctuated with either a stop to fix the truck, a sleep, a crap, a piss, food, gassing up, or just for a chat with a passing truck. I was losing my fucking mind.

At one stage Bantu fell asleep and used my sleeping bag as a pillow. After an hour or so he lifted his head to reveal the entire right side of his face was full of slabbers and so now was my sleeping bag. He wiped his face in the non-wet portion of the bag. He looked at me with a questioning stare, "What the fuck are you looking at?" I gave him my, "In Hong Kong, you would already be

dead!", look.

As we continued on our way a couple of things were quickly becoming apparent. Firstly, Bantu was quickly setting a world record for sleeping. My original thoughts were that he was the relief driver, but nope he was there to sleep, eat, piss, fart and shite, and that was it. You might wonder, well what was I doing, the exact same as Bantu, bar the sleeping; but at least I'd the dubious distinction of paying 600 bucks for the privilege. The other thing I was quickly beginning to appreciate was that Jengis was the toughest bloke I'd ever come across. In our first 24 hours on the road he'd taken two 1hr power

NOT DEAD YET

naps and was repairing the truck every hour no matter what the conditions. At one stage he burnt his hand severely on the engine, giving himself a mobile phone sized burn with a blister sitting about a quarter inch off his hand, it looked like it hurt like hell. The only thing he

did was take off a sock, cut a hole in the top of it for his thumb and pull it down over his hand. Then, he continued on driving. Can you imagine how much pain he must have been in, driving a truck over those roads with the constant repairs? He was a machine. I wanted to ask him at one stage, "So Jengis, do you moisturize?"

We finally made our way through to the town of Altay, which had reached iconic status in my mind, I'd been trying to get there for days. When we got there and I saw that it was one of the poorest, most decrepit towns in the northern hemisphere it felt weird, for days I'd been saying, "If only I could get to Altay everything would be fine!" We pushed on slowly, at one stage passing some folks who'd a puncture in their van. We pulled over to help them, but not only us, so also did the next three trucks that passed. No one can afford to buy anything new there, so everything is run till it disintegrates. Every tube that comes out is patched many times and they use bits of other torn up tubes to shroud the tube at its weak points. The tires are used till they completely shred, simple as that. When the repair was done on the van, there was a conversation around, "Hey, you don't have

a bolt for my front light do you?" The guy spilled out a load of brackets and bolts and without further ado, they all stood there doing a repair to our truck. More people showed up and there was seven or eight people all standing out in the middle of nowhere having a chat and a laugh, no one seemed to be in any rush, they'd no place special to go and all day to get there.

We found our way to a river after dark which Jengis drove the truck through, as you do, and pulled up outside a yurt. Jengis said we need some sleep. It was midnight, so we said we'd start again at first light. So what did we do? We all headed into a yurt which was full of people and went to sleep. I never saw anything like it. Imagine that, some strangers come up, knock on the door, they go to sleep with you and your family in your yurt, and then you make them breakfast in the morning and for the honor they pay you about four dollars. There were at least nine people sleeping in there that night, in a space about the size of my bedroom back home. That's what people have to do to survive, but I've no idea how Jengis knew that this was a yurt which was ok to knock on, there was no sign or anything like that. I made a little faux pas which happened when they told me which cot to get into, note there was already someone in there, in this case a teenage kid who could speak broken English and was full of questions. I said maybe we'd sleep head to toe if you know what I mean? No sooner had I changed direction than the whole yurt was up in a sudden start. Never point your head towards the door in a yurt, it has to be pointing in the direction of the main man's cot. Don't ask why. Just do it.

The second full day on the truck

The next day, soon after starting, we stopped in a small village looking for some welding kit which was surprisingly easy to find. Jengis worked for about five hours welding the truck chassis. In the fenced off area there were four yurts surrounded by scrap metal, two wooden outhouses and two huge piles of Yak poo. There were kids running around playing and having a great time, but looking at them and what little they had, I could feel my heart breaking. One of the ladies brought me into the yurt for some grub, they don't get too many beardy Irish lads around these parts so I was a bit of a novelty. It was a bowl of soup with pasta type things in it and some meat fat and bones, Yum! Not long after we were back on the road, we passed an overturned truck. I knew the drill at this stage, stop, check is everyone ok, do they need help, and only at the point where your certain all is well do you move on again. The key thing to keep in mind is that they don't just stop some times, or when not in a rush, they stop every single time no matter what.

Later in the day we dropped off sleeping beauty (Bantu) at one of the towns, now it was just me and Jengis, I was delighted with the extra room. It had only been fifty hours, Jengis reckoned we'd one more day to go, or said another way, 24 more hours of driving to go. Anyway, with my new found room in the front of the truck I was sitting with my legs spread wider than Galway Bay. Even though I still couldn't open the window, had no A/C, no heating, nor Radio; compared to having to share the space with Bantu, I was in heaven. I was aghast when Jengis picked up a hitch hiker only twenty miles down the track. I thought to myself, "If this fucker is going the whole way to Ulaanbaatar, I'll fucking kill myself!" Luckily he was only hitching to the next town.

On our last full night out in the boonies, Jengis said he needed to get some sleep, two hours. That would run us up to a lofty total of 12 hours kip for the whole journey. At 2am we pulled up to a yurt in the middle of nowhere. He banged down the door till this woman answered, and then told me to go inside where I was faced with the humblest abode I'd yet been in. The woman, dressed only in a robe and severely pissed off after being woken, pointed to a cot where a cat was sleeping. Now a cat in the western world is known for its cleanliness, I don't like em that much, but have to admit they are pretty clean. Its Mongolian equivalent looks more like a fluffy rat. The woman hit the cat a belt waking it out of its sleep and forcing it to retreat to under a bench. She then turned off the light. I couldn't see a thing. I wasn't even in my sleeping bag, so being careful not to point the feet towards the main mans bed, lest I have my throat slit during the night, I stripped and got into the bag.

Next thing I knew I was looking at a pair of green cat eyes, it was the cat meowing like someone was trying to pull off its tail. It was 3am, Jengis was leaving at 4:30am and I was thinking to myself, "Is this oul one going to get up and kick that cat in the nuts or what?" She eventually came over in the pitch dark and belted it. It squealed like fuck and next thing all the kids in the yurt were roaring crying. I parked in my ear plugs and went off to sleep. The yurt was freezing, the people living there were the poorest of the poor so when it came to leaving at 4:30am, I woke the woman up by tipping her on the shoulder, desperately hoping she didn't think I was looking for a shag and gave her about $30 dollars. She looked at the money and thought she was still dreaming and went back to sleep. I went out to Jengis who was busy peeling off the sock he'd wrapped around his severely burnt and blistered hand. At this stage I wasn't surprised when he kicked off a boot, took out a knife, cut a hole in the other sock and put it on his hand. I was looking at this him thinking, "This guy must piss napalm."

A little under 400 km from Ulaanbaatar we hit the Tarmac, I felt like jumping out of the truck and doing a jig but things got worse before they got better. In the course of the next five hours we had no fewer than three punctures. I couldn't believe it, after all those crappy tracks and trails it was the tarmac that was tearing the tires to shit. I did my best to help but, I mostly got in the way. A Mongolian chap stopped to give us a dig out and when we were done came over with water and started washing our hands. He then came into the truck with a bag of cooked sheep bits and we sat there chatting away, eating sheep. Every now and the Jengis would tear off a

NOT DEAD YET

bit which looked like the sheep's nether regions and say, "Mmmmm, very good!"

As we drew closer to Ulaanbaatar I knew the biggest problems were still ahead of me. How would I get the bike off the truck? If I was shaken about so much in the front, the bike must be totaled in the back. Where will I stay? How the hell am I going to get parts for the bike? Where will I leave the bike? Tushig had arranged for his brother to meet me to help me out, would he show?

We drove into the city, the outskirts of which were poor and run down beyond description, and Jengis was on the phone non-stop. We pulled up in a yard belonging to a cashmere sweater producer where our load was getting delivered. It was the first time I realized what we were hauling, cashmere and wool.

I was met there by Saraul, Tushig's brother. Tushig had arranged that he pick me up and bring me to a hotel

with all my stuff and then in the morning bring me back

down to the yard. Tushig if you ever get a chance to read this, you rule all, and I hope one day I can repay your kindness.

I had no changes of clothes and I looked like I had just come up out of a septic tank. I smelt like hell, I was desperate to get a change of gear from my bag, but the guys refused to break the seal on the truck.

Saraul brought me to a hotel which had a shop next door where I bought a 1 liter bottle of shampoo and shower gel and also a box of detergent for my clothes. I checked into the hotel with everyone looking at me like I was a walrus at reception.

I got into the shower and washed the last week off myself. The shampoo wouldn't even lather in my hair until I'd washed it four times. Thankfully I had my laptop with me and the hotel had internet. Three hand shandies later, I was fast asleep.

CHAPTER 32
SCREAMING

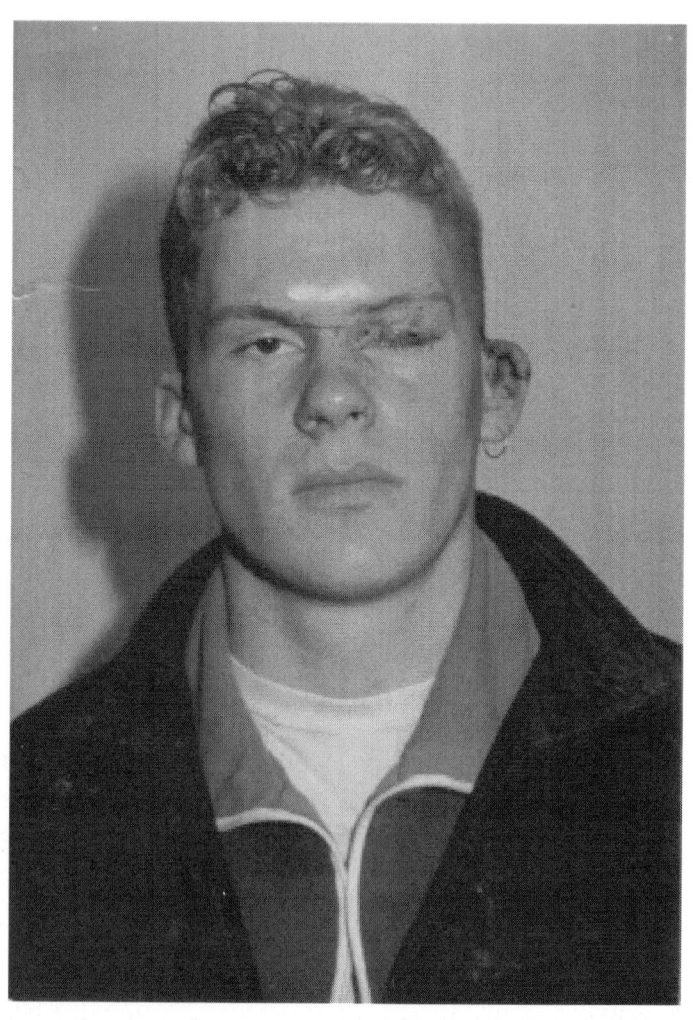

Being a Catholic in Ireland means you're wrong from the get go. Almost the first thing you hear about is original sin, how the very fact you were born means you're guilty of sin, original sin. What a thing to have to carry around with you. You're also taught that you're such a sinner, that the only thing that will save you is Jesus. No matter what you do your screwed, unless of course you embrace Jesus and if he takes a mind to, he'll keep a place for you in heaven. In fairness that's a pretty liberal interpretation of original sin but being a Catholic in Ireland means being guilty, the whole country walks around with enough "Catholic Guilt" to flood the Sahara.

A good kid in school in Ireland was one who sits down in the corner and says nothing. Sit down, shut the fuck up, I don't want to hear a peep out of you. That's growing up in Ireland. Keeping quiet is the Irish way. (Except when there is booze on board) It was cemented through hundreds of years of occupation by the English where you were told "Say nothing to nobody, keep the head down and the arse up!" For decades it was also been the way in business, where the employees of a company said nothing to the managers for fear of being called a rat. Ireland was an economic phenonomen, it never had a boom period from the time the state was founded in 1922 right up until the 1960's. For me, the most comprehensive explanation was the culture, the guilt that everyone walked around with created a massive inferiority complex. Everyone minded their own business, a person who kept themselves to themselves, was deemed a very noble attribute in a neighbor.

There is also a sense of equilibrium, everyone who was born the same is the same. Don't you get too big for them boots! You're just like the rest of us, you're no better. One of the favorite lines my mother used to use on me was "Your good for nothing, except eating, pissing, farting, sleeping and shiteing!" She told us that she would never forgive us for being such evil spiteful children, and she would pray that we wouldn't all end up in hell, for that was what we surely deserved. My granny would threaten us with, "The man on the television can hear you!" We were told we'd be taken away. My upbringing was no different than thousands of other Irish children growing up in Ireland.

In Intel, we used to tell a story about the difference between Ireland and the USA. The analogy used was lobsters in a tank in a fine restaurant. You know the restaurants where you get to point at a live lobster and say that's the one I want. In the USA, if one of those lobsters was almost out, we used to say that the others would push him out and over and cheer his escape. If it was in Ireland, they'd pull him back in and say, "You're going nowhere pal!"

When I was about ten years old my buddy Jason and I used to hang out with this middle aged guy who used to be in the army. His name was Frankie, of course that's not his real name, just the one I'm using for the purposes of the story. At the time I think he was in his late forties. Last I heard he was still alive, which is a pity. For a ten year old this guy was as cool as they came. He had ferocious dogs and carried lots of bullets and war trinkets with him. He even had a necklace with a shark tooth on it, like I said, he was cool. We would meet him in the swimming pool where he worked, he paid us a lot of attention and we liked him. Frankie always told me he liked the white basketball boots I used to wear, especially if they were all polished up and gleaming.

We would go up to Frankie's house and help him count copper coins which he'd amassed over the years in massive jars. He'd give us a few quid which we would blow on cans of coke and sweets. When we were up in his house we'd watch war movies, The Big Red One, and the Green Berets with John Wayne are two that I can remember. Every now and then, Frankie would throw on a porno movie. We were only ten or eleven and didn't get it. Most of what we were looking at was pretty gross. Frankie would look over at us and say "Don't tell me you guys are innocent?" We'd reply no, and continue to watch the movie "Of course we weren't innocent." I asked a man who lived on my road "Do you like Frankie?" Most people knew him from riding his customized bike through the housing estates where we lived. He replied saying "I think he's a fucking child molester, and you should stay the fuck away from him!" I thought that the man just didn't know him, not really understanding what molester meant.

Anytime I was in Frankie's house alone, he would come up behind me and grab my genitals and say "Now don't tell anyone I was doing that." I knew there was something wrong about it, but in Ireland back then you couldn't talk to anyone about it. If you told your parents, they would say it was your fault. Like I said earlier, head down say nothing. I stopped calling up to see Frankie, it didn't feel right. Years later I saw him with another troop of young fella's following him around. This time I was old enough to know what a child molester was. I can still see one of the kid's white shiny bright pair of training shoes. Did anyone ever blow the whistle on him? If anyone was subsequently abused, did some guilt lie with me for not saying something to someone earlier? Years later, as all the Catholic Church child abuse revelations started to come out in Ireland, I could see the same pattern. The kids were too afraid to tell for fear that they would be blamed, that it was their fault, they brought it on themselves. I think society looks at abuse victims like they are somehow broken, that is why no one says anything. There is a famous Irish poem which starts with the lines: Good 'ol Ireland is dead and gone; It's with O'Leary in the Grave.

It's a lament for the passing of the better days in Ireland and on the passing of the poet's youth. The writer never met Frankie. I wonder if he had, maybe the first two lines of that poem might have been, "Good 'Ol Ireland is dead and gone; and may it burn in hell."

If you ever find yourself in a remote place, maybe on a mountain top, or on a remote beach somewhere in South America, or maybe even in a desert in Bolivia and you hear a cleansing scream or a roar, maybe there's an Irish Catholic nearby roaring and screaming into the void. He's telling the world that he is still around, that he is going nowhere and "They can all go fuck themselves!"

CHAPTER 33
GETTING BACK ON THE ROAD

NOT DEAD YET

When they opened the container the next morning I finally was able to understand why Jengis wouldn't let me in the back to check the bike on the journey, it was packed tightly to the roof with bags of cashmere. Never before was a BMW transported in such a comfortable ride. The guys threw down 30 or 40 bags of cashmere and rolled the bike out onto them and down out into the yard. I had a quick look around it. It looked rough, but no worse than when it was packed up and to my complete surprise it started first time. I limped my way to the hotel car park and set about trying to figure out where I was going to take it to get it fixed. I also had to figure out how I was going to get a new shock. I talked with Vait, a German guy who worked in a tour company called Steppenfuchs about what was the best way to get a rear shock to Ulaanbaatar. He told me that if I used DHL, it would take ten days, the quickest way was to get someone who

was flying from Berlin to Ulaanbaatar to bring the part through for me.

The flights left from Berlin on a Sunday. Today was Friday, if I was going to get a part there by Sunday it would be the longest of long shots. I needed someone in Berlin, my mate lived there, but was out of town. I only knew one other guy there who I'd never met, Joe Dilworth (Berlin Joe), I phoned him and told him my problem. Joe was a sound skin and was well up for helping me out. What I needed was a part, and someone to go to the airport in Berlin and convince some random Mongolian chap to take it with him. We thought we'd have no problem getting the part since there are at least five Motorrad dealers in Berlin, and the city is a spares depot.

The part

What I needed was a rear shock for a 2006 BMW GSA. Would you believe that the part was not available anywhere? Normally they can get you a part in 24 hours, but this was an out of stock item due to an apparent worldwide shortage. BMW had used a Japanese company to manufacture them and I guess they had somehow run out. The crunch item here was that Berlin Joe was flying out of Berlin on the Monday, my other buddy in Berlin wouldn't be back till June '12th so this was a one shot deal, and I had to get a shock on Friday/Saturday or wait ten days in Ulaanbaatar. The DHL option also only worked if there was a part available which there wasn't. I talked with Simon Race (Trip quarterback at this stage) and Walter Colebatch about all sorts of alternatives. As it turned out, to get a shock ready takes quite a bit of time, this was a Friday, it was coming into a weekend, and there was little chance of getting it done. Walter gave me Baz's name, a guy who worked for Hyperpro in Holland who said that he would work that night and get me a shock ready by 12 midday on Saturday.

So, now I needed a way to get it to Berlin, DHL country to country on same day deliveries is a no-no on a Saturday. I wracked my brains for someone I knew in Holland who might be able to help, maybe I could put the part in a Taxi, maybe someone knew someone who knew someone, there is always a way! I noticed a fellow motorcyclist Axel Bahr from Germany was online on Facebook, so I gave him a shout and asked did he have any ideas. In one of the biggest coincidences of the century, it turned out Axel also broke down in the same part of Mongolia a while back, on the same bike with the exact same problem! He also resolved the situation in the same way I was doing it. I also had Bar Dunne in Ireland trying to see if he could find a way to organize the shipment from there, none of the numbers I had for DHL Holland were working. After a couple of hours, Axel had arranged for his mate Manuel to pick up the part in Werkendam, Holland, and bring it to Cologne where DHL would same day ship it from there to Berlin and put it in the capable hands of Berlin Joe. These were two guys who I'd never met before, going hundreds of miles out of their way on a Friday evening to bail me out. The same was true of the folks in Hyperpro, all going a mile out of their way for someone they never met.

So now I'd the part, and a way of getting it to Berlin. The thoughts of going up to a random guy in an airport with a mysterious package sounded like something that could get someone jailed, so I phoned the wonderfully fantastic Kate (Kushki Malushki) in Ireland, who had just finished up working in Dublin airport as the marketing development manager for the Far East. She phoned her contacts in Berlin and within a couple of hours, we had cultivated Mongolian Joe, a guy who would take the part from Berlin Joe in Berlin and give it to Ayuntoya, a girl who would carry it through and give it to me in Ulaanbaatar. When Kate came back with the name Mongolian Joe, and the fact that I was working with Berlin Joe already, I just knew that it was going to work. The whole thing kept me up till 5am getting it sorted, some 17 hours after I started. Amazingly, the part arrived at 6:40am on the Monday morning in Ulaanbaatar per the plan. I owe a lot of people a huge debt of thanks for digging me out of that particular hole.

Ulaanbaatar

The lads in Naran BMW did a great job fixing up Sam Gamgee 2 and I was looking forward to getting going again. I wasn't sure if I would go back into the Mongolian countryside or just head north into Russia. Ulaanbaatar is an up and coming city, there are lots of nice hotels with lots of business going on and mining seems to be igniting the country's economy. There's also quite a few foreigners knocking around, mostly tour groups pit stopping on the way to China. Ulaanbaatar is still however, not a particularly good city to hang about in. Walking around at night time, is a serious no no. Most tourists arrive at the airport and the road takes you down Chingis Khan's Avenue into the area with vari-

NOT DEAD YET

ous tourist hotels near the centre, and the main square is nice. Having come in myself on the truck, I saw all the outlying areas and they were in dreadful condition. There were columns of black smoke, open sewers, rubbish tips, it's improving but has got a long way to go. An example is that during winter, where there is little wind around Ulaanbaatar, they say that the air quality is so bad, just living there is the equivalent of smoking 100 cigarettes per day.

Sooner than get into a big story about the city and the things I saw, let me just say this, if you find yourself out that direction, UB is a city to stay a night or two in, if you need to rest up, or get stuff done. At the risk of repeating myself, Mongolia's beauty isn't in its town and cities, it's in its wide open planes and mountains and in the people living in that harsh landscape.

I left Ulaanbaatar that morning and headed north for

the border with Russia. The weather was fine all day and there wasn't a bit of gravel or sand to be seen, just a lovely long straight line of tarmac. The last time I rode the bike, I had been shaken to bits for three straight days. I had to get off the bike a few times to make sure everything was ok, it just didn't feel right to be on a smooth ride again.

North of Ulaanbaatar, Mongolia is green, and it's one of the only locations in the country where they can actually grow crops. The countryside is a mixture of rolling hills and green planes as far as the eye can see. I was thinking about camping or going out and about a bit more in Mongolia but I decided that my Mongolian adventure was over, I'd seen enough and had enough memories to last a lifetime. I said I'd cross the border with Russia and shoot up for Ulan Ude, a city to the east of Lake Baikal, a

journey of about 550 km. Even allowing for a tricky time at the border, I estimated I would be there by 8pm.
I got to the border with Russia at the town of Suhbaatar, and like most remote borders, it was very confusing. There was what appeared to be a checkpoint on the Mongolian side, but it was unmanned. I wasn't sure that I was supposed to stamp out there and no one around me had a word of English. Eventually I found an official looking chap who opened the border and sent me round to this much more official looking building further on up a dirt road. When I got there the computers were down but the Mongolian Customs inspector sorted me out with a handwritten release and let me on my way.
I pulled up to the Russian border and was through in no time. I explained my route to the border guards and where I was off to. I've said it a few times at this stage, you can't overestimate the part that Vladivostok plays in the Russian psyche. It's something they all dream of doing one day and the very fact that I was going to Magadan and Vladivostok meant I was a made man.
With the border crossing done, a couple of things started going against me almost right away. The first was I lost an hour as I crossed the border, so instead of getting to Ulan Ude by 8pm, it would be 9pm, not a big deal but it's always better to arrive early into a city you don't know, especially when you're looking for accommodation.
Then as I was on my way to Ulan Ude, I hit something on the ground and my front tyre deflated. I felt that because I'd hit something and it went down almost right away, I must have shredded the tyre. I pulled off the road but couldn't find anything wrong. What I didn't know was that I'd dented the rim, and because I was running

tubeless tires, the tyre was no longer able to reliably sit on the wheel frame. If I had known the problems this issue was going to cause me further down the road, I think I would have given up and flown home right there and then.

I pumped the tyre up with the compressor and waited for a few moments to see if it went back down, it didn't, so I continued on, gingerly to Ulan Ude.

The countryside was mostly green rolling hills with lots of forests and lakes either side of the road. It felt so good to have the Mongolian roads behind me, and it was orgasmic to be riding on asphalt. In a few days, once I got to the far side of Chita, the asphalt would vanish, but that was still a few days away. As I made it into Ulan Ude the front tyre went down again. "Ah, fuck it anyway!" This time round however, no matter what I did the tyre wouldn't pump up, was it possible I'd picked up a different puncture? I couldn't find any holes, but the tire wouldn't pump up.

It was getting dark and I was knackered tired. I wondered if I could push the bike to a garage or a hotel. While all this was happening, this woman kept trying to sell me a mammoth tooth. I told her, "Look darling I'm trying to fix my bike" and hoped she'd take the hint. But, instead of pissing off, she just kept dropping the price, and to cap it all, it started pissing rain. I asked her did she know where there was a hotel. She said twenty minutes walk, straight ahead. I said to myself "twenty minutes isn't as bad as forty" so I started pushing the fully laden Sam Gamgee up the road with a flat front tyre. There were plenty of young fellas all giving it giggles so I was using the phrase, "Go lick the back of my left one" fairly often.

After an hour of pushing the bike with the constant uttering of phrases like "You'd think that just fucking once, I'd have a poxy fucking puncture on the top of hill and not at the bottom", these guys pulled up alongside and said I was only a few hundred yards from a puncture repair place. "Oh you fucking beauty!" I went in and the guy pumped it up to a big PSI, soaked it with water to see if we could find anything but the bead had been reset and it stayed up. I put it down to the fact that the tires that were on the bike had been abused way beyond what they made for in Mongolia, and once I got a new set on there, things would return to normal.

Oksana, from Moscow had arranged for a set of tires to be in Ulan Ude for me when I got there. A guy called Viktor showed up with them and spent a day with me as we went around Ulan Ude trying to find a shop that had the bit you use to take off the front wheel of a BMW 1200 GS. You'd think I would have brought one with me? I did, but had lost it somewhere in Mongolia. Viktor was obviously a person of some standing in Ulan Ude, he rode a bitchin speed demon motorcycle and no matter which garage we went to, they knew him and gave him full access to their tools. He was a lovely fella and I would have been lost without him. With the tires fitted I said goodbye to Viktor thanking him for all his help and

went for some grub ending up in a Tibetan restaurant. The restaurant was out front but in behind they were hand crafting a Buddhist temple. Most of the people in the restaurant were of Tibetan Origen and the owner even had a photo of himself and the Dalai Lama on the

wall. I talked with two of the workers on the temple, both from Tibet, they were really great company.
The following morning I left Ulan Ude. The good news was that it was very difficult to get lost, once I got on the M55, I could ride it the whole way to Chita. There were no other roads.

Chita

The road from Ulan Ude up to Chita is for the most part in good condition. I had the weather with me, so I was anxious to make hay while the sun shone as it were. It was about 1400 km from Ulan Ude to the turn off from the Trans-Siberian Highway to head north to Yakutsk. The days to get there all blurred together, even looking at the pictures I can't see when one day ends and where the next begins. There are a couple of reasons for it I suppose. Firstly the scenery is very unchanging in that part of the world. There were really just two types, Montana-esqe flat countryside, or hills with lots of trees. When the land was flat, the road stretched off into the distance like a piece of black string rolled out onto a green carpet under a brilliant blue sky. The only variation in the ride came from the constant switching from gravel to asphalt roads. If I die mysteriously at some point and they do an autopsy, a question will no doubt stump the coroner will be, "Now, how do you suppose he got so much dust in his lungs?" When the land was hilly, the sky was blue, everything else was a bright spring green apart from some white clouds and the white gravel path carving its way through the countryside.
These roads are very lonely. You can often go hours with-

out seeing a car or a truck. At one stage I got a puncture and in the whole time it took to strip off the bike, fix the puncture and pack it up again, not a single car passed. Every now and then as I repaired the bike, I'd flick my head over both shoulders to make sure there wasn't a bear heading my direction. Although if it was a female bear that showed up, it was so long since I climbed Mount Crack, I'd have probably tried to shag her.
Every time I would stop for gas the bike drew an ever growing crowd. The more remote I seemed to go, the bigger the novelty a beardy Irish bollix on a BMW became. At one stage I came out of a café and there were eighteen guys standing around the bike. My first reaction was, "Oh shit, what the fuck does this mob want?" I walked up smiling and they looked at me like I was from another time. One of the guys spoke English and said, "You look like you're from Brave Heart, the film". "Oh

you mean Mel Gibson?" I replied hopefully, to which he replied "No the other guy, his buddy, the fat guy" as he motioned to a big belly.

The road from Chita to Tynda in the North has been under construction for years now, and it'll be a long number of years before it's finished yet. Every now and then you pass a tiny village of battered wooden cottages and you can't help wonder, "Why exactly do folks choose to live all the way out here? What do they do all day?" I stopped the first night in a truck stop, pitched the tent and just rolled into the sleeping bag and went asleep. As soon as I woke up, I got underway again.
Every long trip has a day when you do a crazy amount of miles; this was the day for that. I knocked out over 550 miles on a mixture of asphalt and gravel in what seemed like a replay of the previous day.

I was dying for something to come along that I could stop and take a picture of but the pickings were very slim. As it was getting dark I arrived at the turn off for Yakutz, the sign said 1169 km. I pulled in for gas and asked the pump attendant was there anywhere to sleep around here. He gave me directions to a "rough as a badgers arse" bedsit where after a quick wing wash I drifted off to sleep and dreamt of bears.

Tynda

I woke up the next morning to another flat, for a total of three on what was a brand new front tyre. I was riding on a lot of gravel so wasn't sure if it was a genuine puncture or the side wall of the tire was beginning to rupture, or if it was a dent in the wheel frame. One of the guys sitting around told me that 10 km up the road there was a motorcycle mechanic, maybe he would be able to help. I pumped up the tyre and took it slowly down the road but only got 2 km before it was flat again. Even if I could get moving again, at this stage I seriously doubted whether or not the bike would be able to make it to Magadan and thought to myself would I be better off just shooting directly east for Vladivostok. That would be an easy four day ride on asphalt, it would make getting the bike to North America a lot easier and less expensive, as I wouldn't have to ship it from Magadan to Vladivostok. That journey would also be far less hazardous from a safety perspective.
On top of that I started to question my motivation for wanting to go to Magadan in the first place. Was it just because they went there on the Long Way Wound? And

was that a good enough reason to risk life and limb? Wasn't the trip just a "Round the world" trip? Who would care if you went to Magadan? It's not like 99% of people in the world even know where it is, so why the hell are you going there? When Ewan and Charlie went there they had a support crew and more importantly each other, if they got into trouble they would have help. I'd be on my own. This internal monologue had being going on for over 24 hours and I was weary from thinking about it.

I pulled over to redo the pump up routine when a bike came in the other direction. It was Hiro, a Japanese biker who was going round the world on a Chinese built Yamaha, 125cc. As he said himself, the quality of the bike was not too good. Hiro had some tyre weld, but just then I got the idea that maybe the bead just needed to be reset so I hooked up the compressor and just let it rip till it was beginning to overheat and then just waited to see what happened, sure enough it was fixed. (Albeit temporarily)

We started talking and it turned out he had polio which caused him severe physical problems with his legs. It gave me the swift kick in the goolies I needed to cop on. A puncture in a tire albeit in the middle of nowhere, was nothing compared to what Hiro was enduring day to day riding around the world on a 125cc. In about ten minutes I got a great lesson in, "Dude, there are always people worse off than you, so get over yourself and get on with it" on top of that the bike was fixed.

I postponed my decision on going to Vladivostok till I got to Tynda, It was about a hundred miles north of where I was, and I could take some time out over a couple of beers and have a good think about it. Maybe I'd be able to get online and phone a few lads for some advice. Lots of people who write about traveling say that God sends Angels when you're having a hard time. Still others believe that if your keep your karma bank in credit i.e. if you're nice to people nice things will happen to you. Others just think it's all blind luck, and there are lots of times in history where really horrible things happened to really good people and where was Hiro on his 125 that day? Well my two cents is that in ordinary day life, there is something that sends people your way to help you out. I only have to think about all the help I'd received on the trip thus far for me to believe it.

The road up to Tynda leaves the Trans-Siberian highway and starts out on what seems an impossibly thin road, the M56. The M56 has many names, The Lena Highway, the Amur-Yakutsk Highway or the Kolyma Highway and is approximately 3000 km long. The most important thing to understand about the road is that it was mostly built with Gulag slave labour. The prisoners in the Gulags built there way from Magadan out to the Trans-Siberian highway, through 3000 km of remote freezing mosquito infested wilderness and as they died the bodies were incorporated into the road foundations, which is why this network of roads got the name, "The Road of Bones." It is estimated over 2 million people died building the road and almost every km of the road is gravel. I was using these hundred miles up to Tynda to convince myself whether or not the bike could make it, if the tire didn't hold up, there was no point heading further north where there would be no chance to get it fixed. I took it handy and got to Tynda after about 3 hours. I was surprised to find out that 5 km either side of the bigger towns they had laid some asphalt. When all you're expecting is dirt, a bit of asphalt is like a free pint in your local pub, "Oh Jayzus, thanks a mill!" I stopped and asked a policeman to see if he knew where there was a place to stay and he told me to follow him to one, very nice of him.

Tynda got some special attention in my dairy: I'm sitting in what would best be described as a soviet hotel room. The windows are wooden with mosquito traps, and the room is furnished throughout with cheap wooden furniture most of which is damaged. The wall paper reminds me of something I used to see in my grandmothers thirty years ago and to my right is a small picture of a vase of flowers in a broken white frame. The floor is covered with Linoleum and has a brown dusty worn rug thrown down over it. There's a tall brown wardrobe with three white plastic hangers in it and a cracked mirror. The TV is a 16inch portable, the fact that its standalone with no power lead coming from it, means there's little point in turning it on. There's a single bed which Frodo the hobbit would struggle to turn in during the night, and the blankets are many years old and have a sickly dusty feel. Outside it's lashing rain, my worst fear. It could be worse, I could have decided to push on through Tynda today in which case I'd now be caught out in wilds getting soaked. The rain will make many of the stretches to Yakutz almost impassable and the wet sand will accumulate in clumps between my tire threads taking away any traction, rendering them useless. I've been psyching myself out all afternoon since I saw the rain clouds pulling in, whatever chance of getting to Yakutz I had with a dodgy bike, and a dodgy front tyre have quickly disappeared. I was seriously contemplating forgetting about going to

Magadan. Was it time to just cut my losses and go south towards Vladivostok, then try to get to North America from there, maybe to Vancouver. My head had been working overtime since I got to Tynda. I thought to

myself ok its 990 km to Yakutz, three days maximum or two days if you really push it. If you average 50 km/h and ride for ten hours you'll have to camp out one night. If you go slower it'll be two nights. I kept interrogating my decisions by saying, "Why wouldn't you ride for ten hours, and take breaks in between. Even if you're on road for sixteen hours who cares? It's not like there's any towns and cities or places to see on the way, it's all just about getting there." Following that train of thought were the implications if I decided to do it in two days. I'll need to give myself enough time to get to Yakutz in daylight to get the ferry across the river to the city and find a place to stay. So I'll need to make sure I arrive no later than 8pm. If you back up 16 hours from 8pm assuming that's how long it takes to ride 500 km on a dirt road, with a dodgy front tyre, I'll have to leave at 4am in the morning. Therefore I'll really need to do 600 km on the first day, and 400 km on the second. To do 600 km will likely take 18 hours, assuming no problems. (Note, 3 punctures on my front tyre in 3 days so far)

If some of these durations seem a little long to you, keep in mind I was also trying to film it as I went. It all led me to the inescapable conclusion that it had to be done in three days. So the goal should be to just get as far up the road as possible on the first day, and not to even try and do it in two days. I started to look at the Yakutz to Magadan leg and rolled in the same logic, it meant that it would take a minimum of five days. So what was the problem with that? Every inch of me wanted to be in Magadan right then, and for that part of the journey to be over and done with. I was utterly consumed with getting there. No part of my mind was thinking about enjoying it, or staying in the moment, I was obsessed with finishing as soon as possible.

CHAPTER 34
THE ROAD OF BONES

Aldan

From my Diary: The only reason I know where I am is because I asked a guy in a bar what was the name of the town. As it happened he could speak English on account of having studied for two years in Alaska of all places. I couldn't help but wonder how he ended up in a town on a remote offshoot of the trans-Siberian highway.

That day started off bad, just like the day before I had a flattish front tyre. As I was packing the bike there were tons of people all standing around and even at 8am in the morning a heap of drunks had gathered around the bike for conclave. I pumped up the wheel, and not hearing any air leaking, I got on my way. I was expecting a complete nightmare, and set my sights on trying to do 320km. As it turned out the early going was easy and I was delighted. The road was mostly dirt but on account

of the rain the previous night, it wasn't dusty and was very smooth. I couldn't believe my luck as I turned in for some grub with a hundred miles under my belt. The grub in what few roadside cafés there are is poor enough fair. I'd say 85% of the bread that you get doled out is stale. I don't think it's meant to be eaten straight actually, it's more just to thicken up the soup. Mostly I ordered borsch, a kind of stew. I would break up the bread, throw it into it and drop it down the hatch with bottled water, "TGI Friday's it ain't!"
The hotel room in Aldan was a small white room which had no windows and no draft. The bed had a top and bottom bed board so to go to sleep I had to curl into a ball. Normally I'd sleep with ear plugs in, but I found with no windows and very little fresh air, leaving the ear plugs in felt very claustrophobic.

I left Aldan and the sign said 514km to Yakutz. I was confident it would be doable in one day, the local advice said you wouldn't do it any quicker than ten hours. The first 100 km were easy enough going, after that the consistency of the gravel changed and it started to kick the shit out of both me and the bike. I was certain the bike would start shaking itself apart and stuff would start coming off. Anytime I stopped I was inundated with bugs and mosquitos. Did you know that just north of Yakutz, there are over one ton of Mosquito's per square kilometer? Think about how many mosquito's that is. There isn't a lot of things to suck the blood out of in these parts, so when this portly Irish gent showed up, I reckoned I was drawing off about a hundred weight of the fuckers. I used deet 100 as a repellent which is max strength, so you can't use it on your sensitive bits.
It goes without saying, guy's shouldn't spray deet down town (privates). Even if it weren't bad for the John Thomas or town halls we still wouldn't do it, even if it meant we wouldn't get bit anywhere else on our body for the rest of the week. The reason is that every guy harbors in some remote corner of his mind the 500,000/1 shot that "Ivana" the ex-KGB agent just wearing a mink coat with nothing underneath, is going to come into the tent that night and sing a song into his microphone. The down shot of this is that when a guy goes for a number one in these climes, the pork sword becomes the only bit of non deeted flesh in that square km, so a plague of blood suckers descend. "Get off, get off, Yiz bollixes, get off" can be heard echoing across the Russian steppe. Any mosquito who tries to drink from the lad of Don Oisin Alejandro De Corn Hoolio of course pays with his life

with a swift smack. No doubt from a distance all this smacking might look like this lone Irishman was having a hand shandy out in the wilds, not so, I was merely defending myself.

The road up to Yakutz was very hard and slow going with the miles passing at what seemed an impossibly

slow rate. I continued to get the shit beat out of me mile after mile, hour after hour. Every mile you ride you know that if you take your time and go slowly you'll get there eventually safe and sound, but with every mile you get more and more weary and the temptation to go faster and faster takes over. Yakutz was eventually in touching distance when I came across a manky section of road. If you can imagine a track through deep sand where someone had spilt some gravel down to grit it up a bit, and then extend it for 20km - it was awful. I got the bike to the ferry and queued up with everyone else to cross the River Lena and get to Yakutz. Getting on the ferry was a total free for all. It was all done on a sand and mud bank. It looked like vehicles were going to get totaled at any second and I thought to myself people must get injured here the whole time. Once I got on the ferry I was given the rock star treatment by lots of local girls who all wanted to get their picture taken with me. They all had a little bit of English and after the lonely miles I'd endured since leaving Ulan Ude, it was great to be getting some attention.

Then the clouds burst and rain started coming down in sheets as the sky filled with thunder and lightning. I was standing on the boat laughing my ass off, I didn't care, I'd got to Yakutz one of the major milestones of the trip had been accomplished.

NOT DEAD YET

The outskirts of Yakutz look like a nuclear blast site but once you pass this by and get into the centre its like a different place with plenty of modern buildings and hotels. On account of the fact that as a foreign visitor you must register in the towns you visit and the easiest place to do this is in a hotel, the hotels jack up the prices accordingly. The Hotel Lena where I stayed was no exception.

The main square in Yakutz is quite nice, with a big statue of Lenin being the main centerpiece, no different to any other Russian town in that way. The temperature in the city has gotten as low as -89degF during the winter, so the people that live there are very hardy.

The next morning bright and early there was a knock on the door, I threw something on to protect my modesty and there at the door was Bolot, a Yakutian who is very active online helping people who are trying to navigate their way from Yakutz to Magadan and vice versa. We chatted for a while and agreed to meet for dinner later. That evening we talked at length about the Road of Bones to Magadan, where I should stay, how long it would take to complete each section and what I should be worried about. We spent a lot of time marking points on the map where I could get petrol, food etc.

He told me a lot about the area. We talked about the Road and talked about how the "Road(s) of bones" were built out of Magadan. The prisoners would arrive by ship to Magadan which was called the "Gateway to Hell". Bolot told me that the "Road of bones" road starts at Magadan, and ends at Khandyga, but that's merely one section of a "Road of bones" network built by the Gulag prisoners. I was checking the weather forecast for the area and spotted that I'd a three day window where the weather looked promising so I decided that I'd get underway the following morning.

Bolot and I concocted a plan to get me through to Magadan. Step one would be to get back across the River Lena from Yakutsk and start making my way north east on the Kolyma highway. I'd have to ride 350km to catch a boat to take me across the next river which goes south on the River Indigerka for over an hour. This ferry goes twice a day, once in the morning, once in the evening.

It doesn't have a schedule; it just goes when full. If it's not full, it just waits till enough cars and trucks show up and then it sets off. If you miss it, you just have to pitch a tent and wait, there's nowhere to stay. Once I got the ferry across I'd a 30km hike down a road to the town of Khandyga where I'd be able to stay in a guest house which Bolot would arrange for me. Step two would be to ride 550km or so to the town of Oost-Nera where again there was a "hotel" and I could put the head down. It's worth pointing out that hotels in this part of the world are hotels only in the loosest sense of the word, the only similarity they bear to hotels in the west is they have rooms and you pay for them, they are mostly shit holes. Step three would be to take a right turn at Susuman and veer south, down the old summer road and get as far as I was comfortable, pitch a tent for the night, and make my way to Magadan hopefully the next day. All going according to plan I could get there in four days, if the weather got bad or if I had bike problems thing's would take a lot longer.

As we dropped our sixth or seventh beer Bolot got "that" call from the missus, it's so easy to lose track of time when it doesn't get dark and of course when you're gulping away at some tall frosty beers. We called it a night and I headed back to the hotel to pack up. I went through my gear one last time. What exactly hadn't I used yet, and why did I think I would use it in the next couple of days. Anything I could throw away to get the weight down on the bike would help me in the miles ahead.

Khandyga

I got up with a hangover saying the words "What the fuck was I thinking going on the piss when I knew I'd start the Road of Bones today, you'd think you'd have copped on by now you fat bastard!" I had a weather window and really wanted to catch that second ferry so I was in a hurry. Of course, I got lost and spent about forty minutes driving up and down every side street in the town trying to find my way out of Yakutz. I reckoned as long as I was heading North East I'd hit the river which I eventually did.

When I got there, the ferry had a few cars waiting on it. I realized that this smaller ferry wouldn't actually leave until it had a full load either, so instead of being across the river by 9am, it was midday by the time there was enough cars and trucks for the ferry master to go. I'd no idea when or if the second ferry would leave to cross the River Indigerka, it might go at 6pm or wait on traffic, but I knew if I was going to get across that day, I'd better haul ass. The first 40km up the Kolyma highway are in an absolute state. If you can imagine a once gravel road which was ripped to bits by a harsh winter. Now imagine the local council not having the money to resurface it so they just put sand down and then on top of that put lots of big bits of gravel. The bike was washing around like a jet ski. Every km I drove was in constant hope that just up the road things would improve, I prayed that the whole road wouldn't be like this.

Eventually it sorted itself out into a manageable gravel track and I made my way to the ferry, it took about six hours to do the 350 km. I kept asking myself "How has it come to pass, that on one of the world's most god forsaken lonely roads you find yourself in a hurry!"

I finally made it and there were a couple of Lorries, cars and vans waiting so I was pretty sure I hadn't missed it. I wondered was there a Queue? Was I at the back? Would he let me on? Who do you pay? Where is the ferry? The ferry eventually arrived and the 40ft trucks reversed out onto a mud bank and from there onto the ferry while it

NOT DEAD YET

held itself in place using its propeller. Having worked on trucks in a previous life, I was stunned at how skillful the drivers were and thought back to my days trying to guide various drivers, into what we thought were tight spots around the various shopping centers in Ireland. By 6:30pm we were ambling down the river on a gorgeous afternoon without a care world. This was the ferry to take me to the official start of the Road of Bones and it felt like I was heading off to capture King Kong. I think the ferry took ninety minutes, I'd fallen asleep and was woken up by one of the truck drivers. I woke up laughing to myself. I couldn't believe that considering where I was, how far I'd come and what I was about to start, that the only thing I saw fit to do was go for a kip on the boat. I pulled off the boat up a steep gravel bank and passed through a small town where every house was made

of wood thinking to myself, "Please don't let this be Khandyga". I checked the map, I'd still another 20+ km to go so off I went. This section of road was under construction, and when a road which was already one of the World's great fuck stories, was made worse by being under construction you can imagine how bad it was.
It was made even worse by the shadows from the trees which were helping to camouflage potholes and divots in the road. The dust thrown up by the trucks on the road meant at times I was riding blind.
I got to Khandyga where Bolot had arranged a guesthouse for me to stay in. I stopped at a shop and waited for the land lady, Nina to show up, Bolot said she'd meet me at the local shop. While I was there, I met a bunch of locals who could speak a bit of English and told me to be worried about bears on the road. Nina told me to follow their van and we drove to a communist era building on

the outskirts of the town. The room turned out to be an apartment in one of the buildings. We walked in, I got the impression they would be staying but after an hour they left, leaving me in the apartment on my own. The apartments, if they were in the western world would have been condemned decades ago and bull dozed, but in the wilds of Russia, this is as good as it gets accommodation wise.
I hit the scratcher early knowing that I had my first full day ahead of me on the Road of bones.
I was up and ready to go for 7:30am. Nina and Sergei the owners of the apartment came over to drop me round to pick up my bike and show me to the town gas station. I filled up, then got some grub from the market, a lump of ham, a lump of cheese and a round cake type thing which looked like it was filling, and as much water as I could pack onto the bike. Sergei had talked to the local truck drivers and the feedback was that for the first 100 km or so, the going would be ok, after that as the roads started to go over the mountains things could get very bad depending on the weather.
I headed off delighted to be riding on the Road of bones and in my head I was humming at various occasions the theme sound to Star Wars, The Lord of the Rings, Mission Impossible and even a bit of Indiana Jones. There was no doubt about it, like it says at the start of the Conan movies, "These were days of high adventure!"
I was determined to take plenty of breaks, to try and get off the bike every 50 km and make sure I was soaking up my surroundings. I have to admit to never getting the whole, "Stay in the moment" thing. I've ranted and raved about this before but what does it mean? I admit

to being more destination orientated than the average traveller. If you line up the toughest road in the world, I'll do my best to knock it out of the park. The journey orientated folks are back sniffing the dandelions in some meadow or banging their dicks off a rock to make sure they, "Really know what it feels to ride over a rock". There is merit in both, I guess. As my friend Malene put it, where would the world be if Indiana Jones or Frodo weren't destination orientated!?

As promised the early going was straight gravel roads with very few problems and even after a hundred miles I scarcely had a wobble. The going was too easy if any-

thing. I'd my first "hard stop" when I came to a river whose bridge was under construction. The construction teams had laid a trail of gravel over the water and a route to follow to get you back onto the main track. While I was coming across the water and out onto the other side,

I said I'd take a short cut up the side of the bank when the bike got stuck in a massive pile of stones. I did my best to get it out but failed miserably so I stayed there until a guy in a truck came along. With the aid of some construction crew workers we were able to push the bike back up onto the road. I was lucky, someone had come along inside ten minutes, but I was having stretches where I didn't see any traffic for whole hours, I gave myself a mental kick in the bollix for not being more careful and resolved to keep a "drive to arrive" mentality for the rest of the day.

I passed a café doling out what would charitably be described as gruel. When I was leaving one of the girls who cleaned the place looked at how I was dressed as I was getting on the bike and said the words, "Extreme eh?" Well, if the best compliment you can pay a biker is to call him hard-core, the second best is to say he's extreme.

The road started to wind upwards into and around various mountains and for at least a hundred km, I followed a black dusty gravel road with a leafy green border, under a blue sky with mountains popping in and out of the field of view. It was a beautiful day. The only thing that takes away from your appreciation of your surroundings is that you're so focused on the road ahead to make sure you don't come off the bike.

I started to hit lots of water crossings where streams flowed down from the mountains right across the road. At each crossing I got off the bike and walked across to make sure I could get through and there weren't any hidden sinkholes, then walked back, got on the bike and drove through it. God Bless my seal skin socks! The deepest was up to my knees and lasted for only 15 feet or so, the widest was maybe 40 feet but was much shallower, so the going was hard - but doable.

Along the way I passed a few abandoned towns. No one does a "beat up town" quite as well as they do in Far East Russia. Even in Central America I didn't see anything to compare to what lay before me on several occasions, they looked like abandoned gulags. Looking at how decayed some of the towns were, I couldn't help but come to the conclusion that the whole Communist experiment inflicted on the Russian people was a complete and utter load of cobblers.

I passed the turn off for the route down through the old summer road, a point on the Road of Bones where you come to a figure of eight. You can go left or right and the roads meet in the middle near the town of Susuman. You can then go either left or right again and end up Magadan. I took the track down to have a look at the river, if I was able to get across I was going to give this way a shot, but there wasn't a hope in hell, the water was way too deep being well over my hips and a mile over the piston heads, on top of that the current was far too strong. I hung around for about an hour to see if a truck was going to come by but the roads, much as they had been for the last two days were all but empty.

The traffic is diverted down a mud path which leads directly out into the river. Can you imagine that back home? A road where part of the route is to go through a river, it was like some sort of Japanese game show creator drew the map and was chuckling away at the thought of all the people trying to cross.

This is the same bridge that the guys in the Long Way Round came unstuck at, they were able to get a truck to bring them across, I wasn't so lucky. I went down the mud path, the only reason I was able to get back up was because it hadn't been raining in a couple of days. Nothing but a Kamaz truck could attempt the river crossing. It was obvious from the crossing that this way was now only doable in winter when the rivers are frozen, or much later in the summer when the ice water had sufficiently melted and flowed out to sea.

The river, along with many that I'd seen that day, was still loaded up with ice and it was a strange feeling standing

there watching the remainder of the bridge getting slowly destroyed by the onrushing water. I got back on the bike and drove a couple of km up the road to one of the loneliest gas stations on Planet Earth. A couple of guys hang out there with no one around for miles and miles and service the few solitary cars and trucks that pass by each day. There's no human contact at the gas stations, you just pass the money into a hatch slightly bigger than a letter box and they turn on the gas till you've used up what you've paid for.

From that gas station it was another 200 km up to Oost Nera, where I planned to put the head down for the night. The first 100 km of that road, while gravel, was a very fast track, at times I was up to 120 kmph and the bike was still well in control. The only places where the road became difficult were when they were doing construction. I got to Oost Nera around 9pm, filled up with gas again and enquired was there anywhere to stay. The town itself is in terrible condition, so many of the towns and villages I'd driven through in this part of the world were like something from Mad Max II, I felt like I was driving in a country that had just come through a war. Tons of rusting machinery was strewn across the landscape, old wooden houses all either collapsed or on the verge of it, derelict high rises with windows smashed in, you can't help but think, "Surely no one lives here". The hotel was a dump but at that stage all I was looking for was a door between me and the mosquitoes. I checked in through a small hatch and was given a key to a room on the third floor. I walked up the three flights of concrete stairs. Each step was once painted green, and prior to that orange with the area you placed your foot bare through to the concrete stone from use. The room itself had just a net curtain across the window, and the light came from a florescent tube overhead. The toilet in the bathroom was pressed so tight between the wall and bath, that unless you were orange, 4 feet tall and fond of the song "lumpa lumpa lumpadie do", taking a crap was out of the question.

Nature did eventually call and if someone ever got a photo of me taking a dump sitting with my arse on the bowl and my feet in the bath, they could bribe me for all I'm worth. To top things off, the water coming out of the taps was brown, no doubt fed directly from a nearby river, and the room cost $70. Next door a wedding jammed on well into the early hours, it seemed like the whole town was invited.

This was the day when things really started to go wrong. Firstly, the still camera I used for all the riding shots while riding the bike packed in, no big deal I had a spare. But it was smaller than its predecessor and it rattled out of the pocket that I normally kept it in, but not before it had collected 200 or so pictures from the Road of Bones. I still had the SLR, I told myself, but I was sick I'd lost all those photos. To be fair, these weren't just photos. They were irreplaceable pictures of a journey through one of the world's wildest locations, I'm still sick I lost them. Things got a lot worse later. The road itself was very similar to the day before with conditions roughly the same, all gravel, some streams to cross, hills and trees with thousands of mega potholes. The front tire went into a meltdown with seven different deflations that day. Pumping it up wasn't too much of a problem but the Mosquitoes were so thick in those parts I started to go a bit demented with them trying to find any bit of bare skin to feast upon, as I was trying to get the bike back up and running.

I set myself the goal of no matter what problems I was having today, I had to half the distance to Magadan so I would get there the next day, it meant doing ~500km. I'd all day to do it, and any problems I had would just have

to be dealt with. Once I'd the 500km done I'd just find a spot to camp and continue on the next day.

The grub in what few roadside café's there are (maybe 4 locations have food on the Road of Bones), is bad. To

call them Cafés is a bit of a reach to be honest, it's more accurate to say that they are places where you can pay for food which will keep you alive, but give you absolutely no pleasure in the eating of it. There's something about that which isn't surprising when you consider the history of the road.

I wondered how I hadn't got a dose from any of the borsch that I'd eaten, I got my answer an hour after one stop. The Road of Bones was saving it up for the Godzilla dose which was dispatched directly onto the Road of Bones gravel, I didn't even have the time to get into the trees. Thank the Lord God for baby wipes and their soothing, cooling, moisturizing, hypoallergenic, softness

and fluffiness.

I got another mile or two when the second shock wave hit, it felt like someone had stuck a thicket of barbed wire up my arse and was busy pulling it out at 100 km/h.

Without going into too much detail, on both occasions the detonations were so severe I had to take off my motorbike boots, socks, pants and under pants and let it rip completely al fresco. On the second occasion, my ass felt like a car cigarette lighter and I went down to the river to throw some cold water up on it to cool it down. While all this was going on, I was being eaten alive by mosquitos. Can you visualize the scene? Me standing in a river - naked from the waste down with my motorcycle jacket and helmet still on splashing cooling wafer onto my arse. Thankfully these roads are some of the least travelled in the world.

I made it to the turn off for the old summer road, the second loop of the figure of eight, and passed over an incredible mountain pass in the process. After about three hours I noticed the front end of the bike seemed to be rattling more than normal. I stopped at the next deflation and had a look. Sure enough the front shock had blown, "Oh you fucking bastard!" Now I'm pretty sure I should have been focused on my beautiful surroundings. However, the issues with the bike, my stomach (at this stage I was clenching my arse cheeks so hard I was making a button on the bike seat) and the fact that I was so far away from help were absorbing any of the "Gee, it's a nice view" calories.

I'd a decision to make. In all the distance I rode on the old summer road I hadn't seen a single car. The bike was giving me signals that it was on its last legs. If I continued down this road and broke down I'd be stuck so I had no other option but to go back to the federal road, where at least there was some traffic. Towards the end of the day thick dark rain clouds were forming in the sky and it was much colder than previously. I'd gotten a lofty total of 11 km between my last two deflations so I decided to call it a day. I was worried about bears so I pulled off in to an area which looked like it had been flattened out for trucks to pull in to. It was well off the road through a large pool of water and looked like it hadn't been used in months. It looked dry and well drained, I said ok, it's as good a spot as any.

By the time I stopped that night, I was spent big time. I consoled myself with the fact that I could be done tomorrow. The whole night passed without it getting dark. I lay in the tent as it was buffeted by wind and rain. I wrapped up in my sleeping blanket with more layers on me than an onion, I felt as snug as a bug in a rug. Even now, many months later sitting in a kitchen in Donegal Ireland, as I am writing this paragraph there is a storm blowing outside with the wind and rain beating against the windows. I feel so connected with that moment, I feel exactly as I did when I was in that tent (with the addition of some chocolate digestive biscuits and nice cup of tea of course).

It was 0deg while I was packing up the camp to leave the following morning, I had 525 km to go to Magadan. I was pulled a little way off the road and wasn't looking forward to negotiating the huge pool which I'd come through the night before. My front tyre was leaking air from the rim and I wasn't sure how many more flats it would take. My front shock absorber had blown the day before and I'd no idea of the road conditions ahead. On a personal level I was tired right through to my heart. I was coughing like an 80-a-day smoker on account of the dust on the roads, I'd a serious dose of colon blow and had only eaten two slices of bread and cheese in thirty-six hours. I was covered in Mosquito bites and with all the extra punishment my hands were taking with the front shock absorber blown, three calluses had pulled right off, even holding the handle bars felt like I was dipping them in vinegar. No matter how bad I felt I kept thinking of Jengis, the truck driver from Mongolia, the hardest nail I'd ever met, and just said, "Dude, Get on with it!" My thinking at this point was, "Ok, get back onto the road, and go 20 km at a time, if you get to a point where you can go no further, just thumb down a truck and see if you can hitch a ride to Magadan."

So off I went and about 20 km down the road the tyre was flat again and I pulled over to pump it up again. I then tried to start the bike but it wouldn't fire. It would make all the right noises but just wouldn't start. I then

realized that I'd pumped up the tyre without turning on the engine so maybe I'd drained the battery. I pulled out

my voltmeter (first time on the trip it had been used) and checked the voltage, I was getting 12.8V so it should have been ok. I then started thinking can the battery be discharged, still give a 12.8V reading and just not have enough juice to start? You can't jump start a bike without some extra kit, if you just use jump leads to a car for instance you'll end up blowing something, for me previously it was the ABS modulator. I pulled out the battery and said to myself "pull it out, hitch a ride to the next town, and use the trickle charger to charge it up and then come back and go again". When you're stopped by the side of the road with a dodgy gut, a dodgy bike and flicking your head regularly over each shoulder to check for bears while swatting a couple of million mosquitoes, it is easy to start to lose the rag.

Just when I was about to implode, a trucker stopped who was a great help. I jacked up the battery to his while I had it pulled out of the bike and he revved the shit out of the truck, I put it back in but still no joy, we both came to the conclusion that the battery was good. So what the fuck else could it be? This is where fate stepped in to save me one more time. Anyone who knows me will tell you I'm useless at fixing stuff, really useless, and it's true. I'm good at other stuff though, some examples will spring to mind eventually. Really the only way I learn is when something shafts me, so if a part has caused me to break down before, I will always know how to fix that. Three days before I left Ireland I was driving down the M7 when fuel started spraying out the fuel injector line of the bike, and doused my legs from knee to boot. What it turned out to be was one of the O-rings had perished and the seal was gone. When I brought the bike up to BMW to get it repaired, I had a conversation with one of the mechanics about fuel pump controllers. I already knew they were a common failure item so I was getting one as part of my spares kit, but the mechanic showed me how to replace it. I whipped out the spare part, replaced it and the bike fired up, "Oh you fucking beauty!!!!" Some good comes out of everything, who would have thought that anything positive could ever come from being doused with petrol? The other good that came out of it was that there is now a Russian truck driver who thinks that I'm the best trouble shooter of engines in the Northern hemisphere. He was looking at me like I was MacGyver! Y'know one of those looks that said, "How the fuck did you figure that out! Dude! You know your stuff!" Of course I lapped it up joking, "Anything broke on your truck you'd like me to take a look at while I'm at it?"

For the rest of the day I scrapped with the bike through umpteen tire deflations, dodgy bike handling on account of the front shock being blown, and eventually I made it to Tarmac just outside Magadan. I rode up to the mask of sorrow got off the bike and looked out at Magadan harbor below.

I'd done it. The second Death Star had been destroyed. Two months and two days after leaving Ireland the mission was accomplished.

NOT DEAD YET

CHAPTER 35
MAGADAN TO VANCOUVER

I checked into the Hotel Ocean, not too far from the sea front in Magadan Harbor. It wasn't long before I found out that my boat wouldn't sail until the 21st of June, almost a week later. I looked around Magadan and asked myself what would I do here for a week? I still didn't know how I felt about getting there, I didn't have any great sense of accomplishment. This would end up being the third long layover of the trip, the first in Barnaul Russia waiting for tires, the second in Ulaanbaatar waiting for a shock absorber and now in Magadan waiting for a boat. I thought long and hard about the road ahead, and to stop myself getting overwhelmed I broke it into small stages.

Step 1 Get the boat booked to Vladivostok from Magadan - Take care of all the customs formalities - Strip all the gear off the bike which you can replace in a Walmart in Canada, Note I also had to fly from South Korea to Japan so getting the weight down would greatly reduce the cost - Get rid of any flammable and pressurized items in the luggage - Make contact with the shipping agent in South Korea, tell them what you want, when you think you'll be there - Make contact with BMW in Vancouver, book the bike in for service / repair - Book flight to Vancouver - Book motorcycle insurance for North America

Step 2 Spend ~6 days on the Russian Freighter to get to Vladivostok and survive it!! - Get to Vladivostok on Sunday June 27th - Find the place where you buy the ferry tickets in Vladivostok to take me and the bike to South

NOT DEAD YET

Korea, hopefully it would be open on Sundays - See if you can purchase ticket for the ferry from Zarubino to South Korea for Monday 28th, if you can't book it for Wednesday 30th (Leaves 3 times a week)

Step 3 Ride to Zarubino - Clear customs and board ferry, sail for 19hours - Arrive in Sokcho, South Korea - clear customs etc. - try and find the bonded truck - Take truck to Seoul - Crate bike and ship it - Find a place to stay - Fly out to Vancouver on the 3rd of July

Step 4 Get a place to stay in Vancouver - Clear the bike through Customs - Bring the bike to BMW for Wednesday 7th July - Collect the bike on the 9th of July - Start riding north for Alaska on the 10th of July. It would be a 20 day long logistical nightmare.

There is very little to do in Magadan really, it's not a place that anyone would ever go to whose not on their way to somewhere else if that makes sense. It's a way point, a place to get to where you can pass a night and then continue on your journey.

The fog and wind in the town is relentless as it streams in from the bay and what can start out as a lovely summer's morning, can feel like a December morning by lunch time. I slipped into a routine while there. I got up when I woke, had a shower and checked for emails from home. Then I'd walk up the steep hill to the town centre after first looking to my right out to sea. The view changed constantly depending on which way the wind was blowing. I'd walk till I came to a bakery which sold bread rolls which always had fruit and cheese in the centre. From there I'd walk another couple of hundred yards to a small

café where they played the same record every day and I'd have two cups of black tea. They'd Wi-Fi and I'd pass a couple of hours checking on the news from home and looking up the scores in the World cup.
After that I'd continue down the hill to the centre of the town which is centered about a huge white church with golden spires. I'd loop round the square and make my way up the hill again taking a meandering route back to the hotel.
The first boat I was due to travel on was a Russian cargo ship run out of a very run down office, which I was sure I saw a couple of rats wiping their feet on the way out of. It crushed any lingering hope that it might turn out to be a nice voyage for me. I knew at any moment Russian customs could get awkward and torpedo the whole plan and leave me languishing for days so I just had to take one day at a time, there was no point in planning beyond the next day. I was filled with frustrated form of nervous anticipation.
It was a freighter and not used to taking any passengers so where would I sleep? What would I eat? How much stuff would I bring food and drink wise? What would the crew be like? What the hell was I going to do on a Russian freighter for six days?
The one thing I was really looking forward to was night time on the boat when hopefully I'd be able to look up and see countless stars if I was lucky enough to get a clear night, or maybe catch some sunsets, maybe even see a couple of whales.
The big day arrived and I headed down to the docks to get on the boat. At this point there were lots of things that could go wrong. If customs got awkward it would

be a deal breaker, maybe the Captain of the ship would get awkward, or maybe the ship was over booked. I knew I wasn't "On the ship" until it left the port. The first thing that went onto the boat was all the containers and then some cars and 4x4's were loaded on top of those into a sealed area. Next thing my bike was winched on board with four straps, a very nervous moment for me. Then I was told to come on board and went into a small wooden paneled canteen area where I was told to wait. I wondered if I'd be bedding down there for the next six nights. I then asked one of the crew where I'd be sleeping. There was some too 'ing and fro 'ing with another member of the crew and next thing I was brought to my own Cabin. I thought to myself I don't think I'm supposed to be here, I'll probably have to pay extra or will get turfed out once we get underway.

As it turned out, these were to be my quarters for the next five nights and six days. It had a bed, a chair, a sink, and a table, with a toilet down a corridor and even a shared shower down stairs. It even had a poster of a girl ripping her T-shirt off. It might not sound like luxury but compared to what I was expecting this might as well have been a suite at the Ritz. I got my next big "woo hoo" moment about an hour later when I found out the ship cook would be cooking the meals. There would be breakfast at 8, lunch at 12, and tea at 4 and dinner at 8. I donated all the pasta and noodles which I'd packed to the cook. We left the port of Magadan at about 3pm and headed out of the harbor on our way south. The crew told me that the ship would cover roughly 300 miles every 24 hours. If we had good weather we would be in Vladivostok by Saturday (this was Monday), if we had

stormy weather it would be Sunday.
One of the ship's crew, a chap called Igor spoke English. A couple more of them had a few words so at least I'd have a few lads to chat to. Igor even said he'd give me a tour of the boat once we got out to sea, it was like all my birthdays were coming together. I set about understanding if there were any ship protocols that I needed to worry about. For example where was off limits or don't go on deck when the radar is running, that sort of thing. The last thing I wanted to do was piss off any of the lads that you'd be sharing a fairly confined space with for the next six days.
I hit the scratcher that night rocked to sleep by the movements of the ship as it sailed its way south though the North Pacific Ocean. I was really looking forward to seeing some wild life and especially the night sky as we were going to be so far out to sea. It'll be just like Columbus I told myself. The chances of all of the above happening took a downturn on the first night when around 9pm the fog moved in. It felt like we were sailing in a cloudy glass bottle with nothing changing in any direction, no matter which way you looked all you could see was a wall of mist.
I scolded myself severely for eating a whole bag of fruit and nut mix the first day I was on the boat, it meant I'd no goodies and badly missed something to have a chew on, or a bottle of soda to drink. There was cold tea, coffee or water on the boat, and that was it. It's a strange thing. The idleness made me think about food more. When I was on the road I didn't really think about food at all, but now I was on the boat with a lot of time to kill, I was thinking about nose bag a lot more. I've always

been partial to fodder, and found myself thinking about Banoffie pie, even more than the topless girl who was in the poster in my cabin. For those of you who don't know what a Banoffie pie is, let me explain. You take sweet meal biscuit and bind it together gently with caramel. On top of this biscuit caramel base you put a thin layer of soft caramel. (Are you foaming at the mouth yet?) That done, you take a couple of bananas, not green, but not going brown either, yellow, and chop it up and put it around the base. (Ah yes! You see now where the Banoffie name started eh?) Well, from there you whip up some fresh cream. (Now if the thought of taking a bottle of that satanic instant spray stuff out comes to your mind, head off the down the shops and buy a cactus and stick it up your backside!) Like I said freshly whipped cream. You then cover bananas with the cream and this is really the only point at which there is flexibility in the recipe, you may or may not add a sprinkle of chocolate chips. Pop it in the fridge for the amount of time it takes to boil a kettle of water to make some tea. Make sure there's enough water so you can make yourself at least two large mugs (In Ireland we'd call a large mug "Tae" (tay)), and if its drunk with either a large cheese sandwich or Banoffie its best drunk in large slugs as opposed to sips. It's very important you keep the head down when you're eating it, or a goose will come through the window and rob the plate of pie. Cut yourself off a slice of Banoffie at least the width and length of a DVD cover case, and wolf into it like you're expecting a baby. Make sure you take the aforementioned large slugs of "tay", the heat will prevent the cholesterol in the cream turning you into a solid before you finish.

NOT DEAD YET

Igor was a great guy and the voyage would have been a lot less interesting if it wasn't for him. He brought me to every corner of the ship, and gave me a shout if they were expecting to see land or anything interesting and I got the impression he enjoyed practicing his English talking to me.

That night there was a full moon and it lit up a vast tract of the ocean. I went out and stood there looking at it soaking up the moment, I had to keep telling myself "Dude, you are out in the middle of the North Pacific Ocean on a Russian Freighter". The seas seemed to be much heavier, and the wind was blowing hard. The feeling of standing out there on top of all that black water was exhilarating. You can't help but think some tentacles will jump up out of the sea and drag you in, or a shark will jump up and pull you in when you're leaning over the edge. The air was fresh and crisp and I savored every breath of chilled air pulling it deep into my lungs, it was a wonderful feeling.

I was surprised to find out that there were actually some women on board, five all told. Two old ladies, one ship cook maybe about 25, and two who were in their early thirties. As usual men (all men?), yeah all men (except those who putt from the rough) do the "I would" and "I wouldn't" filtering routine. I was finding my "I wouldn't" list which included all five on the first day, was already down to three as I sat eating lunch at noon on the third day, with one other moved into the "I might if I'd ten pints on" category.

Throughout the boat you can feel the vibration of the engine and the propeller which rotates at 112RPM. It never gets any faster and while not in port, never gets any slower. In a way, it sets the rhythm for the whole boat. The meal times are the other metronome for ship activity. The meals were ok. Breakfast was normally two eggs, bread and tea. One morning it was milk, barley and bread. Yes, that's right, it's a long way from a bowl of Cereal, some toast and a cup of coffee. At that stage I was in a "Food is food" mode. As long as it prevented me from feeling hungry, I'd eat it. Lunch always started

off with soup, bread and then it was rice or potato and some form of meat. This was normally the biggest meal of the day and while it lacked a lot in taste, it was good ballast and filled you up, which is mostly what I look for in grub anyway. The 4pm meal was tea and bread with something else, one day it was two tinned peach halves, the day before it was three small slices of cheese and another day it was an orange. Dinner again started with soup and bread, and finished with a small second course of two meat pies or two bits of minced meat with some potatoes.

Igor was also responsible for buying the food for the ship which they bought every 45 days. If they buy in Russia it normally works out at $5 per day to feed a sailor, which is pretty good going I think. If they buy in Singapore it is over $10, and about $4 if they buy in China, it all depends on which route they are running. The bread is baked every day on board, and as you can imagine there is no dairy whatsoever. Any milk that's knocking around is all made from powder. The butter is a margarine type thing, and isn't bad. All the sailors clean their plates, i.e. eat all their food and never ask for more. There seems to be an appreciation that to make the boat profitable the rations have to be what they are, and also that the girls in the kitchen put the effort in to making it for them and they did their best, so they should eat it.

After every meal I headed out for a lap around the boat. If the weather was good I'd stay out for a long time grabbing a chair and sitting looking out at the ocean which on that ship was only a few meters away.

That part of the voyage was much like being on a flat straight road I think. The view never changed but because I didn't have to concentrate on riding the bike, my mind was able to drift off in a million different directions. Sometimes that's a good thing as you remember funny stuff that happened to you when you were younger, but other times you do the whole "coulda shoulda woulda" routine on yourself.

The weather changes incredibly quickly in the North Pacific, albeit the almost ever present constant was the fog surrounding the ship. If we did get blue skies or a clear view, you had to make the most of it, it wouldn't last. Igor took me down to the engine room, It was like being in the World War II German movie "Das Boat". The noise was deafening, everything was covered in thick black grease and the heat had you sweating in only a couple of minutes. I was stunned by the size of it occupying three decks of the ship all there to feed rotations of the propeller shaft.

The girl in the poster in my cabin started to drive me nuts. Her blue jeans were torn in many places and shredded at the waist. Her fly was at half-mast and no matter how much I used my Jedi Powers I couldn't get it to go down any further. On my fifth day at sea, sex was jumping into my head every couple of minutes. Can you imagine what it must be like to work on a nuclear submarine where they go out for six month stretches? The only thing that stops me thinking about sex is food. The grub at 4pm always had the potential to be the most disappointing. One day it was tea, bread, and one peach from a tin. That day it was tea, bread and a small bowl of tinned pilchards. If you read that and in your head said the word "yum" you're a fucking penguin. No other creature save a tom cat would be into it. I looked into the bowl, and wouldn't have been more disappointed, if it was full of rat's asses. I was thinking to myself that the number one way to guarantee that you're never kissed for the rest of your life is to start the day with any form of tinned fish, kippers, pilchards, sardines, all food of the devil. If you know anyone who tucks into tinned fish in the morning there's a good chance you are talking to a hermit, or someone who lives alone with a couple of cats. The last day on the boat started under nice blue skies and we finally had a view of land off the starboard side. Another passenger and I had kept a constant vigil hoping to see whales or some other forms of sea life. As much as we'd seen was a couple of very distant seals and one whale a long way off. Mostly we'd just seen seabirds and the crew reckoned they always show up like clockwork when the kitchen has prepared meals and are throwing away the leftovers.

As we pulled into Vladivostok harbor the first thing I asked Igor was, "What is the story with the heat?" Igor told me its normal for 30deg + that time of year in Vladivostok. After the cold air out to sea and the chill of Far Eastern Russia, I was sweating bullets. We got to Vladivostok by 4pm, and then waited in line to be unloaded. It was 8pm by the time the bike was winched off the boat. I was sad to leave the boat, I liked it a lot. There's something very comforting about the routine on a boat, even though before I got on it, I thought it would be like a prison, being confined to such a small area for such a long time. Igor had some time to kill before his next shift started at 12 Midnight so he got me through customs, ordered me a taxi, got in it himself and took me up to the Hotel Vladivostok. He couldn't have done more to help me. He was a great guy.

Vladivostok

Checking into the hotel in a pool of sweat with the usual mountain of paperwork to fill out was a pain, but I was happy I'd completed part one, I was in Vladivostok. From there I'd to find my way to Zarubino, then to Sokcho in South Korea, then to Seoul, then Japan, then

Vancouver. As expected, I missed the opportunity to get the ferry from Zarubino on the Monday, so now had a few days to kill in Vladivostok.

Vladivostok is a great town, pure and simple, in my opinion the best town I'd been in while in Russia. It's called the San Francisco of Russia and it's a good comparison. The town is built on hills at the end of a peninsula and no matter where you are, you've a view of the sea. The architecture doesn't feel like Russia, and walking around the town feels more like being in Italy or the south of France. It's also the home port of the Russian Pacific Fleet and as we were coming into the harbor way off out in the distance, there were tens of naval vessels engaging in exercises. I know I've been going on a lot about Russian women but you could easily mistake the city for a cat walk. One morning I was up early to buy my ferry ticket and I passed a couple of hundred women walking to work in outfits that you could get arrested for wearing in the US. The outfit which seemed to be en vogue was a light colored backless dress, I'm serious though, lads and lesbian ladies, if thou go'est to Vladivostok, forget not thy bucket to catch the foam from your mouth.

I think everyone who arrives in Vladivostok in the summer says the same thing, "Jayzus it's roasting!" and given I'd brought mostly Arctic type gear, I was cooking. I stopped by the Vladivostok Train station where the most famous train journey in the world begins, the Trans- Siberian which runs the whole way to Moscow. Believe it or not it was finished in 1903 and it runs for 5,777 miles crossing seven times zones. I'm not sure but I think you can ride a train the whole way to London now with the

Channel tunnel etc. with only a few train changes.
As you look out from the dock behind the train station there are several navy vessels and a hospital ship with the odd cargo ship passing by your field of view. There are lots of seats laid out and it seems to be the place to bring a bird, if you want to slap the gob on her. All the kissing going on coupled with the aforementioned scantily clad Russian crumpet would drive you demented. I met three Swiss guys, three of them called Marcus, and one called Peter. They had driven there in an older Toyota land cruiser and two gnarly looking Africa Twin motorcycles. One of the Marcus's was a mechanic and made lots of modifications to the bikes and the land cruiser and fair play to the equipment, it got them there surviving Kazakhstan and Mongolia.

Earlier in the day I'd also met a German chap called Denis, who'd ridden across the Trans - Siberian Highway on a 650, he was on his way to Japan. The lads were giving me serious style points for going to Magadan and doing the Road of Bones. The Swiss lads went for a very interesting strategy when picking their gear, it was all old. One of the motorcycles had 160,000km on it. Their thinking was that the older the gear they have the easier it would be to get parts for in Mongolia, Kazakhstan and Russia. They steered a mile clear of anything with complicated electronics simply because if it went FUBAR, they'd have no way of getting up and running in the more remote areas.

We went out for some grub and beers and shared stories from the road and had a great laugh about the Russian Lonely planet phrase book. In the book it doesn't describe how to say, "Can I have a chicken sandwich" but does translate phrases used during sex including "Don't worry I'll do it myself". I'm 39 years old, and I've yet to use the phrase "Don't worry I'll do it myself" much less heard any girl saying it to me!

The two phrases which give away which gender the writer is of course: "Do you have a condom" (Yeah, like that's something a guy would say!) and the gag reflex inducing, "There's no greater happiness than being close to you"

The phrase that was the most thought provoking I think was, "Use your tongue". Don't you think it's an awfully forward thing to say to someone?

It was great hanging out with the Swiss lads, they were great fun. We even took time out to go to an up market strip club. One of the Marcus's didn't come, I thought he had moral objections but it turned out to be because they didn't show enough bush. We all talked about where we thought the best looking women in the world were from, and we all circled in on Russia. The vast majority of my mental energy was being burned on my front wheel, would it hold out long enough to get me to Zarubino and on to Korea? I hadn't a clue. My mind had been completely and utterly preoccupied with my front tyre since Ulan Ude. I was praying it would hold out till Zarubino, it was only 200km away and 90% of the journey was on asphalt. My big worry was that I would have a deflation and wouldn't be able to reset the bead with the compressor. I left Vladivostok in the rain after saying goodbye to the three Marcus's and Peter; they were a great bunch of lads. There are almost no signs as you're leaving Vladivostok to tell you which way you're going but because it's on a thin peninsula, as long as can see the sea on either your right or left side you have to be heading north, south would put you in the water very quickly.

There were several police checks leaving the area, not surprising when you consider the amount of freight that comes through Vladivostok, but they only wanted to see the passport and the vehicle import document, so there was no real hassle, but if you're coming this way give yourself plenty of time. I got to Zarubino just after midday, at which point I started handing out cash like I was at a wedding. First off, it was 250 rouples to a clerk, some form of a tax which allows you into the port, no problem. Then I went to the passenger terminal and paid 700 more rouples which was the Terminal tax. Then a woman who looked very like my mother came out from one of the main offices and asked for my paperwork. She vanished with my stuff, came back with some forms for me to sign, then went off for a while and came back with even more forms, and then there was lots of waiting.

Some friendly customs guys came along and checked through the bike. I'd a bunch of stickers on the back of the bike which I'd collected as souvenirs as I traveled , one of them was from Canada, so this dude, who was just standing there starts arguing with me and the customs guys, that I wasn't from Ireland, that I must be from Canada. I pointed to the other stickers and said, "So am I also from Ireland, the Czech republic, Germany, Utah, Cody, Nevada and Route 66 also?" For whatever reason, because the Canada sticker was on the reg plate he wouldn't shut up. I could see that a seed of doubt was starting to grow in the customs guys heads. I was thinking to myself, "Who is this fucker and why the fuck wasn't he drowned at birth and why doesn't he just fuck off!", he was just a guy waiting on the ferry with nothing else to do. I pulled off the Canada sticker and said, "Now, Happy?" and mumbled, "You bollix!" under my breath. With that done, the customs guys seemed happy and let me through.

I rode the bike up onto the ferry, unloaded my carry-on

bag and then went back to the ferry terminal to go through customs again, this time as an individual. I kept saying, "Dude, you and the bike aren't out of Russia till you're actually in Korea!" Customs and bag check was a breeze, and then I went on board. I'd taken advice and got a first class cabin, which was a cabin with four beds, a sink, and a microwave. Otherwise you can find yourself sleeping in an area with up to twelve other passengers on the floor. With the boat journey scheduled to take twenty-two hours I said I'd treat myself. The ferry was supposed to leave at 6pm, it eventually pulled out at 9pm but then went back to pick up two late arriving containers, so at 11pm we were still at the ferry dock. I kept saying to myself, "Told ya, you ain't out of Russia till your on the South Korean mainland!" I got talking to several Russian guys who were working in South Korea and we shared a bottle of Vodka. I stopped drinking in the wee hours and as I finished up for the night, we still hadn't moved. The good news was that none of the three other beds in the cabin were taken, so I'd the place to myself and after watching the movie Ghost Town on the laptop, I nodded off to sleep. What time we eventually left at, I don't know.

Sokcho

The next morning I walked up to the viewing decks and had a look around, there was just sea visible on all horizons. The closest country was North Korea and the ferry was taking a very wide berth from it. I went up to information and asked what time the ferry would arrive in Sokcho, they said 3:30pm. That meant there was no way I'd make it to Seoul to ship the bike, I'd miss my connection with the customs truck, so what would happen now? We pulled into a well-manicured harbor in South Korea and I made my way through customs and immigration control. I was the first Irish guy they'd seen coming through that border crossing apparently because on all of their cheat sheets of how to deal with visitors from various countries, nowhere did it mention Ireland. I looked around for someone to give a high five to, "First Paddy through! woo hoo!!!!)

Wendy Choi, a girl who works with Air Korea, gave me a call and said I could stay in the drivers hut till 2am, which would be the new time we'd be leaving for Seoul, I was already tired, the very thought of it had me groaning. The truck driver was mad keen for me to hit the scratcher and go asleep but it was only 6pm, I thought to myself no way I'm going to kip now, so I told him I'm was off out for a walk and that I'd be back in a couple of hours. We'd be leaving at 2am and the little metal container office was no place to hang out for eight hours. At one stage, I walked into the container with my boots on, the two lads who were in there let a screech out of them like a lion had just clamped its jaws around their hind quarters, "Ok, I get it, no shoes on in the house and it's a big deal". The lads even spent a minute or two cleaning the floor after me, it wasn't even dirty. I went over to the shops and bought them some Pepsi to make up for it. The contrast between Russia and Korea was incredible. Even though the last town I stayed in while in Russia was one of that country's best, Vladivostok, South Korea in my opinion, was way ahead of it. The big difference from a traveller perspective is that, "Trust" is back on the table.

When I went into the shops it was like back home, take a basket walk around and put stuff in it, then pay for it up at the checkout, as opposed to having to point at what you want, pay for it and only then, is it passed out to you from behind a counter. We were able to leave the bike outside with the van out in the open all night, there was

absolutely no hassle and the truck driver told me, "No need to worry, it'll be fine."
When I booked into a hotel in Seoul, a key was handed over, "You can pay tomorrow when you're leaving." In Russia checking into a hotel with all the associated paperwork was a real drag and unless you were fully paid up in advance, no one would have anything to do with you. I reminded myself that it was Russia that was the outlier, most of the world operates differently, I just been in Russia for so long I'd forgotten.
The signs in South Korea we're all multilingual and there was a huge variety of every type of shop. That said, there were no way near as many fine women there, so it all balances out I guess. I made my way back to the container and we closed the door and all the windows to get the head down. The container was full of Mozzies so we spent a full thirty minutes lapping round the room, whacking the shit out of anything that even remotely resembled something that could fly. We had a fan and a TV in the corner of the container and the driver seemed to want to go to sleep with the TV on which was playing back to back lessons in some form of back gammon. Then he turned off the fan and went off to sleep snoring, the sound was similar to the mating call of a Moose. Slowly the heat rose in the container, and the Mozzies which hadn't been killed earlier came out and started sucking like calves. It wasn't long before I was soaked with sweat and itching like a whore from all the bites. The clock struck 2am, and we got into the truck and drove off for Seoul. It's about 3-4 hours to get from Sokcho to Seoul and it was dark the whole time we drove so I can't tell you what the countryside was like, except to

say that we crossed a lot of rivers.

We hit the outskirts of Seoul at dawn, it's a massive city with over 10 million inhabitants. We got to the crating company just as it started pissing rain. The guys got a forklift, and lifted a pallet up to the back of the truck. I got on the bike and waddled back onto the pallet all while the rain teemed down. We got in and the lads built the crate up around the bike. I was 40 kg heavier than we had budgeted for, the final weight also included the weight of the crate, something I'd overlooked. I stripped off what I had intended to ship with the bike and brought it back to the truck. When all was said and done with the craters, the van driver was kind enough to drop me to a hotel close to the airport.

I can still remember checking in. The last time I'd washed was in Vladivostok and since then I'd slept on a ferry and in a metal hut without washing. I was dragging the bowels of what was in my panniers behind me as I trudged off the rain soaked streets of Seoul into the hotel. The receptionist looked at me like I was a talking horse.

The cost of an extra bag from Korea to Vancouver is expensive and I had a lot of stuff which was for Arctic type conditions, it was time to dump it. I was also tired of looking like a BMW had puked up on me so I ditched the blue jacket and enduro boots, I wouldn't need them in North America. It was time to start riding in Jeans and a jacket. Looking back now, it was a stupid move but when you travel alone you never get a chance to get a second opinion and constantly make mistakes. From Seoul, I'd 3 flights, 2 train rides, a bus ride, and two taxi rides before I'd get to a place to stay in Vancouver. It was all just lines on a sheet of paper for me at this stage. I'd been in project management mode since I damaged the front wheel in Ulan Ude and only ever let myself look 24hrs ahead on the plan.

After a shower, knowing I'd be traveling for way more that 24hrs, I emptied a can of deodorant onto my armpits, under my man boobs, above my love handles and anywhere else I could deodorize without burning the balls off myself.

I left my hotel in Seoul at 6:30am on July 3rd, 2010, (That time and date is important for later!) to catch a flight to Osaka in Japan. From there I flew to Haneda airport in Tokyo. Continuing on from there I had to take a two hour train ride to the other side of the city where Narita airport was situated. Scrambling from there to catch the flight to Vancouver, we took off at 6:30pm Tokyo time. The flight to Vancouver was roughly eight hours and got me into Vancouver at 10:30am, July 3rd, or put another way, 8 hours before I left Tokyo, on account of passing over the international date line.

The whole way, I had either middle seats or was crammed in like a sardine, but I didn't mind. A couple of years ago if someone had shown me this flight schedule, I'd have passed out, but like I said before when you've gone through the full suite of Central American borders, nothing seems difficult anymore.

The big swing in time change set me up for the worst dose of Jet lag in recorded history. Up to that point I'd crossed eleven time zones but always while riding the bike, so an hour here and there does no damage, but that lark of arriving before you left was a bit too much for the constitution to bear. My gut was also feeling the effects. In the one length of pipe between my O-rings, I'd Russian grub from Zarubino, Korean Ferry grub, Mainland Korean grub, three different airplane food offerings, airport food in two Japanese airports, and the final straw was to throw some Vancouver grub into the mix. It was way too many different types of bacteria for my body to assimilate and I nearly broke the porcelain throne when I got to the hotel.

NOT DEAD YET

CHAPTER 36
VANCOUVER TO VALDEZ

Clearing the bike out of customs was about what you'd expect when dealing with the public sector. I went in on the Monday morning and the chap in Air Canada said that customs had a hold on it. I asked was there any more information than that. He said no, so off I toddled to customs. The customs guy said to come back tomorrow or the next day. I asked was there a problem to which he replied no, and that I should ring Air Canada the next day to see if it had cleared. So that was it.
I went back to the hotel and went off and did some Vancouver tourist stuff while I waited. The bike cleared the next day and the Air Canada warehouse guys gave me a hand removing the packaging, the warehouse lads were a great bunch and we'd a good laugh de-crating the bike. I pumped up the front tyre for the gajillionth time and headed off back to my hotel. The next morning I dropped the bike off with Pacific Yamaha BMW. The bike needed some major work including a new front shock, new tires, all the fluids changed, new brake pads, new spark plugs and a new air filter. For good measure it also needed new grommets on the sump guard, which was the same problem Joe had way back on the first day of the trip ten months earlier.
While I was waiting on the bike to get fixed up, my buddy Shelley Williamson (note the two e's in Shelley, she tells me "it's a thing") took me round Vancouver to replenish some of the cheaper bits and pieces I'd thrown away in Seoul. We spent most of the day lost, eventually I bought a GPS and we were lost no longer but we'd a good laugh. Shelley, a keen biker had spent most of her life up in the Great North West so had plenty of route tips.

NOT DEAD YET

A day or so later, I collected the bike which cost a small fortune to get back on the road and drove to the town of 100 Mile House, on the way passing through the astonishingly beautiful Joffre Lakes provincial park.

It was the first day since way back in Mid-May that there wasn't something wrong with the bike, something had been up with the bike for almost two straight months. That day there was nothing, everything was perfect. The roads were full of bikers, mostly Harley riders. I heard there was a convention in Vancouver, so no doubt they

were all heading to that.

The last time I rode the bike for the whole day was when I got to Magadan, I can remember how difficult it was and how much nervous and physical energy I was burning trying to get there, averaging about 50 km/h. In contrast, riding in North America really was about as relaxing as it gets. The road surface was flawless, there were plenty of places to stop for gas and something to eat and you can be pretty much guaranteed that at the end of every day, you'll be able to find somewhere to stay. You don't have to worry about stuff getting robbed off your bike, or the cops stopping you without cause, everybody speaks English and most people are quite friendly, it's a doddle. That's the part I think I was missing, that sense of not knowing what was going to happen next.

I met two guys who were filming a movie as I was parked up staring out onto a lake, it was called The Big year. It starred Steve Martin, Owen Wilson and Jack Black. They shouted over to me, "Hey buddy…you hungry?" My ears pricked up instantly and next thing I knew I was chowing down on a beef sub, "Great to meet you guys!"

The next day I rode up to Quesnel on the Caribou highway, stopping a little short of the town and staying in a roadside truck stop come motel, called the Alamo Diner. I don't know why, but it gave me an intense feeling of being back in Russia. That evening I rode up to the town and had a walk by the river. All day I was bored out of my mind, there hadn't been a whole pile to see and by 4pm I was starting to fall asleep on the bike. At this stage I was asking myself, "Where are you going? To Alaska? Why? You were there last year." I had no good reason to be heading North, I was wandering.

I saw a sign outside a bar called "Murphy's" with the words "Try our famous ribs." "It has to be an Irish bar" I thought to myself, so after a quick shower I walked through the door with a serious goo on me for some ribs and a few beers. All the restaurant seats were taken but there was a seat available at the bar, so over I went. The bar was circular and all the seats were taken with working men, all out for a beer after a hard weeks work. Everyone was friendly and at varying times there were seven or eight of us jumping in and out of the conversation as the topic of conversation varied from Obama to the Gulf. I stepped up from the stool to loosen my belt after a few beers and a whole mess of wings when one of the guys said, "Hey, your belt is on funny". I said, "What?" Well, my buckle was to the right with the bit that goes into the buckle to the left. Have a quick look down at your belt, which is it? Buckle to the left or the right? I said, "How do you mean? There's no one way to have your belt, surely the buckle can be left or right?" With that, a straw poll began of the lads at the bar and sure enough I was the only one who had the buckle to the right. They asked me if I was left handed which might explain it, or maybe that's how they did it in Ireland. You can probably tell we all had a few beers on at this stage, but this is going somewhere. With that firmly out there as this weekend's "odd" thing, one of the guys ventured, as if to break the silence, "I shaved my balls last night" to which there was stunned silence. The guy, whose name was Ger, was a big hairy chap who worked painting lines on the roads for the government. The barman led the group with, "What the hell did you do that for?" One of the other guys then butted in with, "Oh C'mon Blake, it's not like you never shaved your balls before". The barman retorted with a "Hell no, I never did no such thing!" So there we were, listening to Ger explain that his wife had asked him to do it. One of the guys asked "So just your balls, or the whole kit and caboodle?" Ger replied, "The whole kit and caboodle." A round of questions kicked off but the one that got the most mileage was, "was it itchy?" This was answered by one of the other guys, "Nope, not really it grows back pretty quick". Everybody turned and looked at him with a glance that said, "So I guess you shave the meat and two veg too!" The question was eventually asked of me, "Did you ever shave your balls?" I replied a truthful, "Nope!" I did say that I've trimmed downtown when it was starting to look like a burst couch, which got a good laugh round the bar. The last topic ended up being the most controversial. Do you sit or stand when you're wiping your backside? There was comfortably a minute of silence before anyone would volunteer an answer on this one. Most of the lads were over 40, so it would be a dreadful thing to admit one way or the other, and find out you were the stray sheep after so many years. The first sentence that was offered was, "Well, girls sit, I know that!" That answer was greeted with much nodding of heads and general agreement. Ger offered, "I stand". No one, however seconded it, given he was the first one to venture he had shaved his balls, he wasn't a safe horse to back at this point. Next thing, we had a qualified, "Sit" from one of the men at the bar. "I sit, because in my line of work, I end up using public toilets and you can see over the doorway, so I don't particularly like anyone to know when I'm wiping the holiest of holies." A qualifying question was asked, "So at home, do you stand or sit?" He replied, "I sit." The bartender said that, "If you sit you're a girl, or just too damn lazy to stand up and do it", to which Ger countered, "Say you've got a heap of plop between the cheeks, if you stand well now it's just squidgeed between your cheeks, gonna take you a week to wipe it!" The barman said, "Hmmm, that's a good point"

At the end of the discussion, our little conclave summed up as follows: Belts should be worn with the buckle to the left as you look down (Reason: Because most women are right handed, add raucous laughter) Down town should be kept neat and tidy, but shaving is extreme. It might get cold. As for sitting and standing, we ended up with a" 50 – 50 split" for "standing to sitting" with a strong signal to sitting, if you had lots of sisters. As for whether or not who should decide on which is correct, we said that it would be best left to the United Nations. On a further point we all agreed that Lindsay Lohan "would get it" but Sarah Palin wouldn't, not even with ten pints on board.

I continued up the Cassiar Highway, and made my way to the town of Stewart. Stewart is famous for many things, mostly because of its proximity to Hyder in Alaska and several glaciers which are in the area. You'll need to look at a map to see it, but this part of Alaska has no road network, and the town is only serviced by the one road out of British Colombia, the 37A. The reason I went there is because it's a great location to see salmon spawning which draws bears from all around that location. On the Hyder side of the border they've built a viewing area over a river where the bears walk to collect salmon which have come up the river to spawn. It's an incredible sight. The Bears only have to open their mouth to catch a salmon. After leaving Stewart the road is long and lonely the whole way up to Watson Lake in the Yukon Territory. I couldn't help but feel that the road was a mirror of the road up to Yakutsk from Tynda.

Just a little bit mental

I said earlier that riding around North America after the trials and tribulations of Mongolia and the Road of Bones was very hard to adjust to. I was feeling bored and restless. I'm not saying that the Great North West is boring, it absolutely isn't, its just that compared to Mongolia and Far Eastern Russia where every single mile is a constant source of worry and stress, it's totally doable and a huge step down in the adventure stakes. Of course you could go off hiking into the wilderness in British Colombia and the Yukon and have the adventure of a lifetime, you just cant ride a BMW in there.
One night while sitting in a motel in Whitehorse, just for the fun I wondered how much it would be to fly myself back to Mongolia."Hmm, $2,000 to fly from Whitehorse to Vancouver, Vancouver to Beijing and then Beijing to Ulaanbaatar." Ah but where would I park the bike? The motel owner turned out to be a biker and told me I could leave my bike and all my stuff there if I liked. Then I wondered would I be able to get a visa, I looked it up and they do a limited service at the airport. I thought to myself "If I went, I know I'd get a visa, the Mongolian customs guys are easy to deal with." (I do not recommend this, always go with a visa) Then I wondered, if I flew back there, would I be able to rent a 4x4 and ride round the country for a week, to try and get it out of my system. Yes, sure enough there were multiple vendors offering to hire 4x4's on package tours, etc.
Three days later I was back in Ulaanbaatar after a hellish combination of flights. I drove south of UB and stayed in a yurt motel by a lake. I had planned to drive around

for four days to try and get back into the wilds but I was so tired from the flight that I couldn't even move for two days. Two days after that it was time to head north to another Yurt Motel and then head back to Whitehorse. It was a bad idea to go, not for the first time I was caught up in the romance of going back and didn't comprehend just how bad the jet lag would be. The only moment that sticks in my memory is one night when there was a full moon. I was lying in the yurt listening to the wood crackling as it burnt in the stove. I left the door of the yurt wide open and through the door I could see the moon reflecting on the lake. Just for a moment, I thought to myself it was worth coming back for.

I got back to Whitehorse too tired to breathe and couldn't help notice how the amount of cyclists seemed to be totally eclipsing the motorcyclists, I met tens of them who were going to do the whole Pan American. It's hard to feel like a studly biker when you see guys cycling your route with a big smile on their face. Can you imagine what your ass would look like if you cycled from Alaska to Argentina? I don't think you'd need a nut cracker come Halloween, that's for sure.

Along the way I met a couple who had just got back from fishing and the girl had caught a Salmon so big she could hardly lift it. As I was riding along my head was all over the place. In a perverse way, I still missed the hardship from Mongolia and Russia. North America is so structured and organized with everything working just the way it should, that it can all start to feel repetitive and predictable. I'd give myself a good kick in the hole every time I'd catch myself thinking it and say something suitably chastising like "Shut your pie hole ya dopey bollix, there's guys all over the world who'd love to be doing what you are." I told myself its all part of adjusting to being back in the West. I caught a lot of rain on the way up through the Yukon, but still managed to pick up a few nice pictures along the way.

It was a pain to be riding through spectacular countryside when all you could see was the rain on your visor and the road ahead, but on average I had been very lucky with the weather on the trip so I wasn't in a position to complain. As the day wore on, I stopped every hour or so for a coffee to get out of the rain in the process meeting a whole host of unusual characters. The first chap I met came out of a shop drinking a cup of coffee which he was holding in a very deformed hand. I mean really deformed. He only had two large fingers and that was it. He swapped the coffee from the right hand (deformed one) to the left and held it out for me to shake it. The fingers were way longer than you'd expect and almost wrapped around my entire hand and it was a little wet. It was so gross, but I checked back any exclamations or weird looks. I'm sure this guy actually enjoyed weirding people out with it, he was smiling just a bit too much. Next thing a guy showed up riding a Harley, he was after coming up from Washington State but was born in Michigan. He came over and shook our hands, mine first, and Johnny two fingers next. Well, he wasn't as good as holding onto his emotions as I was and no sooner had he the fingers in his hand, he said, "Y'know something, I think I'm gonna puke, that hand is some vile shit!" In fairness, we all burst out laughing, the guy went onto explain he was born with his hand like that but it didn't hold him back. He said he used to shake hands with the left hand but now enjoyed people's reactions to it in a weird sort of way. Neither of us bucked up the courage to ask, "So what the fuck is the wet feeling?" When he was gone we both scuppered off and washed our hands like they'd just been raped. The big news up there at that moment was that the Top Of The World Highway had been washed out, which meant there was only one road in and out of Alaska, the Alcan highway. The rain had been so heavy that it had created a flood which washed a whole section of the road away, and the local consensus was that it wouldn't be opened again till september. It wasn't a big problem, but it would mean having to go back down the same road I just came up when it would be time to head east again.

After a couple of hundred miles I got to Destruction bay, one of the more scenic areas on the Alcan highway, the water in the lake was so blue it had me saying to myself "Man, that doesn't look real!" I crossed the border into the US and stopped off for some gas. While I was there a guy tapped me on the shoulder and said, "Hey I know you, I'm following your blog". He introduced himself as John and invited me back to his place where we nailed a couple of Guinness's and two pizzas and talked away for a couple of hours about bikes and road trips. I said good luck to John and thanked him for his hospitality and then set about trying to find the motel where I'd stayed previously in Tok. The owner and I had really hit it off and had a great night the last time I visited and I was looking forward to seeing him again. I found the place and saw him but can you believe he didn't remember me! I went up to him and said, "Hey! How's it going! Remember me!" To which he replied a slowly drawn out, "Yeeeaaaaahhhh" which if you had subtitles running under it would say, "Haven't a fucking clue who you are!" It was a bit mental I thought. I had often remembered back to sharing a couple of beers with this old timer in Alaska and it was firmly filed in the "good times" folder in my brain, and the fucker didn't even remember me! It's not like I'm a normal looking fucker, a 6ft 4inch fat bastard with an Irish accent with a mouth, riding a bike to fucking Argentina with a big fuck off beard. How many of those do you get calling that you can't remember one who you went drinking with only a year previously?

The ride down from Tok to Valdez was a great day out. The sun shone for most of the day and some of the views available from the Thompson pass as you cross over the mountains and on into Valdez were beyond belief. Once I dropped down from the mountain pass the clouds gathered in and the rain started and barely stopped until I crossed back into Canada a few days later.

Valdez is a fishing town and it's also an oil terminal, the terminus for all the oil that's pumped down from the Arctic Ocean. With the amount of boats out fishing it's hard to believe that any fish would make it upstream to spawn but apparently fishing is prohibited until there are for example 5,000,000 salmon gone up the river, at which point fishing is allowed to start. It's turned on for a finite period of time, and then turned off again and the general consensus is that the authorities here do a very good job managing it.

The setting for the town is about as scenic as it can get with snow-capped mountains on all sides, the only downside being the architecture of the buildings in the town, which is pretty bovine. I met an Ozzie couple who I hung about with for most of the time I was there. We went out for dinner and then went on a boat trip into Prince William Sound. The weather, as you have to expect in Alaska, was wicked and the trip was a mix of looking for wildlife and taking a trip out to the Colombia Ice field. The Captain spent an inordinate amount of time looking for puffins, a bird about the size of a can of diet Pepsi with a yellow beak. The risks he was taking, bringing the boat in really close to the cliffs and into the entrance of sea caves seemed grossly disproportionate to the reward. I doubt you'll ever be hounded to show a slide show of your pictures of the lesser puffin, like most of the rest of the passengers I was firmly in the, "Take her out to sea and let's see if we can see some whales!"

side of the house. Mostly we saw seals, seagulls, some whale tails, and even the much sought after lesser puffin. Even though the weather was crap it was a really good day out. That evening we went out and had some fish and chips and had a good chat about how we'd ended up there.

It was time to start thinking about going home. I plumbed in Valdez to New York on Google Maps, excluding using the interstates and including a diversion south into Montana and Wyoming, it had me pegged at a little over 5,000 miles.

CHAPTER 37
VALDEZ TO NEW YORK

NOT DEAD YET

I had originally planned to do the Dalton highway again, but having done it in 2008 and with the weather forecast as gloomy as I'd ever seen it, I decided I'd Iron butt it the whole way to Burwash Landing in the Yukon, a distance of about 475 miles. I left Valdez as I'd arrived, riding out up over the pass in a fine drizzle. The Thompson pass was covered in fog as I went over and the mountains were nowhere to be seen. "No problem", I'd a lot of miles to do today and I'd seen it all in the sunshine on the way down, so I couldn't complain.

After a hundred miles or so I stopped for gas and met a Danish Couple (Mini and Moose) who were out touring Alaska and the Yukon. There were doing it rough and as we talked they shared a tin of spam from the local shop. From there I continued on up to Tok, stopped for more gas and a bite to eat and kept going up towards the Canadian border.

I got to the Canadian border and passed through continuing onto Burwash landing where I stopped for the night. It's a small motel and RV park beside a lake. It's a lovely setting, perched on the banks of a beautiful lake but run by a grumpy oul fella. Much like Watson Lake the location, so many miles from anywhere with so little in between, means that this is one of the "default" locations where you stay on the Alcan.

In the restaurant there were five other guys all sitting at tables by themselves, all staring down into their dinner. It reminded me of when I used to go on business trips to the US from Ireland. The folks at home would think, "Oh its well for you heading away to America". The reality was that when you got there, you were alone. They were all staring into their dinner, wishing they were someplace else.

I went out for a stroll and pointed my face east. It wasn't hard to find as the sun was setting behind me. About 12,000km "that way" I reckoned was Ireland, I was feeling good. I was on my way home. The next day I passed an overturned truck which had been transporting fish. There were tens of people helping themselves to the fish before the load went rotten, one of them offered me a three foot long salmon, I looked at them and pointed to the bike and had a giggle.

Watson Lake has really only two reasons to stay there, one is that it's a long way to the next town, so you kind of have to stay there and the other reason to stop is the sign

forest, which seemed to have doubled in size since I was there the year previously. In 1992 it had 10,000 signs, now it is closer to 100,000. It's very unusual and if you're coming this way, well worth stopping for. Other than that, Watson Lake is an overpriced transit town. I left very early the next morning in the bitter cold. It doesn't really matter how good your gear is, when it gets cold up in these latitudes, after about an hour you're going to be freezing too. I stopped off for a coffee to get some heat and met a biker who had just retired from truck driving and was now driving around North America in a fairly aimless direction. He had his dog with him which he kept in a little suitcase bag. We went inside, murdered about five cups of coffee each and wished each other well as we went our separate ways.

As I was making my way down the Alcan in the general direction of Fort St John I was getting Deja Vu up the yin yang from when I was there in 2008. If you're lucky enough to get the weather there are few places in the world which can match the rugged landscape of these parts. I was in a nice rhythm, leaving where I stayed very early - getting about a hundred miles under my belt, then stopping for some breakfast. I'd then do another hundred miles, stop for a coffee, you can guess the rest of it.

The weather for the next two day was supposed to be terrible so I resolved to try and make it the whole way to Fort St John, which would mean covering 1500 miles in three days. A bizarre situation occurred in a roadside cafe one morning, I'd stopped for coffee and this chap in the opposite table was ordering breakfast. The waitress was from Quebec and could speak perfect English but had a thick French accent. The guy, who was from somewhere with a very shallow gene pool, couldn't understand her. I offered to help and I found myself translating

English between two people who were both speaking English.

Once you get to the end of the Alcan Highway you start to get back onto the Canadian prairies. The roads are straight and long with a couple of chipmunks being the peak highlight for 500 miles.

I met three riders from Michigan on the road, two of whom were retired and one was working as a police officer in Detroit. We first met at a construction zone on the highway where we all had to park up for twenty minutes and wait for the pilot car to come back. It was pretty obvious that their chief worry was bears. One of them seemed to be going on like bears occupied every thought in his head, what to do if you saw one, whatever you do don't run, raise yourself up so that bear thinks your bigger than him. What he didn't notice was that a bunch of RV's had pulled in behind us. A lady, deciding to make some use of the delay on the road, took out her dogs to take a leak on the road. The biker dude caught the sight of a moving black animal (the lady's dog) in his peripheral vision and he thought it was a bear, in the process letting a wild screech out of his lungs. When he realized it wasn't a bear he started whooping and hollering like he'd won the lottery. The other bikers and I were rolling around laughing at him. I met them again later on when we stopped for breakfast and they were a great laugh. They told me a lot about Detroit, not a town I'll be visiting soon based on their advice. We chatted for a good while and had a good laugh and said our goodbyes and wished each other well.

That night I went to see Inception, with Leo De Caprio. It was the first movie I'd seen in the Cinema since I'd left

Ireland, Fort St John didn't have a whole pile else going on so it was as good a way as any to pass the time.
You start to see the mountains again as you turn off for the town of Grand Cache. I remember coming this way before with Jolly Jim Green in 2008 and I went to the same cafe as we'd stopped in, as a kind of a salute to old trips and good friends. Well, Jim, it's still a shit cafe!
Alberta
I stopped in Hinton, more specifically in Tim Horton's for a Crystal Meth Donut (apple fritter) and a coffee and got talking to a biker and his wife. I told him who I was, where I'd come from, etc. I told him I'd be done and dusted with traveling mid-august, remarking that the fun was almost over. He replied dead pan, "Well you must be getting married!" which brought a round of laughter from both us and the adjoining tables. I told him that I was in this part of the world last year and the year before but never saw so many Harley's on either visit. It turned out it was due to the Canadian Dollar's strength against the US Dollar, everyone was buying them apparently. While the road down to Hinton is relatively unremarkable, I enjoyed it immensely. The sun shone and the air felt fresh and clean the whole way, I didn't have a care in the world. I'd covered 3000 km in four days. My ass was wondering what exactly it did that was so wrong, to deserve such punishment.
I drove down from Hinton to Jasper and on into Banff on the Icefields Parkway. This road is quite possibly the world's most scenic byway. Even though it was my 5th time riding that road I was still muttering, "Holy Jayzus" under my breath as I rounded bends and was continuously confronted with views you really can't believe are

in front of you. The road was teeming with bikers. I was there a little under a year previously, albeit in August at the start of the project and there wasn't a sinner on the road, although the weather was terrible back then, which probably explained it.

By about 3pm my scenery bucket was full and I was done. I couldn't see another beautiful mountain, brilliant blue lake, I was full up. I pulled over and got a cabin, purchased a six pack of beer and sipped the evening away as I watched the sun set behind the mountains.

The next day, I'd cross into the last country of the trip the USA, via the Montana border. This was the 27th country of the trip. Canada, USA, Mexico, Guatemala, El Salvador, Honduras, Nicaragua, Panama, Colombia, Ecuador, Peru, Chile, Argentina, Ireland, Wales, England, France, Belgium, Holland, Germany, Czech republic, Slovakia, Ukraine, Russia, Mongolia, South Korea, Japan (3 hour train ride, and two internal flights so it counts!), then back to Canada and now finally, the USA.

I could feel the end coming on, almost like I was in a gorgeous warm bath but I had accidentally kicked the plug out and no matter how hard I tried I couldn't stop the water running away. Not sure why I used that analogy, it's a long time since I was able to fit into a bath. The whores who design baths and bathrooms obviously aren't aware there are people over 6ft tall in Ireland. Y'know when you'd see a scene in a movie where a dude is shagging a woman in the bath, you can always hear me saying, "That'll never happen to me!" I've always been very envious of small people who get to take those bubble baths, y'know the ones where you can't even see any water, just bubbles. I'd love to go in with a huge bucket of freezing cold water and throw it over them, roaring something appropriate like, "Where did you put my duck!?".

I rode south towards the border with Montana and had

picture postcard weather the whole day. It was my third time riding Glacier National park and the first time that it wasn't lashing rain so I'd an incredible time. Given the time of year the roads were full of RV's and I started bumping into people who were starting to make their way to Sturgis, the world's largest Biker convention.

Hungry Horse

As the evening was wearing on I decided to head for Hungry Horse where I'd a very strange experience. I stayed in the same Motel as Ewan and Charlie did (again) and there is a scene where it shows the room they stayed in so I went over and took a still of it. Next thing, a woman came down to me and asked "Why are you taking a picture of the door?" I told her why. Then she said that her sister had died in that room a year to the day ago and that she was here to kind of say a last farewell. They were going to put her sister's ashes in the river nearby and they were going kayaking to say good luck. After someone tells you something like that you can't really just say good night so there was nothing else to be done but get a six pack and get all liquored up. She was nailing the vodka like it was apple juice thankfully I finished up before the world started spinning.

I've asked a lot of people who I've met on the road what is their favorite state in the USA and in any top three, Montana is almost always there. This was my third time to visit it, and I know I'll be back.

I left Hungry horse a little after 9am and took a mean-

dering route in a southerly direction. I wasn't in any rush, the goal today was ride until my ass hurt, then find a motel, get a six pack and watch the sun set.
I threw away my Alpine stars riding pants, they'd a hole in the crotch which was great for cooling down my "Town Halls" but the pants were water proof and were too hot for the conditions. I switched to jeans and one of the first things I noticed was, I was getting about twenty wedgies a day. I must have stopped 20 times to pick the shorts out of my crack.
The sun shone all day and in a couple of places the sky almost looked burnt, it was great to be out riding in it. I kept telling myself, "Dude, you could be in work!"

Beartooth Highway

Towards the end of the day I was on the Beartooth highway again and everyone who I talked to was recounting the story of a family that were mauled by a Grizzly bear that night just outside Cooke City. They were cooking in a campground and the bear came up and attacked them. The Beartooth highway is one of the most scenic routes you can imagine, and the towns either end of it Cooke City and Red Lodge are wall to wall bikers, mostly Harley's.
The people I was meeting this time round in Montana were a wary bunch, friendly up to a point but the conversation always seems to dry up pretty quickly. I was still having a ball just riding around as I moved on into Wyoming. I skirted through bits of Yellowstone Park under blue cloudless skies without a care in the world. The last time I was there I almost X-rayed the place I

took so many pictures, in some ways I used to think that I had to get the picture to prove I was there. As you ride around Yellowstone you can see queues of people all doing the same thing, waiting to stand by the sign while they get their picture taken, isn't it crazy? Can you imagine the conversation, "So where did you go on holiday? We went to Yellowstone." "I don't fucking believe you, you're a liar, prove it!" At which point the person whips out the picture and says, "Ha Ha, see I've got a photo. Now stick that where the sun don't shine"

Cody Wyoming

I made my way to Cody Wyoming where I stayed for the night and met some really cool folks (Mr and Mrs Pat

NOT DEAD YET

Murphy would you believe!) who had travelled all over the world including Russia and large parts of Africa. We went out for Mexican grub and yapped the whole night away about all sorts of things. The next morning I needed to get back on some rough roads, it was time to ante up on the adventure side of the trip so I took some dirt roads which led to a variety of geological centers.
The clutch seemed like it was acting up so after an hour I said I better get back on the asphalt. The rest of the day revolved round riding through beautiful canyons, I really didn't know that Wyoming had so much stuff going on, and compared to the regions around Yellowstone park, it's relatively empty, with almost no traffic on the road.

Mount Rushmore

I passed through some really tiny towns, "Emblem" with a population of ten was two blinks of the eye, and "Shell" a little further on, a mere flick of the head to the right and left. With all the straight roads I'd been riding, my rear tire was squaring off big time, I suppose it had 11,000 km on it since it was changed in Vancouver, so it was due a change, I was looking at it wondering, "Hmm will it make it to Minneapolis?", where I planned to get it serviced.
Anytime I stopped for a cold drink and there was a biker there, I asked their opinion just by way of making conversation, the general consensus was that I was fine. The second problem was my clutch, every now and then it was sticking, either it wouldn't go into neutral or wouldn't change gear and eventually it started making a whirring noise. The bike had over a lot of miles on

NOT DEAD YET

it and after the punishment it had taken over the Pan Am, Mongolia and Far eastern Russia I reckoned it was shaping up to shit the bed at any moment. I decided that I couldn't go through any small towns, I had to try and minimize any and all clutch movements and just hope and pray it would get me to Minneapolis. So, what followed was two excruciating days on the Interstate. It was straight, hot, unchanging and unbelievably boring.
With the clutch in such bad shape, I had to skip the Bad Lands but did make it to Mount Rushmore. Let me say what every person who has ever seen them says, "Jayzus they're way smaller than they look on TV." Rushmore is close to a town called Keystone, which is a place where Capitalism vomited all over a town. You have never seen so many hotels, arcades and souvenir shops in your entire life. After that, I just kept on riding hoping Sam Gamgee would hold together. It was only 1800 miles. C'mon Sam, hold together.

Sioux Falls

The folks living in South Dakota are a very friendly bunch, any interaction I had with any of the folks I met along the way were all very cordial and friendly, I was taken aback by it actually. I had travelled extensively in the US either on road trips or on business, and I didn't realize there was a place this friendly in the US.
I made my way to the town of Sioux Falls and while I was in getting a milkshake, I met a guy called Jon who was also driving a GS. He and a few buddies were over in nearby bar having a few beers and invited me over and a group of seven or eight of us sat outside making the

most of a seemingly never ending happy hour. There was a real mixed crowd in the bar, everything from 21 year olds right up to seniors, well over 70. There were lots of bikers coming and going outside and nobody seemed to be overly concerned with getting stopped for drink driving. One of the lads was telling a story of how he got really drunk and as he was driving home was puking to his side while he kept on riding, every now and then he'd throw his head to the right and throw off a puke. We were all howling laughing. The guys were telling me that every road in the state either runs north to south or east to west, the whole place is one big grid. It was a great night and I retired back to the motel before I got too drunk.

Minneapolis

The next morning I went to Minneapolis. The guys had directed me to Leo South, a BMW dealer on the way north to Minneapolis and I stopped there to get a new back tyre, an oil change and to figure out what the hell was up with the clutch. The guys took me straight in and of course when I tried to show them what was up with the clutch, the bike behaved itself like there was never a problem. We talked it over and said it might just have been a bit of dirt, or something which shook itself loose. It sounded good to me and I went up to Minneapolis to visit my buddy Mike Bond and his family. I got to within three miles of where I needed to get to in Minneapolis before the clutch packed in big style. It wouldn't change gear and the gear lever was just flapping in the wind. As always happens when you break down, there was a pile of traffic behind me, all looking at me like I was buttoned up the back. I managed to get the bike to neutral and back into first gear and the bike bucked like it was a rodeo horse till I got to a motel.

It was a Saturday and I'd be stuck until the Monday at the earliest. If you have to change a Clutch in a BMW motorcycle you're talking a minimum of a $1000 and that's just for the labour so I wasn't looking forward to the outcome. I talked to the guys and told them that the bike only had to make it to New York, and then another 100 km from Dublin airport to Portarlington, they were the only remaining miles the bike will ever see, so if they could keep the cost to a minimum that would be a big help.

While I was kicking my heels I hooked up with my buddy Mike. We worked together for two years with Intel in Portland, he left there to become a doctor and is now based in Minneapolis. I was telling him about the bribing routine in the Ukraine, "So is this a big problem ? Or a small problem?" It became the running joke for the weekend. I asked him whether or not he got to do many TUBES as a doctor. He said, "Tubes?" I said, "Yeah, Totally Unnecessary Boob Exams." Dan McKenzie, a biker from Southern Minnesota popped up to say hello while I was in Minneapolis. While he was there we even found the time to fix a woman's car, in fairness it was only the battery but when I'm retelling this story to my grandkids, it'll be an engine rebuild done with our bare hands. I got the bike back and the mechanic went through the problem, explaining that it wasn't fully fixed but it should be enough to get me home.

While I was in Minneapolis I got a mail from Bob Aalbue in Chicago saying to come on over and stay in his place. Bob was one of the soundest men you could meet. He invited a couple of his buddies over to share a beer and we'd a hoot. One of his buddies, Will, was a police officer who used to serve with the army and had some great stories about Europe and Honduras as well as lots of great climbing stories. Bob's missus, Cindy was a great laugh. She told a great story about how she heard I was coming to stay. Bob out of the blue said to her that there was a guy coming to stay with them for a couple of days. She asked for how long and he said, "I don't know, a couple of days." She asked who was the person who was coming, to which he replied, "I don't really know, some biker guy". She then asked, "When will he get to Chicago?" to which Bob replied, "I'm not really sure". Her final question was, "What is the guy's name?" to which Bob replied "I don't know how to pronounce it!" We stayed up supping beer till almost 1am which was a good innings when you consider we started at 7pm. Bob and Will were planning a run up to Churchill in Canada which involved a 150 mile trek over train tracks, I wished them good luck with that one. The next morning Bob escorted me to the interstate and I was on my way again.

Southern Illinois, Cleveland and Ohio

The next day when I pulled in to get some gas I noticed the final drive was sweating oil, "You bastard!" This trip was ending almost exactly the same way it had started with multiple bike problems.

The states in the USA get very small the further east you go and every couple of hours I passed through another one; Illinois, Indiana, and then Ohio all passed through my rear view mirror in less than a day's ride. My plan was to take highway six the whole way into New York, it would mean I could go slowly and preserve the final drive and it would also get me off the interstate.
When I passed into Ohio I couldn't help but notice the amount of insanely fat bastards knocking around the place. Now I'm carrying a fair bit of storage myself, so normally I'm not one to talk, but all of these people were a minimum of a hundred and fifty pounds overweight. Several had to be strapped at the knee, some couldn't even fit into the chairs in the restaurants and one person I saw had to be pulled out of a booth in a diner. Highway 6 was turning into a nightmare as I passed close to Cleveland, it was quickly becoming the world's largest

suburb and by the time it got close to the city of Cleveland it was a parking lot so I got back on the interstate to get the city behind me.

The countryside in this part of the world is nice enough, it's not particularly photogenic though and you never really see anything that's worthy of taking a picture of. I remember remarking to myself, "Dude you just passed through the entire state of Indiana and didn't take a single picture." I could of course have stopped and found nice things to see and do in these states but I just wanted to finish. That combined with the fact that the bike was unhealthy, had me making a B-line for New York.

I stopped for the night in Fremont and got a note from Chris Dawe in Pennsylvania, a biker from ADVRIDER, offering me a place to stay when I got there. I took him up on the offer and arrived in his place in the early afternoon.

Dallas PA

Chris has hosted lots of motorcycle travelers in his time and knew exactly what I was looking for, some cold beer, somewhere to wash my clothes, some grub and a great chat. Chris lives with his Mother who is 84 years old, although her outlook and the way she talks and goes about day to day living is more like a 30 year old, she was great company. Chris stuffed me full of grub and beer and was a great host. Later on that evening we took the bikes out for a spin round the lake and then out the back of his house where he has 88 acres to burn your bike around in. The sun was setting over a nearby forest and it was a beautiful summers evening. The two of us remarked to

each other "Man, this is the life!"
I only had 160 miles to go to New York, the clutch felt

like it was going to go any second and I kept on thinking I heard the final drive making some strange noises. Surely both of them had another 160 miles in them?
The plan was to ride to New York in the A.M. Chris rode with me to the interstate and thankfully the bike seemed fine. It was 90 degF, the heat was murder so I pulled over for a soda which is when I noticed the final drive had leaked out what remained of the oil in it, or close to it, I reckoned. Thankfully it was beside a garage and there was a mechanic close by. I gave him a shout, he said he didn't know much about motorcycles, especially BMW's but Bob Aalbue had given me a procedure for filling up the Final drive. With that in hand we filled it up and did a botch job to get me to New York which at that point was less than ninety miles away.

New York

I got back on the road and as I got closer and closer to New York I'd love to say that I was welling up with excitement, but I wasn't. There were too many bike problems to enjoy the ride to the finish line. The clutch was acting the bollix, the final drive was making me very nervous, and the heat meant that if I hit traffic, the bike would be overheating in no time.

As it happened, it was the George Washington Bridge

that was my eventual undoing. I hit the tail back from the bridge which was about two miles long and with all the clutching involved in riding through stopped/slow moving traffic the clutch finally went tits up, on no finer place that the George Washington bridge in rush hour traffic. The only thing that saved my blushes was that one of the lanes was coned off to traffic so I could just move the bike over to the side.

I checked the clutch oil, there were no leaks, then checked the hose down to the connection point, it was fine too. I did the glorious mysteries of the Rosary hoping it was just air in the line and tied the clutch lever the full way back hoping the air would come to the top. The bike was also overheating with the heat so the break would at least get that cooled down. After about ten minutes and 50,000 Glances at "Ponse features" from passing New Yorkers, the cops showed up. I told them I was broken down and I explained the story but made out like it just happened so I didn't have to answer the, "What the hell were you doing taking a limping bike into New York City traffic" question. They asked where I was from, where I had been and in fairness they were great.

I told them I was 15 minutes from home. I only had to make it to the "ship-my-bike" guys in Long Island. I told them pointing at the bike, this may still go, it may still be rideable in a couple of minutes and I told them what I thought the problem was. Fair balls to them, when I started the bike and was able to get it in gear they followed me down the Long Island Expressway till I got off on the road to ship-my-bike. The bike spluttered and jumped as I drove up to the shipping company, it had got me to New York. I stripped off the clothes I was wearing, gave myself a wing wash with some baby wipes and the lads in ship-my-bike dropped me to the train station where I'd catch a train into Penn Station, New York. As I was buying the ticket I noticed an Irish bar across the street. I toddled over, sat up on a high stool and wet the back of my throat with two celebratory Sam Adams. After the beers I took the train to Penn Station and got a Taxi to East 63rd street where Derval O' Connell, a friend of mine, had organized a place for me to stay. I hadn't seen her in over 20 years so we'd heaps of gossip to catch up on. After spending a week hanging around New York doing all the touristy stuff, the only deed left was to fly home to Ireland. About a week later the bike arrived at Dublin airport and I rode it home to Portarlington, a distance of about a 100km.

Once home I gave it a quick clean and put it in the conservatory beside Sam Gamgee 1. I didn't want to really scrub it, I kind of like the idea that there's still some dirt on it from Far Eastern Russia and Mongolia.

CHAPTER 38
GOING HOME WITH WHAT I LEARNED

I set myself the target of writing this chapter in less than twenty minutes, if what I learned wasn't at the top of my mind, well then I probably didn't learn it that well, if that makes any sense.

What goes around comes around

The first thing that comes to mind is, "What goes around comes around." If you can keep your "karma bank" in the black by doing your utmost to have positive interactions with the people you meet, it will come back to you over and over again. It's been said before and is worth repeating, broadly speaking, if you are nice to people, guess what, they'll be nice back to you. You're probably thinking to yourself, "I don't need to go round the world to find that one out, I already knew it", but while traveling around the world, I found I was reminded of it at almost every turn. Ask yourself every day "Did I go out of my way to help someone today?" If most days the answer is yes, happy days are just around the corner.

You are better than you think

When you start something very big, it's easy to feel overwhelmed by the whole thing. Sometimes it's the thought of the enormity of "it" that stops you starting in the first place. If however you stay focused on the goal, take things one day at time, one task at a time and constantly try and learn as you go, you will get there. When you put yourself to the test you'll surprise yourself, you'll never believe how strong you are. If you happen to be reading this book you're reading about a failure, i.e. failing to make a documentary about riding around the world on a bike. The fact that you're reading this proves there is always some good that comes from failing: So fail on!

Smiling is attractive

There isn't a person in the world that doesn't look better when they smile, and people are attracted to people who smile a lot. I guess everyone wants to be around people who are outwardly happy, it cheers us all up. By the same token hanging around with a grumpy bastard all day will just drag you down. The amount of difficult situations where the mere fact that I kept smiling got me through it is beyond count. So how do you get yourself smiling? Constantly think of things to be grateful about is a good way to start, after that I always try and remember funny scenes from movies in my head.

Don't let fear stop you

The world is not nearly as dangerous as people make out. The papers and media are always looking for the sensational story and love to exaggerate bad situations. The best example I can give you is Mexico. The Paranoia north of the border is skirting on hysteria. If you were to believe the stories you'd never leave the USA. The truth is that it's a wonderful place; just don't hang round the border. Remember its ok to be afraid, hell if you weren't a little afraid there'd be something wrong with you. When it comes to traveling my advice is not to travel at night, it's when the bad guys come out, always try and get to your destination before dark.

Politeness is the lubricant that will get you through
There is an old saying that the "Squeaky wheel gets the oil", which is true, but remember, you eventually just fuck out that wheel and change it. People want to be talked to and treated the right way. If you walk round with a sense of entitlement or a sense that you expect to be treated a certain way, life is going to be one long series of upsets. People will be nice to you, if you are nice to them or if they're paid to be nice, or if they're angels. You're entitled to fuck all bar the air you breathe, so be nice, be polite and you've got a shot.

If you're wrong say you're sorry.

People don't know how to say sorry. They might say something like "I'm sorry I did that, but you were doing this and it made me do it!" They might also say, "I'm sorry" and follow it up with a "Hey I said I'm sorry, why didn't you say you're sorry!" The best of the lot is "I'm sorry" and when the affected person says, "What are you sorry for" and they reply "I don't know, I'm just sorry, you seem pissed at me." Another example is to say you're sorry, then justify why you did it by talking a whole pile about all the shit you had going on, how you were feeling as if it somehow absolves you from doing the "thing". I think that saying sorry has to be done as an open and closed event, you have to say it without any expectation of reciprocation. You have to take the time to figure out what you did wrong, what was the impact, and how did it make the other person feel. Then you have to wrap it all up in a sentence which makes the other person feel like you really mean it.

My example:
Hi Joe, I'm so sorry the project didn't work out. I walked out on you and the project and robbed you of the chance of fulfilling you dream of making a production for TV. I was an asshole, I'm sorry and I feel terrible about it.

The End

FAQ'S

How much does it cost to do the Pan American Highway?

I don't think its possible to do it well for less than $30,000. Before I start, let me say that the internet abounds with stories of people who travelled the world on a shoestring, its possible but I don't advise it. The chief costs come from shipping the bike. If you have to go across the Atlantic twice for example, that will run you $4000. Shipping the bike from Panama to South America will run you $1,000. Allowing for inflation and unforeseen import taxes, budget $6,000.

As your prepping you'll hear stories from guys who have friends working down the docks who can get a bike into a container for nothing and then you can just pick it up when you get to wherever your going, its all horse shit. You will likely need 3 sets of tires and 3 bike services with oil changes and maybe two break pad changes. If your riding a BMW, you'll need to budget $4,000, this will give you some headroom for any unforeseen repairs and cost of parts that you may bring with you up front. Do research to find out the most common parts which fail and if you have the room, bring them with you. Again, if your riding a BMW - the labour alone on the bike is $100 an hour. They are a good bike, but they ain't cheap to maintain!

Gasoline is relatively easy to calculate, just work out your total miles and take an average cost of $5 per gallon. Budget: $4200. 30,000 miles / 30mpg = 1000 gallons * 5 dollars. If your doing the Pan American you'll end up doing about 25,000 miles - anyway you get the gist - its pretty easy to work out.

Bike insurance (Third party), Travel Health insurance and border insurance for the bike: Budget: $800

Flights: This really depends on where you are shipping your bike, working from Ireland or the UK: Budget $2500 to cover 2 transatlantic and the Darien gap hop. Already, were up to $17,500.

Now, Calculate the excursions you want to take while traveling. Whale watching, Machu Picchu, National parks, theme parks, boat rides, museums, attractions. In 6 months your going to do plenty - Budget a minimum of $2500, if it sounds a lot, its less than a $100 a week on activities and day trips, its not that much. There is no point riding all the way to Cuzco and then skimping with your coppers and not going to see Machu Picchu.

Now the variable component of the trip starts. Traveling in Canada and the USA if you want to stay in hotels and motels I think you need to budget $80 a day. In Mexico about $50 a day, In Central America, $40 a day and in South America about $50 a day. If you go to hostels its a lot less and if you plan to camp (not advisable in Central America), its even cheaper.

Similarly when it comes to grub, most folks touring in the USA would do $10 for breakfast, $12 for lunch and $20 for dinner to include some beer, make sure the budget includes beer! The same would go for Canada. It's a lot cheaper in Mexico, Central and South America so you need to work out your durations. How long will you stay in each country. I've met some folks who ate out of tins the whole time they traveled, it really depends on if you want to travel with a bit of comfort or not.

Maybe your thinking of couch surfing, think wisely. If you get a name as someone who is bumming his way round the world looking for free food and accommodation, you'll be found out, people don't like freeloaders. Maybe your thinking of using charity to pay for the trip. I've heard of people raising $20,000 for traveling and only donating $5000 to charity, using the rest to pay for the trip - Karma will catch up!

Realistically the only way you'll pay for the trip is to work very hard for a long time and save up the money to go. Along the way as your saving pick up all the stuff you'll need and research your route properly. Most people will take up to 10 years to save up for something like this, its worth it! The best commitment I can give you is that you'll do your trip 3 times. Once while your planning it, once while your doing it and again when you come home. So take the time to plan it well. You may meat some loonies who'll tell you "oh no just go with the flow, let the road take you where it will" - but every trip has a start, middle and end. If you don't at least have a route with some rough durations you'll miss out on seeing some of the worlds great destinations and you'll make a complete balls of your budget.

How long did it take to prepare for the trip?

If its your first ever trip and your doing a Pan American, at least 6 months, thats assuming you have a day job. You could do it in less than 2 months if your at it full time.

Which country did you like the best and why?
For the ease of it, its hard to beat the USA. You could

spend your life touring around it and never run out of things to see. Valdez in Alaska, and the Bonneville salt flats are two of my favorite places on earth. Mexico would be the cultural highlight with so many ruin sites. For being utterly different, Peru, Bolivia and Northern Chile stand out because at times it was like I was on Mars, and the friendliest people by far were in Colombia.

Do I need Visas?

For your country you'll need to check it out for specifics. The countries along the Pan-American highway require no visas other than the normal tourist visas that you would have to get if you were traveling there (assuming you are staying less than 90 days in any one country). That's the same for anyone in North America or Europe. Do the research, use websites like Horizons Unlimited, UKGSER's and ADVRIDER. They have forums which are very helpful but only take advice from people who've done it.

Should I learn Spanish before I go?

Yes, it will help enormously. Just being able to order food or get directions will make your travels much easier.

What is the best bike to take on the trip?

Any of these will do the job:
BMW 1150 / 1100
BMW 1200 (Don't recommend the 2005/6 Models)
BMW 650 Paris Dakar

KTM 990 Adventurer
Kawasaki KLR 650
Suzuki Vstrom
That being said - You can do it on any bike. Remember - a lot of people cycle on push bikes around the world including up and down the Pan-American highway - if they can do it on a bicycle - you can do it on any motorbike.

Can you recommend shipping companies?

I've used three companies on multiple occasions and always found them very good.
For Outward bound from the USA - Shipmybike.com
For Outward bound from the UK, Ireland or mainland Europe - James Cargo, London.
For Panama to Colombia, or Panama to Quite - Girag. Note they fly out of Tocumen airport and its much cheaper to get to Bogota than Quito.

How much did it cost to ship the bike?

Budget $2200 for transatlantic, and $1000 for Central America to Colombia, $1900 for Panama to Quito.

What Medical provisions did you have?

I had multi-trip travel insurance - it covers for 180 days of travel. I also had a first aid kit and 2 doses of general purpose antibiotics. Loads of companies offer this type of cover to capitalize on the world wide backpacker market. (Try www.vhi.ie)

NOT DEAD YET

What about insurance for the bike?

I used motorcycle express. Note - you won't get anyone to cover theft or fully comprehensive. This is just third party liability so you can drive in the countries legally that you want to pass through. In some of the South American countries you also will have to buy third party insurance at the border, but don't worry its quite cheap. Its critical to understand, if your bike gets robbed or your in an accident, there is no insurance in the world that will cover the replacement of you bike, especially in south America. I've had people pester me for months on travel advice and then not go because they were afraid of their bike getting robbed. This is the primary reason I seldom stayed in big cities, there is far less chance of hassle in the countryside.

What type of Panniers did you use?
Touratech Zega Panniers- in general they have very good gear, its expensive but its well made.

Where did you get your maps of Russia and Mongolia?

Stanfords - UK - Do not go to Russia without a good map! Beware with Stanfords, they cost a fortune to ship maps outside the UK - so start with Amazon.com
What sort of Rider gear would you recommend?
I would whole heartedly recommend BMW rider gear (Ralleye 2 or 3 suit) While its very expensive - it will save your life and last you a very long time - that isn't true

of other gear I've tried - e.g. I went through 3 different pairs of pants which ripped at the crotch. My friend Tom Victory put it best when he said that they are a ten year suit. Another point to think about is that if you look at a lot of the folks riding the Dakar, even though they aren't riding BMW's, they are wearing this rider gear.

If I was to do a trip and write a book and make a documentary would I make any money?

No! The genre is way too small, but don't let that deter you.

Can you recommend a good camera?
If your going on the trip of a lifetime I highly recommend buying a camera that will take high quality pictures - you are going to need to spend a few quid. For best results / price ratio, I recommend the Nikon D5000 - excellent pictures - and you can pick it up for under 500 quid.

How did you backup your images while you were traveling?

I brought a 1TB WD Portable drive and copied the images onto it. These days you can also buy space on Google Drive and upload your pictures and videos to the web as you travel if you can get an internet signal. This is obviously way better than people have had to deal with in the past. They key thing to keep in mind with your pictures is that you need a physical backup and a geographical backup - for example so that all the photos aren't just stored on the hard drive of you PC - Use Google Drive or Picassa and make sure you upload them full size.

For the videos you posted online, what camera did you use and what editing s/w did you use to cut the movies together?

The videos were shot with a Canon HFS100 and Canon HFS200. I used Final Cut Pro X to put the movies together. The action shots were filmed with a FLIP ULTRA HD.

Can you recommend any websites for people who are thinking of doing more research and planning?

These are the ones I continually use.
http://www.advrider.com
http://www.ukgser.com
http://www.horizonsunlimited.com

Would you do it again?

In a heartbeat!

Is there anything you should have taken but didn't?

I'd recommend bringing a kindle. You can load hundreds of books onto it and they don't need much power, they stay on for days. You'll end up in a lot of places where there is little to do and a kindle would be a great way to spend the time. Second, I'd bring some tubes for the tires.

Do you recommend camping?

In Canada and North America you can camp as much as you like - there are facilities near all the big parks so if you have the room to bring the gear, go for it. In Mexico and Central America I don't recommend it. In Central America it's not safe but the other point is that accommodation is very inexpensive so why would you bother? It's better to get up and have a shower than trying to find a river to hang your balls in. In South America, there are no facilities but there are such huge empty spaces it shouldn't be a problem, except for Colombia and Bolivia.

Do you have any tips for prospective motorcycle travelers?

Always have $1000 dollars somewhere for emergencies. Pack it in a place where no one can find it. If the shit hits the fan, it can save your life.

Scan all your important paperwork and have a copy of it online for example on gmail or google drive. If you lose your documents these will be a life saver. This includes copies of all your credits cards front and back. If you lose them and you need to book a flight this will help a lot.

Never ride a motorcycle at night in remote areas. There is too much wildlife, if you hit it while on a bike its all over. Also in poorer countries the road conditions can deteriorate very quickly, if you cant see the road your in for a world of hurt. If you do get caught out at night pull over and wait for a truck to pass you. Then follow the truck, you can use it to clear your path of animals and people or any other hazards which may be on the road.

Spend a little time to learn the key phrases you'll need in the country your visiting. Being able to order food and place to stay will be invaluable.

Spread positive Karma. Do everything you can to be nice to the people you meet, it'll all come back.

Get a good rain jacket and pants, these are brilliant not just for the rain but keeping off the cold, you wont wear the pants much but the jacket will be seldom off.

Always take a crap before you leave in the morning. Have a couple of cups of coffee, normally a great way of getting things moving. There is nothing worse than being two hours from anywhere bursting to use the loo.

Always use ear plugs, riding a bike is very loud on your ears, and the effects are cumulative. Get in the habit of doing putting them in.

If you wear glasses, get prescription sun glasses that wrap around and fit comfortably in your helmet. You can protect your eyes not only from UV by doing this but every insect imaginable.
Bring a good moisturizer. It's not gay. The wind will play havoc with your face and most of the time you'll be walking around with a face redder than a baboons arse

otherwise.

Upload your friends contact information online, if you need them for anything it can save time. Similarly if you want to burn an afternoon writing postcards its great to have the addresses handy.

Keep people at home apprised of where you are by using a blog or Facebook. If worst comes to worst, at least they'll know where to start searching.

Bring something that cures itch, you'll be eaten alive by mosquitos at various points, its inevitable.

Bring a Kindle and load it up before you leave. Great way to pass the time when you passing through the worlds crappy towns.

Bring a decent multivitamin. Your diet won't be great so its easy to get run down.

Make sure your set up with online banking so you can keep an eye on your credit cards and bank balance. This is especially important if you cards get stolen. Also make sure you tell your credit card company that your going traveling and to what countries and when so they don't put a stop on your card when they see a transaction coming in from Colombia.

Use your credit card to get money at ATM's, obviously this is only if you load up your card to a positive balance, this is the cheapest form of foreign exchange you can get.

Key point to remember, don't put too much onto it because the banks only insure you stolen card for buys that put it in the red, so if you have money on the card and it gets used up fraudulently, they don't cover that.

Bring a light durable laptop. Lenovo are doing some very durable laptops which can withstand all manner of vibration. Its a great way to keep in touch with family and friends and plan your days ahead.

Bring a portable hard drive and back up your pictures and videos regularly.

Bring a spare key for the motorcycle.

Get all your teeth in great shape before you leave, you don't want to have to deal with that crap when your away. Bring an electronic toothbrush, they do a far better job of cleaning them

Never drink the water from a tap, only a bottle. Your arse is precious.

Always order hot food in second and third world countries, absolutely no salads. What they are serving might not make the locals sick, but it will create a tornado in a lily livered westerner's colon.

Test yourself every day. Do the things you wouldn't normally do, this is your chance to be the person you always wanted to be. Don't let fear stop you.

Find me on Google+ where I've uploaded all the route information and literally thousands of pictures from the trip.

Printed in Great Britain
by Amazon.co.uk, Ltd.,
Marston Gate.